ICE CREAM

ICE CREAM

THIRTY OF THE MOST INTERESTING SKATERS IN HISTORY

TOLLER CRANSTON

& MARTHA LOWDER KIMBALL

National Library of Canada Cataloguing in Publication Data

Cranston, Toller
    Ice cream : thirty of the most interesting skaters in history / Toller Cranston; with Martha Lowder Kimball.

ISBN 0-7710-2332-4

1. Skaters – Biography. I. Kimball, Martha Lowder. II. Title.

GV850.A2C74 2002   796.91'2'0922   C2002-902354-8

Published simultaneously in the United States of America by McClelland & Stewart Ltd., P.O. Box 1030, Plattsburgh, New York 12901

Library of Congress Control Number: 2002107048

We acknowledge the financial support of the Government of Canada through the Book Publishing Industry Development Program for our publishing activities. We further acknowledge the support of the Canada Council for the Arts and the Ontario Arts Council for our publishing program.

Line drawings throughout by Toller Cranston.

Typeset in Berkeley by M&S, Toronto
Printed and bound in Canada

McClelland & Stewart Ltd.
The Canadian Publishers
481 University Avenue
Toronto, Ontario
M5G 2E9
www.mcclelland.com

1 2 3 4 5   06 05 04 03 02

To Chuck and Alice Zetterstrom and
Gavin and Sandy Lowder,
siblings and siblings-in-law extraordinaire

M. L. K.

To Horst and Stefanie Tutepastell,
my two very special friends for life
and friends and supporters of all artists

T. C.

CONTENTS

A WORD TO THE READER

Toller Cranston, throughout his long and ever-so-tortuous skating career – alone among his peers, or so it seemed to him – hungered after historical and anecdotal knowledge of the great figure skaters, past and contemporary. What, specifically, were their skating gifts? Who were they as people? What drove them and defined their personalities?

With his unquenchable curiosity, Toller ferreted out what information he could from any casual witness willing to throw light on the talents and private lives of historically important skaters. Anyone whom Toller engaged in one of his "little chats" knows that the one-sided interrogations resembled scenes from the Spanish Inquisition. Sensing his responsibility as a living repository of institutional knowledge, he stored the data in a private mental archive that became the backbone of this book.

Toller chose – sensibly, I think – to feature skaters about whom he possessed extensive knowledge and preferably whom he had known well as individuals. Thus we offer informed but highly personal impressions, not a comprehensive history of the sport's most significant practitioners. You might argue for the inclusion of Gillis Grafström or Ulrich Salchow, for example, but neither of us ever met those skaters. You might also reasonably point out that we never met Sonja Henie either, but Toller *feels* that he knew her, and that's what matters.

The skaters included in this book all made a strong impression upon the figure-skating world, and perhaps upon the larger world in general. They contributed to the development of the sport, whether through commanding athletic prowess, unusual aesthetic characteristics, influence on the formal rules, or sheer force of personality. They reflected and illuminated their times and environments. Certainly none of them could be called boring, which is the deadliest sin in Toller's catechism. In many cases, the greatest weight was given to those skaters who elevated figure skating to an art form.

Occasionally, however – one might call this the *Time* Man-of-the-Year syndrome – skaters were included because they altered the course of the sport in a way that may have been negative as well as positive.

Certain skaters didn't receive the honor of a full chapter within these pages simply because they had already made modest to major appearances in either *Zero Tollerance* or *When Hell Freezes Over, Should I Bring My Skates?*, Toller's previous books. Among the many who fall into this category are Christopher Bowman, Lu Chen, Ekaterina Gordeeva and Sergei Grinkov, Katherine Healy, Janet Lynn, Brian Pockar, and Paul Wylie.

Certain other skaters, notably Brian Boitano and Dick Button, demonstrate their importance by leaping in and out of other people's chapters.

We ordered the entries chronologically by birth year. Pairs skaters and ice-dance teams are listed according to the earlier date of birth. You may notice that Tonya Harding follows directly behind Nancy Kerrigan, as she often did as events unfolded. That was a fortuitous twist of fate for us as writers (though Kerrigan might disagree).

The first-person "I" throughout the book is, of course, Toller's utterly unique voice. Anything aesthetic, sensory, emotional, exaggerated, opinionated, or redundant comes from him. On the other hand, anything chronological, organized, or fact-based, including the footnotes, comes from his humble co-author. We tell you this so that you will know whom to blame when you disagree with the opinions expressed or when you find factual errors.

We hope that Toller's subjective and capricious decisions regarding whom to include and whom to omit will prove controversial and thought-provoking. What is figure skating, after all, without heated and self-righteous disagreement? Take your blood-pressure medicine, and begin reading.

Martha Lowder Kimball

Dear Toller
"Only you will
compete with my legend"
Sonja
Nov 4th '66
Los Angeles

CHAPTER 1

SONJA HENIE

The Steel Showgirl

Sonja Henie was born on April 8, 1912, while a freak snowstorm blanketed her native Oslo, Norway. Wilhelm and Selma Henie provided their daughter with a loving home and all the benefits old money could confer. The family owned a hunting lodge, where their second-born child took avidly to skiing at age four. She transferred her new skills to the ice a year later.

Sonja's first love was ballet. The great Anna Pavlova herself advised the Henies that their gifted daughter should study classical dance. Young Sonja had dramatic flair and a love of musical interpretation. Those qualities stood her in good stead when she began to enter, and win, figure-skating competitions.

Sonja was privately tutored in order to be free to study and train abroad. By the age of nine, she was the Norwegian champion. The ballerina on ice, famous for her freestyle performances, won the first of ten consecutive world titles in 1927, and the first of three consecutive Olympic titles in 1928. Since she was sometimes favored by a glut of

Norwegian judges, it was Sonja who inspired the rule that specifies only one judge per nation on any panel.

Contrary to the custom of wearing ankle-length skirts, Sonja was permitted, because of her youth, to compete in knee-length costumes. That allowed her to launch a jump in her first Olympic appearance. Her derring-do scandalized the elderly and conservative gentlemen who headed the International Skating Union (ISU), the body that governed both figure and speed skating.

After turning professional in 1936, Sonja transformed herself almost overnight into a legitimate movie star, while continuing to perform on ice in a variety of extravaganzas, including her Hollywood Ice Revue, produced by Arthur Wirtz until 1951. She ultimately starred in ten movies produced by Darryl F. Zanuck for Twentieth Century Fox between 1937 and 1945: *One in a Million, Thin Ice, Happy Landing, My Lucky Star, Second Fiddle, Everything Happens at Night, Sun Valley Serenade, Iceland, Wintertime,* and *It's a Pleasure.* She also made *The Countess of Monte Cristo* for Universal-International and, with her third husband, Niels Onstad, produced a travelogue, *Hello London,* featuring her skating.

Sonja was married three times: to American sportsman and millionaire Dan Topping; to wealthy American businessman Winthrop Gardiner, Jr.; and to Onstad, a Norwegian shipping mogul and art-lover. She died in 1969 of aggressive leukemia while flying to a hospital for therapy. She was fifty-seven years old.

$\qquad$

I f I were to select the greatest female figure skater of all time, I would consider Sonja Henie the number-one contender. Her competitive credentials are so astounding, particularly in light of the early age at which she achieved them, that skating history can offer no equal. In fact, no one has come close. The appealing, blonde, and dimpled Norwegian won her first world title in 1927, at the precocious age of fourteen.

The competitive fields were small then and the outdoor conditions rigorous. Few spectators attended skating events during those days before television and the big ice extravaganzas arrived on the scene. Simply through the force of her personality and the strength of her will, Sonja pushed figure skating into the mainstream.

Michelle Kwan, a twenty-first-century phenomenon, is certainly, in my opinion, one of the most brilliant female skaters of all time. Yet if one compares her straightforward career to Sonja's multifaceted trajectory – world and Olympic competitions, film success, touring shows, product endorsements, great wealth, famous lovers, and multiple husbands – Michelle (and anyone else, for that matter, with the possible exception of Katarina Witt) is simply not in the running.

Sonja was probably the first "professional amateur" in figure skating. Eric Zeller, a famous German skating coach and a Henie acquaintance, told me once in Garmisch-Partenkirchen, a Bavarian town that both Sonja and I knew well, that Henie *père* had an effective trick in his bag. He would let it be known to an exhibition promoter that his talented and famous daughter, billed to headline the evening's entertainment, did not presently feel well enough to skate. However, a certain fabulously expensive silver tea service that she had seen in a shop window might make her feel considerably better and allow her to rise to the occasion. Sonja lived comfortably on the family's earned and inherited wealth, but never tired of acquiring more. Greed was one of her less attractive qualities.

Today the promotion of talented children is generally the province of the "skating mother," an infamous breed. In Sonja's case, Mr. Wilhelm Henie was the captain of the ship. He shrewdly managed every detail of his daughter's career until his death just a year after Sonja finally turned professional. In all my research, I never heard a shard of revealing information about his wife.

Sonja, though proficient enough in executing the eighty figures that were required in her day, shone brightest in free skating, which she imbued with a sense of dance at a time when most skating was stiff and formal. She performed famously to *Les Sylphides* and Camille Saint-Saëns's "Dying Swan," fancying herself the "Pavlova of the Ice," a title that enthusiastic journalists were happy to award her. Although her comparatively simple technique must be understood in the context of the limited technical vocabulary of her times, she demonstrated one ability the likes of which has not been seen since. She could run on her toe picks, forwards or backwards, without any obvious physical effort.

My understanding of Sonja Henie is somewhat fragmented, the result of dozens of questions asked of people who knew her, coupled with some personal reflection. My first memory goes back to the early 1960s, when I watched Sonja, a bona fide movie star, on screen in a number of old Hollywood films.

She had approached Hollywood immediately after winning her tenth world title and subsequently turning professional. Ice was then foreign to Hollywood (except as it appeared in afternoon highballs). Sonja's acting skills were as yet untried, and her English was heavily accented. For those very sound reasons, she was offered only one skating scene in a movie in which someone else would star. Sonja flatly refused, insisting that she could carry a movie on her own. Her audacity paid off. She got her way.

When Sonja skated for film, she seemed removed from the familiar and prosaic ice-arena environment. Her fictional settings were always ballrooms, palaces, or mystical alpine scenes. Beginning with *Sun Valley Serenade*, the sets featured black ice. Years later, when I performed in my own filmed specials, all ten of them utilized black ice, an exotic and highly reflective surface. However, the black ice in Sonja Henie's movies was much blacker and more mirror-like than my own.

Miles White, a costumer who had designed for Sonja and later designed for me when I mounted my own Broadway ice show, informed me that the secret to creating *her* black ice was in perfusing the water with India ink before freezing the surface. Whenever Sonja filmed scenes on black ice, Miles told me, he was obliged to keep multiple copies of each of her costumes on standby in the event of a wet fall that would leave her costume badly marked.

One of Sonja's great contributions to the sport of ice skating was the natural theatricality that she brought to it. Her shows were great spectacles, with the most lavish costuming and careful attention to music, pageantry, and lighting. Although the star possessed a difficult temperament and often cursed like a sailor, she was knowledgeable and totally committed to the excellence of every technical aspect of her projects.

In 1975, I collided with Sonja's ghost, or at least with her energy. I was given the candy-floss-pink dressing room that had been specially designed for her during her ice-show days in Detroit, Michigan. She demanded, and received, full star treatment, something I admired and tried to emulate. Although those accommodations had become rather sad and tawdry, in my imagination they were still grand, glittery, and Hollywood rococo.

In 1978, I unsuccessfully tried to cajole Al Grant, then vice-president of Madison Square Garden in New York City, to produce Toller Cranston's The Ice Show. In the course of our conversations, I asked Grant to name the top three performance highlights he had witnessed at the Garden. He replied that he couldn't come up with a number two or three, but number one, by a country mile, was Sonja Henie's performances in her Hollywood Ice Revue.

Renowned Holiday on Ice choreographer Ted Shuffle, now deceased, had been a chorus boy in that show. He told me that Sonja's ability to endear herself to audiences was hardly accidental. She used a number of theatrical tricks. First, she glued rhinestones onto her eyelids. Then, at the risk of temporary blindness, she stared directly into the spotlights. As a result, when she looked out into the audience, each spectator thought that he or she had made direct eye contact with the *grande dame*.

Sonja went to elaborate pains with her makeup. According to Canadian skater Andrea McLaughlin, Sonja did not apply it directly to her body in the usual way, with a powder puff or a sponge. Instead, she had herself dipped into a vat of candy-floss-pink liquid makeup that had been specially created for her. When Andrea showed me a sample of the color, I found it grotesque. Andrea assured me, however, that under exactly the right lighting conditions (which the star, of course, demanded), Sonja's entire five-foot-three, 110-pound body glowed like a perfect Georgia peach. The tint of the potion, manufactured exclusively for her use, became known as "Sonja Pink."

John Routh, another chorus boy in her show, recalled for my amusement that Sonja liked to be carried through the backstage area with warm, moist towels wrapped around her legs. They were removed only seconds before she was to burst through the curtains. Those towels kept her million-dollar muscles warm and limber. The prodigious amount of physical effort that Sonja exerted each day stretched her limits, necessitating frequent massages and other soothing tricks of the trade.

Sonja placed no small value on her talent and importance. Her arrogance could be stunning. Once, according to John Routh, just before the second half of a show, a young fan brought Sonja a dozen roses. She accepted the bouquet, took a big sniff, and threw the flowers onto the floor. Before disappearing through the curtain, she announced to the astounded fan, "Roses are for stars. Orchids for Sonja!"

Exotic orchids were one of Sonja's passions. She once sent to Hawaii and imported a planeload of the delicate blossoms for a party she planned to host in her Hollywood home.

Don Watson, ex-manager of the now-defunct Ice Capades, served as a font of Henie information during the time when I guest-starred with that company. I was forever grilling him for anecdotes. According to Don, when Sonja was flying high, she was probably the most famous woman in the world, Hollywood's number-one box-office draw. Her annual New Year's Eve party held at her mansion on Delfern Drive was *the* party of the year. Any Hollywood bigwig or up-and-coming movie star who failed to receive an invitation virtually had to leave town to save face. Sonja's parties were as lavish and glamorous as any Hollywood could produce. At a time when only movie stars owned swimming pools, Sonja's pool was filled with ice swans topped with coronets of candles.

Although she frequented the highest levels of Hollywood social circles, Sonja was far more comfortable with the homosexual chorus boys who appreciated her sense of melodrama and her bawdy, high camp humor. Many a drag queen patterned his persona after hers. During the after-show midnight hours, chorus boys cajoled Sonja to display her jewel collection. The private horde included fabulous ensembles of rubies, diamonds, emeralds, sapphires, and pearls.

Sonja believed that, after her death, the collection should be displayed under hermetically sealed glass like the British crown jewels. Talking to John, I was reminded of a newsreel that I once saw in a movie theater as a child. The report described Miss Henie as one of the richest women in the world and revealed that a jewel thief had robbed her in an elevator at New York's exclusive Waldorf-Astoria Hotel. Robberies were standard fare in the life of a star who insisted on traveling with a sack containing thousands of dollars worth of jewelry.

Sonja's life, however, had a dark and controversial side. Prior to the 1974 World Figure Skating Championships (Worlds) in Munich, West Germany, Morris Chalfen paid me a visit at the Toronto Cricket Skating and Curling Club. Chalfen, proprietor of the European Holiday on Ice company, a dyed-in-the-wool ice-show impresario who had produced a number of special engagements for Sonja, had come from Minneapolis, Minnesota, to see me. He thought that a similar sort of production could be mounted in B-class arenas. The object was to star me as a male Sonja Henie. The reference to B venues, rather than A, struck a sour cord and offended my ego. Morris and I did not make a deal.

However, during our conversation in the lobby of the Cricket Club, I learned many things about Sonja. One recollection that he shared related to her relationship with Adolf Hitler.

Not long before the 1932 Olympics in Garmisch-Partenkirchen, West Germany, Sonja gave an exhibition at the Berlin Sports Palast. Important Nazis attended, from Hitler to Göring to Goebbels. Upon taking the ice, Sonja skated to the section of the arena where they were seated, gave the distinctive Nazi salute, and shouted, "Heil Hitler!" That enthusiastic gesture surprised and offended much of the world.

Although Sonja later emphatically denied any pro-Nazi political leanings, from that time on, and for many years to come, her global reputation was that of a Nazi sympathizer, or perhaps even a collaborator. In truth, she was simply politically naïve and drawn to power and glamor. Failing to understand why she shouldn't, she maintained a long-standing friendship with Hitler that became increasingly awkward as world events unfolded.

However, that friendship resulted in one notably fortuitous outcome. At a luncheon that he hosted for Sonja and her parents at his hideaway, the Eagle's Nest near Berchtesgaden, Hitler gave Henie a photo of himself in order to thank her for presenting a charity skating exhibition. Later, when the Germans invaded Norway, the Nazis targeted the Henies' country house, Landoën, as potential headquarters, and a group of officers arrived in a chauffeured limousine to confiscate the property. When the colonel in charge discovered the inscribed photograph of the Führer, resting in a silver frame on the family's grand piano, the house was saved from German plunder. None of the Henie properties was ever damaged. Perhaps not surprisingly, with her flair for stage managing, Sonja herself had thought to order the photo placed in such a strategic location.

Once Sonja began producing her own ice shows, she was forced to compete at a financial and logistical disadvantage against her former producer, Arthur Wirtz, who had sewn up the major arenas and replaced her with principal skater Barbara Ann Scott of Canada, the 1948 Olympic champion. In 1953, Morris Chalfen offered to rescue Sonja's ice revue by taking it to Europe for an extended tour that would begin in London, England, and eventually culminate in Oslo.

Because of her pro-German reputation, Sonja was terribly apprehensive about performing anywhere in Norway. Besides, she had done little to aid the Norwegian war effort. She expected to be *persona non grata* on her native soil. When eventually she relented and made the trip, she was greatly relieved to find Oslo ready to receive its prodigal daughter (by then an American citizen) with open arms. Sonja was all the rage during that run. She sold out the open-air Oslo sports stadium, standing room included, for an entire month.

According to lore, when the curtains parted for the show's opening, torrential rains abated, and the skies remained clear until after the finale. Norwegians dubbed that phenomenon, which characterized the show's entire run, "Sonja weather."

Chalfen told me that he received a telephone call, if not from Sonja herself, then from someone within her organization, asking what to do with all the Norwegian kroner that Sonja had earned. Chalfen arranged for two small-time thugs to smuggle part of the vast fortune out of the country and bring back American dollars in exchange. Sonja's faithful secretary made international runs as well. According to legend, when the smuggled kroner hit the European money market, the Norwegian economy fluctuated dramatically.

Lucky stars seem to shine directly above certain individuals' heads. Sonja must have been one of those fortunate people. Chalfen informed me that an important modern-art collection became available for a song at a time when Sonja was one of the few people flush enough to purchase it. On a whim, and without any profound artistic knowledge, she bought the collection of works by modern Expressionist masters. Once again, she struck gold. The collection was to become perhaps her most stunning investment ever, based on a decision that had rested primarily on luck. Those paintings are on display at the Sonja Henie, Niels Onstad Art Center just outside Oslo, where they can be viewed by anyone so inclined. Sonja's trophies and medals reside there as well.

Even under her lucky star, however, Sonja's life was neither as fortunate nor as uncomplicated as it might superficially have seemed to be. She was a lonely woman. The mantle of global stardom weighed heavily on her shoulders.

True, she was indefatigable. She could exhaust as many as five partners per show, while remaining as fresh as a daisy. But she was equally hard on her partners off the ice. Casual sex, with everyone from celebrated movie stars like Tyrone Power to various skating companions, was one remedy she adopted to kill her emotional pain.

At the reunion of great Canadian skaters, A Legendary Night of Figure Skating, held in 1999 at Toronto's new Air Canada Centre, I met one of Sonja's skating partners, Michael Kirby. He provided some interesting insights into her character. According to Michael, who has written a book of memoirs, Sonja chose her partners not for their skating abilities but for their looks and personal appeal. A partnership didn't last long unless the male performed in bed like a virtuoso. To my great disappointment, Michael swore to me that he and Sonja had never made love. But the star stopped speaking to him as a result, and he was soon her ex-partner.

Based on many reports, Sonja abjured the company of women. She was truly comfortable only with men. Jinx Clark, a secondary principal in

Sonja's show, was one of the few female skaters Sonja liked. I met Jinx in 1975 and dined with her at her home in Colorado Springs, Colorado. In the course of our conversation, I concluded that Jinx must have been somewhat similar to Sonja herself. She let it slip that she could lay claim to a handful of ex-husbands, and though a woman of a certain age, she continued to ride a Harley-Davidson motorcycle. It seems quite understandable that Sonja would have preferred women like Jinx to others who lived more conventionally.

Carol Heiss, an American, won the 1960 women's Olympic championship in Squaw Valley, California. After the Games, while Carol was working with the Three Stooges on a frighteningly terrible movie, Sonja visited the film set. Carol, Olympic gold medalist though she was, meekly asked Miss Henie for her autograph. Sonja delivered that autograph coupled with the remark, "You're very good, my dear, but you'll never be a star." Then she departed in a cloud of mink.

Probably the best biographical skating documentary that I ever saw was the Henie film produced in 1994 by the Norwegian Broadcasting Corporation. Curiously, I watched that documentary during a skating engagement in Hong Kong for promoter Ted Wilson, a fanatic collector of skating films. One fragment looms in my memory. Vivi-Anne Hultén, one of Sonja's competitors, revealed that, even as a child of ten, the Norwegian exuded such charisma and projected such a larger-than-life persona through her performances that all other skaters in her wake felt like mattress stuffing (my paraphrase). No performing artist, no matter how experienced, can compete with such manifest magic.

The exact details of Sonja Henie's skating technique have been lost from twenty-first-century memory, preserved only on aging Hollywood celluloid. But her personality continues to eclipse that of every other skater in history. In the final analysis, it is the personality of a great performer that remains most memorable. Through the force of her character and her grand ambition, Sonja Henie changed figure skating from an esoteric pastime for the few to an international passion. For that alone, we must remember and revere her.

Landover, 1985

CHAPTER 2

LUDMILA AND

OLEG PROTOPOPOV

✍

Paganini and His Violin

O leg Protopopov was born on July 16, 1932. During his preteen years, he survived the Nazi siege of Leningrad, Russia. It wasn't until the relatively advanced age of fifteen that he began figure skating.

Ludmila Belousova, born on November 22, 1935, became interested in the sport as a child upon seeing Sonja Henie skate in the film *Sun Valley Serenade*. Thus it has always been; one generation influences the next. Ludmila wanted to dance on the ice as Sonja did in her movies. In time she would, but she didn't begin until she reached age sixteen.

The couple met in 1954 at their Moscow training rink and married three years later. No pairs coach would agree to teach them. They were well beyond the age when Soviet sport students were considered malleable. However, they possessed sufficient talent and motivation to train on their own.

Oleg and Ludmila entered their first Worlds in 1958 in Paris, France, where they placed thirteenth. Reaching the silver-medal position in 1962, for three years they remained stuck there behind West Germans Marika Kilius and Hans-Jurgen Baumler.

The Protopopovs achieved dominance in their sport in time for the 1964 Olympic Games in Innsbruck, Austria, where they won the first of two sets of Olympic gold medals. By the time they received their second in 1968 in Grenoble, France, Oleg was thirty-six, Ludmila, thirty-three.

They brought to the ice fluid, balletic movement that melded perfectly with classical music. They were able to perform their precise moves slowly and dramatically, with superb edge control. They took particular pride in their death-spiral variations, which they renamed life spirals and enjoyed demonstrating to audiences.

Following the 1969 Worlds in Colorado Springs, the fiercely independent Protopopovs refused the Soviet government's request that they stop skating and become national coaches. Instead they turned professional and joined a domestic ice show. In 1979, during a European tour, they sought asylum and defected to Switzerland.

In their forties, fifties, and even sixties, the Protopopovs continued to train regularly in order to perform at carefully selected venues, including the World Professional Figure Skating Championships in Landover, Maryland, and the Jimmy Fund Dana-Farber Cancer Institute benefit at Harvard. Right up until the new millennium, the couple thrilled audiences with their artistic lines and athletic control. In their eternal love story, Oleg played the role of Paganini. The lovely Ludmila was his finely tuned violin.

⅋ᛏ⅋ᛏ⅋ᛏ

I n 1965, my mother took me to see the world tour of champions when it played the Montreal Forum in Quebec following the Colorado Springs Worlds. A child's first impression of anything invariably is more profound and memorable than subsequent experiences. There were so many wonderful skaters at the Forum that day. I feel as though I can still remember the entire show, including what costume each performer wore. Perhaps the following impressions don't seem to relate to the Protopopovs, but collectively they served as the warm-up act for the pièce de résistance.

The French champion, Nicole Hassler, stunned me with her ability to spin. It was so phenomenal that her three-minute exhibition number consisted almost entirely of three spins. She performed no jumps and practically no linking choreography. I had never seen anything like her routine.

I also remember watching the young Czech, Ondrej Nepela. Still virtually a child, he already competed at the world level and could execute double Axels. Years later, I would often beat Ondrej in free skating. In 1965, that very idea was unimaginable. Ondrej eventually won the 1972 Olympic gold medal in Sapporo, Japan. Those were the first Games held in Asia. Tragically, Ondrej would die of AIDS-related cancer in 1989, becoming one of the first figure skaters to succumb to that growing epidemic.

One of Ondrej's teammates was a phenomenally tall and slim Czechoslovakian woman named Hana Mazkova. I had never seen anyone with so much natural talent. She could leap, suspend herself in the air, and seemingly hover above the ice before landing.

Petra Burka from Canada, the 1965 world champion and the daughter of my future teacher, Ellen Burka, also skated with a mechanically flawless virtuosity that I, in my relatively unskilled state, found disturbing.

There were other impressive exhibitions, but one performance towered above the rest. World ice-dancing champions Ludmila and Oleg Protopopov skated last, in the position of honor. They performed to "Meditation" from Massenet's *Thaïs*, costumed with elegance and refinement. Oleg wore a black skating suit with a touch of white at his throat. Ludmila wore a perfectly simple V-neck dress in an electric shade of fuchsia.

Just before the Protopopovs began their performance, the audience became hushed, awed by the skaters' regal presence and aura. I interpreted that stillness as the crowd's acknowledgement that something great was about to happen. The audience paid Oleg and Ludmila the supreme compliment of watching their entire performance in silence. The only sound of which I was conscious was the thumping of my heart as I sat in the upper tier of seats, thoroughly transfixed by the spectacle.

At the end of the number, everybody, including me, stood and applauded madly. That was my first experience of a standing ovation.

Canadian audiences, as knowledgeable and generous as they are to
skaters, often leap to their feet too easily and for all the wrong reasons.
Standing ovations should be reserved for performances like the one I witnessed in Montreal. It was almost a religious catharsis, as though we, the
audience, had been specially chosen to experience something divine.

Oleg and Ludmila gave many encores, but it was that first performance of "Meditation" that I will never forget. Years later, on a more
analytical level, I would cite that same experience as the first time I ever
witnessed the perfect and equal balance of sport and art. That ideal of
combining sport and art was to become the driving force behind my own
career, whether I was conscious of the fact in the early days or not.
Unfortunately, at least for me, that approach came with an enormous
price tag.

Oleg and Ludmila dominated pairs skating for almost a decade. Every
time I saw their performances on television, it appeared to me that they
stood in a class by themselves. They shared a profound understanding of
figure skating as an art, and they arrived at each world championship with
new moves that allowed them to dance upon the razor's edge of creativity. Anyone who saw this pair during their amateur heyday was aware of
their unique nobility and their god-like presence at center ice.

At the 1967 Worlds in Vienna, the Protopopovs performed their
competitive program on an outdoor rink. As I watched them on television, the sky poured down heavy sheets of rain. I was fascinated to note
that Oleg and Ludmila glided onto the ice holding an umbrella that
matched their costumes.

The Protopopovs won many world titles and two Olympic gold
medals. However, their amateur career ended on a somewhat sour note
when fellow Soviets Irina Rodnina and Alexei Ulanov defeated them at
the 1969 Worlds in Colorado Springs. Knowing Oleg as well as I do now,
I suspect that receiving the bronze medal severely wounded his ego and
rankled for some time. That world event was the Protopopovs' last
amateur competition.

In 1974, before I knew the Protopopovs personally, I won the world
free-skating title in Munich, an accomplishment that contributed to a

major change in how international judges and fans viewed me. Afterward I received a telegram from the Soviet Union, signed by Oleg and Ludmila: "Dear Toller, thank you for continuing our art." Receiving that telegram was one of the greatest thrills of my skating career and perhaps of my life.

Years later, Oleg and Ludmila told me the painful and heart-wrenching stories of their poor treatment by the U.S.S.R. once they turned professional. The Communist regime was at its most totalitarian. Even Olympic gold medalists were small cogs in the great Soviet machine. When the Protopopovs stopped competing, three choices were available to them: coaching, performing in a Russian ice show, or leaving the ice altogether. Those great classical artists were obliged to perform in a commercial ice show that probably featured bears and chimps and other elements that would surely have been anathema to both of them.

In 1979, the Protopopovs made international news by defecting from Mother Russia. For some years, they occasionally had been allowed to leave the Soviet Union to skate as special guest stars with a tiny, provincial ice tour in West Germany. The thought of defecting to the West had germinated in their minds for years while they strategized and waited for an opportune time. After seeing the Protopopovs make frequent border crossings without incident, customs officials relaxed their vigilance.

At last, taking as many personal and household objects with them as they could, Oleg and Ludmila flew to West Germany. By the time the announcement of their defection reached the world press, they had petitioned Switzerland for political asylum. The news rocked the figure-skating world. Any defection by the Soviet Union's big cultural stars (whether Rudolf Nureyev, Mikhail Baryshnikov, Natalia Makarova, or Alexander Gudunov) was a painful slap in the face of the Communist system.

The Protopopovs, had they not defected, would eventually have evaporated into obscurity. By rising again like two phoenixes from the ashes, they became huge American box-office attractions. They chose to remain based in the small Swiss town of Grundenwald, but for the next decade they performed primarily on North American soil.

I believe that Dick Button brokered the Protopopovs' lucrative Ice Capades contract, and he did so quickly in order to capitalize upon the global publicity that their defection had created. They became principal stars. At the same time, I was a guest star with Ice Capades. We happened to meet in Philadelphia, Pennsylvania.

Oleg is a supreme skating fanatic. When it comes to unconscious eccentricity, he is in a class by himself, leaving the Gary Beacoms of this world – and even me – far behind in the dust.

He astounded ice-show managers by personally measuring each surface with a tape measure, right down to the millimeter. I was accustomed to visually checking the lay of the land and adapting to a new surface quite easily. I generally preferred fewer square feet, because that involved less work. Oleg, on the other hand, craved Olympic-sized rinks, perhaps because of his inability to exorcise his amateur frustrations.

The Protopopovs, who were consistently kind to me, invited me out for dinner one night after the show. That was a special thrill. I remember dressing to the nines, presuming that we three great stars would dine in Philadelphia's grandest restaurant. Imagine my surprise when the Protopopovs created that dinner on a hot burner in their hotel room and served it up on plastic plates.

Although Oleg, Ludmila, and I shared similar figure-skating philosophies, we were 180 degrees apart in our views of how to live, dress, and spend money. Oleg and Ludmila had arrived in the West without a dime. They were smart enough to know that the time to earn money had arrived. They wanted to save as much of it as possible in order to secure their future.

Soon after the Protopopovs' dazzling defection to the West, Dick Button invited them to perform at the World Professional Championships in Landover. At many of those competitions, I played a dual role: performer and CBC commentator. When the Protopopovs first appeared, I felt that the tsar and tsarina of Russia had arrived. All the other skaters were extremely excited, and the press corps lined up for individual interviews with the royal couple. I in turn lined up for my fifteen-minute audience. Although Oleg and Ludmila have always been charming to me, as their interviewer I felt like a kindergarten student questioning the school principal. Oleg knew how to hold court. He did not answer questions. He pontificated about the true art of skating.

The Protopopovs offered the finest example of classic, refined pairs skating. It was not so much what they did as how they did it that set them apart from everyone else in Landover. The audience would surely have stoned any judge who failed to hold up a perfect 10.0. Although Oleg and Ludmila competed in Landover for a number of years, they neither equaled nor surpassed their first appearance, when they cast a mysterious aura over judges and spectators.

Oleg, to my surprise and horror, typically underwent a metamorphosis between the practice sessions and the competition. Possessing little hair, he dragged out a rather frightening blond toupée. The makeup he applied was fantastic and theatrical, *à la* Ballet Russe de Monte Carlo circa 1920. Although diplomacy was never my strong suit, out of respect I kept silent. Nobody else ever said a word to Oleg either.

Once, Oleg's blond toupée plopped onto the ice at the end of the couple's routine. With great dignity, Ludmila plucked it up and returned it to its rightful resting-place. The audience let out the tiniest, most respectful, titter. Upon witnessing the incident, I vowed never to wear a toupée on the ice, even if all my hair had fallen out. I would interpret my baldness as a divine omen to retire immediately, if not sooner.

When I was casting skaters for my CBC television special "Strawberry Ice," I very much wished to hire the Protopopovs as special guest stars. The producers offered Ludmila and Oleg $10,000, plus first-class accommodations, if they would fly from Switzerland to Toronto to perform a two-and-one-half-minute number for that multimillion-dollar television special. How could they afford to pass up such an opportunity?

Oleg refused the offer, citing the inconvenience of my timing. He didn't want to compromise their period of rest. I accepted his decision, although I was disappointed. I later learned that Oleg approached daily living with scientific meticulousness. Absolutely nothing could interfere with his prescribed regimen. Both Oleg and Ludmila were well into their fifties by then, but that was not the point. They wouldn't bend their draconian rules of skating discipline for any reason. Perhaps that explains their success and longevity.

Oleg and Ludmila, above and beyond their skating abilities and their stellar track record, possessed a strong intellectual curiosity, coupled with

devout passion for their fellow skaters and for all the important international competitions. Because of my position as a CBC commentator, I also
harbored those interests. Sharing that common denominator over the
years, we often met as friends to discuss the idiosyncratic nuances of bad
judging and great skating.

I observed that Oleg was as anti-Soviet in his evaluations as I was
pro-Soviet. It is accurate to say that we were diametrically opposed in
our understanding, in particular, of pairs skating. I presumed that Oleg
couldn't bring himself to endorse a Soviet team because he subconsciously considered himself and Ludmila the superior interpreters of the
art. To demean other Soviet pairs was to enhance his self-image. Perhaps
I am mistaken, but it seemed to me that this otherwise intelligent and
mature man was not immune to superficial resentments and touches of
professional jealousy. Ludmila was kind, gracious, and not without her
own opinions. However, when it came to pairs skating, her views almost
without exception mirrored Oleg's.

The Protopopovs remain so devoted to figure skating that, like hospital patients connected intravenously to a blood source, they simply
cannot and will not live without the sport. Their passion is pure and
unadulterated. Oleg told me on a number of occasions that his greatest
desire, when death knocks on his door, is to die in the act of skating.
Ludmila would probably follow suit on the spot.

Once, at the National Gallery of Art in Washington, D.C., I saw two
Rembrandt portraits, one of a man and the other of his wife. I studied
both portraits and tried to decide which one I would choose for myself
if I were offered that gift. The choice was impossible. Considering their
matched sizes, quality, emotional content, and technique, it would not
have made sense to hang one without the other. The couple seemed inextricably connected.

Some say that when couples grow old together, they begin to resem-
ble one another, both in personality and in physical appearance. Thus
it was with those portraits, and thus it is with the Protopopovs. We
know them as an inseparable pair, on and off the ice. They are a single
person. Their extraordinary emotional rapport has always been evident

in their performances. No other pair in the history of skating has achieved their degree of intellectual, emotional, and physical synchronicity.

Time marches on and youth vanishes. At the 1997 Worlds in Lausanne, Switzerland, I was delighted to see Oleg and Ludmila at a reception at the Olympic Museum. I ran up to embrace them as if they were distant members of my family, complimenting Oleg upon his youthful appearance. He whispered in my ear that the secret formula for young skin was to sleep well and then splash fresh urine all over one's face. I assured Oleg that he looked great, but that I would be looking older each day without that magical treatment.

Several years later, while I was in Mexico, a courier brought me a package from Switzerland. It contained a special cassette that I put into my audio system. I heard Oleg's voice proffering various musical selections that he felt would be suitable for my latest choreography. I was extremely moved, and my mind swam with decades of memories involving the Protopopovs. What Oleg did not know was that I had retired from figure skating. There would be no more comebacks for me.

The last time I saw the Protopopovs, we were all in Lake Placid, New York, for the famous Labor Day show. It was September 2000. I had been invited to serve as announcer. Oleg and Ludmila, my elders by two decades, had been invited to perform.

I watched them from the shadows as they glittered together under the spotlights, seemingly unchanged from the first time I had seen them. They received the only standing ovation of the evening, bringing back memories of their ovation in Montreal thirty-five years earlier. The three of us had come full circle together.

No skaters ever have given more to the sport of figure skating than Oleg and Ludmila Protopopov, and none ever will.

CHAPTER 3

LUDMILA PAKHOMOVA
AND ALEXANDER GORSHKOV

Art Trumps Sport

L udmila Pakhomova, born in 1950, was the daughter of a Soviet pilot who shot down twenty German warplanes during the Second World War. In the same focused way, Ludmila shot down English domination of ice dancing.

Alexander Gorshkov, born in 1947, was Ludmila's husband and partner. A weaker skater, he was content to present his flashy, energetic wife.

The April 1971 issue of *Skating* magazine painted the colorful struggle that took place at the European Figure Skating Championships (Europeans) in Zurich, Switzerland: "The Dance competition was skated in a tense politically-tainted atmosphere. Rumour had it that authoritative circles had warned the Soviets that their spectacular approach did not fit the requirements of ice dancing. It developed into a battle between the English classic school of tradition and the demonstrative Russian school of expression."

The Russian school won in a five-four split.

Ludmila and Alexander were the first Russians to win a world title and the first to invent (with their coach, Elena Tchaikovskaya, in 1974) an international dance, the Tango Romantica. Theirs was a classical presentation, influenced by the Russian ballet tradition.

ℰℰℰℰℰℰ

I have always believed that sharing historical anecdotes about major players in the figure-skating world is important to the development of young skaters. Because the world moves quickly, most skaters today, I'm sorry to say, are aware only of their own generation.

It is as necessary to understand Ludmila Pakhomova and Alexander Gorshkov as any other skaters who appear in this book. In my view, they are the most important ice-dance team of the twentieth century, with Jayne Torvill and Christopher Dean placing second.

My first Worlds as a competitor took place in 1970 in Ljubljana, Yugoslavia, where I met such historically significant skaters as Irina Rodnina, Alexei Ulanov, Beatrix Schuba, Gabriele Seyfert, and Janet Lynn. The lord of ice dance at the time was American coach Ronald Ludington. He had trained many superior teams and was the prime exponent of the fresh, athletic American style. I had become particularly aware of Ludington's influence during my summer training at Lake Placid. He taught virtually every important ice-dance team in the United States – and the teams were all clones of one other.

In Ljubljana, Ludington's star pupils were the American team of Judy Schwomeyer and James Sladky. The behind-the-scenes buzz touted Schwomeyer and Sladky as gold-medal shoo-ins. As the new kid on the block, I was surprised that no other results were even considered. The Americans' style showed a certain mathematical and technical perfection. I likened them to an automobile whose high price reflected its smooth-running engine, not its appearance.

In the hair-splitting ice-dance finale, Schwomeyer and Sladky placed second, while the judges awarded the gold medal to the Soviet team, Ludmila Pakhomova and Alexander Gorshkov. I felt that nobody in the audience but me understood the full import of what had happened. That competition had not been about technical superiority. It had hinged on the battle between sport and art. Art had won.

Ludmila, although her husband partnered her, was basically a one-woman band. Her presence and gift for dramatic self-expression, coupled with extreme musicality and originality, compelled attention. Neither spectators nor judges watched Alexander when he performed.

Ludmila and Alexander won again and again: in Lyon, in Calgary, in Bratislava, in Munich, and in Gothenburg. Behind closed doors, other skaters referred to the elegant but rather stiff Alexander as "the waiter," because he basically just stood on two skates and presented his sensational wife.

Each year, in competitions and exhibitions, Ludmila's inventiveness enthralled and transfixed spectators and judges alike. During the early 1970s, I skated exhibitions in Moscow and Leningrad a dozen times or more. The Soviet Union's stable included numerous fabulous skaters, but, no matter who performed, Pakhomova and Gorshkov closed the show. It wasn't unusual, at the end of a three-hour presentation, for Ludmila and Alexander to offer four or five encores.

Ludmila had the splendid body of a ballerina, although her face was not particularly attractive; her partner was probably prettier than she was. Alexander's aristocratic and handsome visage, however, did not compensate for the fact that he couldn't skate well, while Ludmila was the most fascinating performer I had ever seen. She underwent a physical metamorphosis on the ice that made one think her the most divine creature on God's earth. For me, her pure and heartfelt passion was almost unbearably beautiful.

Once, after skating in Graz, Austria, a stop on an exhibition tour, I informed the entire cast of skating luminaries that I had decided to conduct a séance in my hotel room that evening. Many skaters arrived for the event, even some who didn't speak English. Ludmila and Alexander sat front-row center.

I dimmed the lights and pretended to enter a somnambulistic trance. I confess that my nerves nearly failed me, because I didn't possess any psychic ability that I knew of. However, the lark somehow became high theater and ultimately terrified many of the spectators.

I called upon Sonja Henie's spirit for assistance. Then, in what I passed off as Sonja's voice, I expressed exactly what I thought of each person in the room. Ken Shelley, American champion, was so enamored of my performance that, when I requested that Sonja give a sign of her presence, Ken released one of the most enormous farts in history. With that, the rabble cracked up. I assured everyone that Sonja was truly with us, though the channels had been temporarily blocked. An aura of serious purpose redescended on the room.

Finally I addressed Ludmila and asked her, in "Sonja's" voice, if she was aware of the important revolution in ice dance that she had inspired. Did she understand the importance of her role in the sport's history? Ludmila was one of the victims who bought my schtick. The séance ended with her running out of the room in a flood of tears of awe, followed by "the waiter."

In those days, my lack of credentials placed me at the bottom of the international pecking order. After the séance, however, my profile rose to such a level that I was treated with great deference until the end of the tour.

Ludmila and Alexander won the first Olympic gold medal ever awarded in the sport of ice dance, at the 1976 Games in Innsbruck. After the Worlds in Gothenburg, they retired.

My own life was in turmoil then, and my future did not seem bright. I performed my Worlds exhibition as Canio from *Pagliacci*, because I felt that I had become the tragic fool of the opera. Just before I began to skate, Ludmila came running up to the boards to watch me, even though it was clear that she was still preparing to dress for her own performance. That afternoon, the tragic fool skated only for Ludmila. She knew who I was, and I knew who she was. Nobody else understood.

Not long after her amateur glory days, Ludmila died rather quickly of a terrible cancer. I heard that thousands of people attended her funeral, as though she had been a head of state. Perhaps she had been.

Ludmila Pakhomova, consciously or unconsciously, revolutionized ice dance, single-handedly changing it from a nondescript sport into pure art. The acid test for any great artist is whether the spectator can detect honesty and sincerity in the performance. With Ludmila's death, the figure-skating world lost one of its greatest artists. I can only imagine how she would evaluate ice dance today. I suspect that she is turning over (artfully, with pointed toes and wrists lightly flexed) in her grave.

With Sarah Hughes, 2002

CHAPTER 4

PEGGY FLEMING

❧

A Role Model for the Ages

N amed for the song "Peg o' My Heart," Peggy was born to Doris and Al Fleming on July 27, 1948, in San Jose, California. One of four sisters, she nevertheless grew up a tomboy in the family's idyllic rural setting. At the end of 1957, a new skating rink opened nearby. Doris saw its ad for a special introductory offer, and Al, who already loved the sport, packed up his girls and took them skating. For Peggy, it was love at first skate.

When Peggy was eleven, the family moved to Pasadena. Not long afterward, she lost her new coach, William Kipp, in the airplane crash near Brussels, Belgium, that killed the entire American figure-skating team en route to the 1961 Worlds in Prague, Czechoslovakia. For a while, Peggy's desire to skate was greatly diminished. Later she became one of the foremost young Americans to rebuild the sport, with the help of a succession of coaches: John Nicks, Peter Betts, and then, in 1965, Carlo and Christa Fassi, two of the coaches who had been imported from Europe after the crash.

That year, in a giant leap of faith, Peggy and her entire family moved to Colorado Springs so that Peggy could train with the Fassis at the Broadmoor World Arena. She had already won the first of five consecutive national titles in 1964. Two years later, under Carlo's direction and with Bob Paul's choreographic work and instruction in the aesthetics of music and dance, she added the first of three world gold medals.

The pièce de résistance was the gold medal Peggy won at the 1968 Olympics in Grenoble, France. She wore a chartreuse dress, a nod to the color of the liqueur produced by the monks at the local Grande Chartreuse Carthusian monastery.

Peggy turned professional after the 1968 Worlds in Geneva, Switzerland. She influenced the next generation of little girls as she floated like a good fairy through many television specials and select arena performances. Later she educated the television-viewing public as Dick Button's perennial foil in the ABC broadcasting booth at competitions.

Even as an expectant mother, Peggy served as a role model. An article about her experience with childbirth and young motherhood appeared in a magazine distributed to pregnant women across America.

In recent years, Peggy has offered a more profound contribution to American life by going public with her breast-cancer battle, detailed in her autobiography, *The Long Program*. After a needle biopsy and a lumpectomy, and while still waiting shakily for a verdict from the pathologist, Peggy managed to perform with Robin Cousins in "A Skater's Tribute to Hollywood." Following further surgery and lymph-node biopsies, she learned the good news that the cancer hadn't spread.

Several news outlets leaked the word of her cancer before Peggy had informed family members and friends. It was the thirtieth anniversary of her victory in Grenoble, on the night of the men's short program in Nagano, when CBS announced the news to the Olympic viewing audience. Peggy withstood with characteristic grace the world's intrusion on her privacy. Following radiation and Tamoxifen treatment, she has been cancer-free for more than a full Olympiad.

Peggy and her husband of more than thirty years, Greg Jenkins, son of an Olympic gold medalist, live in Los Gatos, California. They have two grown sons and several grandchildren.

Cℰℒℰℒℰℒℰ

T he 1961 plane crash of Sabena Airlines Flight 548 near Brussels devastated the figure-skating world. Above and beyond the personal horror of that terrible accident, America, always a dominant force in figure skating, lost its entire international team, a team that had taken years to develop.

Various lesser talents like Lorraine Hanlon, Barbara Roles, and Monty Hoyt attempted the next year to fill the shoes of the great champions who had been killed (including three members of one distinguished figure-skating family, Laurence, Maribel Y., and Maribel Vinson Owen), but it was not until Peggy Fleming emerged that America once more sent a major competitor into world competition.

A French-Canadian family kindly took me, a tiny skater who lived in suburban Montreal, to view the 1965 U.S. Nationals in Lake Placid. Lake Placid Village was a major skating center during the summer months. Nationals took place in February, however, when the remote Adirondack hamlet was sparsely populated and racked by the harsh elements.

The women skated earlier than the men that year, so I did not see the ladies' competition. I did witness the men's final event, in which Gary Visconti defeated Scott Allen and Tim Wood in a surprising upset. Wearing a strange and odious-green jumpsuit, Gary performed with great verve, managing to smile non-stop for the duration of his five-minute program. I remember thinking that, if the athleticism of his routine didn't tax him physically, surely the effort to smile so much must take its toll.

Although Gary's victory was significant, the talk of Lake Placid was the fabulous new female champion, Peggy Fleming of Pasadena, California. Following the men's long-program event, Peggy performed an exhibition to "Ave Maria," wearing a simple white dress. Her brunette hair was adorned with an extremely wide headband of the type that was to become one of her trademarks.

"Ave Maria" today is a hokey musical choice. It has now been done to death by every known skater, including me. However, Peggy's version was totally gorgeous. I was convinced that she would soon become a major force in the world of international figure skating. A star had been born.

Ellen Burka, a former Dutch champion and my future skating coach, had emigrated with her husband from the Netherlands to Canada. To support herself, she taught figure skating in Toronto, Ontario. By her own admission, the teacher's greatest teacher and most important influence was her daughter and pupil, Petra, the 1965 world champion. Peggy Fleming was Petra's major rival.

Above and beyond pure talent, Peggy enjoyed some formidable advantages over Petra. In good old American style, wealthy people sponsored her, influential supporters and television networks rallied to her cause, and an entourage followed her everywhere to attend to her whims. That sort of concerted, across-the-board support was virtually unknown in Canada. Her coach, beginning in 1965, was Carlo Fassi. Carlo was a competent teacher – but a veritable genius at international manipulation and figure-skating politics. Even Peggy's mother was formidable. Doris Fleming will go down in history as the most notorious skating mother of all time. Together, all those influences constituted a powerful war machine.

At the 1966 Worlds in Davos, Switzerland, Peggy, then a two-time American champion, defeated Petra Burka. Ellen, as Petra's coach and solitary sponsor, decided then and there that her daughter no longer had a promising future in amateur skating. Petra immediately turned professional and signed on with Holiday on Ice in Europe.

Ellen was and is both intelligent and wise, but I believe that Petra, a phenomenal skater and solid competitor, should have continued as an amateur, because she might quite conceivably have given Peggy a run for her money. It was convenient for Peggy when her nemesis retreated from the battlefield.

In 1967, Peggy won her third U.S. title.

The 1967–68 season was an Olympic year, so the results of the various national championships were critical to ambitious competitors hoping to make the team. My own performance at the 1968 Canadians in Kerrisdale, B.C., was among my most controversial, and the results were certainly the most personally devastating. My free-skating program caused a major sensation, but I received marks ranging from first place to last. I finished fourth overall and therefore did not make the Canadian

Olympic team bound for Grenoble. I limped back home to Baie D'Urfé and sank into a deep depression, feeling that I had deserved a place on the team.

The next week, I watched the U.S. Nationals on ABC's *Wide World of Sports*. Televised skating was rare in those days, but I was lucky to witness, despite grainy reception on our small black-and-white set, two sensational long-program performances. One was the phenomenal routine with which John Misha Petkevich won the men's bronze medal behind Tim Wood and Gary Visconti. The other was Peggy Fleming's winning performance. Peggy skated like the wind, simply without flaw. She completed two double Axels. Through my tears of self-pity, I tried to explain to my mother that my performance in Kerrisdale had been no less spectacular than Peggy's and John Misha's. I suspect that she didn't believe me.

Peggy went to Grenoble and immediately won the two-day school-figure event. East Germany's Gabriele Seyfert placed second, followed by Austria's Beatrix Schuba. Ellen Burka possessed a profound knowledge of the art of school figures. She told me years later that Peggy's ability to perform them under pressure was remarkable. She described Peggy's tracings as neat and tidy. In those days, of course, the outcome of the compulsory-figure event was disproportionately weighty.

Dredging up the whys and wherefores of competition results can be an unpleasant and unpopular exercise. Peggy's winning free-skating per-formance at the Grenoble Olympics was highly overrated. The routine contained several major flaws, including a fall on the double Lutz, a poorly landed double flip, a popped double Axel, and an omitted double Salchow. Still, Peggy's artistic marks consisted of an unbroken string of 5.9s.

Two other splendid skaters, Gabriele Seyfert and Czechoslovakia's Hana Maskova, finished second and third overall. As jumpers, they were far superior to Peggy. However, Peggy enjoyed such enormous support, and her mystique was so persuasive, that Gabriele and Hana, although both were from influential Communist countries, stood no chance of beating America's superstar, even if they had skated on their heads.

Peggy won another gold medal at the 1968 Worlds in Geneva, where the Olympic scenario played out again. Gabriele and Hana skated rings around Peggy from a technical standpoint. If the Geneva footage could be dredged up from the depths of international skating archives, the world would see an example of the sort of injustices that have been committed over the years at world and Olympic events.

It would be interesting if an entirely objective panel of experts were to view the footage of important competitions of the past and render verdicts based entirely on what they saw on film. I'm convinced that, with few exceptions, the gold-medal winners would have to turn over their prizes to more deserving competitors. Such a review will never occur.

In the years after Grenoble and Geneva, Peggy's major competitors, Gabriele and Hana, both knew personal tragedy. Gabriele won two world titles, in 1969 and 1970, but because of the East German government's fear that she would defect, she was put out to pasture, a virtual state prisoner.

Hana was killed in a car accident in France soon after joining Holiday on Ice. The official cause of death was listed as drunken driving, but many people, including Olympic champion Ondrej Nepela of Czechoslovakia, were certain that Hana's death had in fact been a murder. According to rampant rumors, she had been involved in cloak-and-dagger espionage.

Peggy, after her amateur glory, embarked in 1968 upon a dazzling professional career. She signed long-term contracts with a television and motion-picture production company and with NBC television and radio. She starred in big American ice shows and became the first figure skater to be featured in one-hour television specials. Eventually she also became an ABC staple in the broadcast booth.

With her beauty and her many titles, Peggy was a huge box-office attraction. My one recurrent disappointment was that she didn't maintain her technical skills. Once, I went to see Ice Follies in New York with Dick Button, former Olympic gold medalist. Peggy was the star of the production. She skated her number, gorgeously dressed and made up, while a pianist played a grand piano that had been rolled out onto the ice. The glamorous setting created a certain impression, but the content of the program was hardly challenging. I don't recall a single jump.

Backstage, Dick asked me what I thought. I expressed myself in no uncertain terms, as I am wont to do. When I returned Dick's question, he cagily made no comment.

Over the years, Dick and I have shared a certain way of viewing figure skating. Unlike me, however, Dick has always been loath to express extreme opinions. He has left that ugly chore to others.

For years, I was forever bumping into Peggy at various international competitions and exhibitions, even in the great theatrical show Ice at Radio City Music Hall, where Peggy and I co-starred with Robin Cousins. I felt then that Peggy was resting comfortably on her laurels. Perhaps, though, my opinion was too academic, too narrowly concerned with technical excellence.

What Peggy did do with great success was contribute in a dramatic way to the evolution of skating as a genuine art form, a medium of beauty and elegance. She was the first female American champion to bring true refinement and glamor to the ice. Even today, when Peggy is mentioned along with other internationally acclaimed skaters, her name is accompanied by adjectives such as *lovely*, *balletic*, and *graceful*.

Peggy's greatest claim to fame, in my view, was her image. She was not only beautiful and glamorous, but she presented an entirely new figure-skating body type, demonstrating a marked contrast to the heavyset, athletic, European workhorses who had long reigned over the sport. She also offered a refined, demure demeanor, a soft voice, and a stable lifestyle, worthy of imitation by little girls everywhere.

Since 1968, the United States has produced a great line of female skating champions. The most telling fact of all is that every one of them has been influenced and inspired by the artful style of Peggy Fleming, on and off the ice.

Circa 1976

CHAPTER 5

JOHN CURRY

❧

Master of Classical Expression

J ohn, the youngest of three boys, was born to Rita and Joseph Curry in suburban Birmingham, England, on September 9, 1949. Early in his life he developed a passion for theater, encouraged by his father, a self-employed precision engineer, who often took him to see musical comedies. John constructed a model theater and played out stories in miniature, concocting the scenery, costumes, and lighting.

What John truly wanted to do, though, was dance, something that his father expressly prohibited. In time he transferred his passion to the ice, without ever leaving behind the balletic and dramatic underpinnings.

When John was seven years old and just beginning to take skating lessons with Ken Vickers, his mother nursed her husband and John's brother Andrew, both of whom suffered from tuberculosis, in a part of the gracious family home that was ruled off-limits to the two healthy brothers. At one point, John believed that Andrew had died, but that nobody had thought to tell him about it. Going to the skating rink became a welcome escape from this unnatural house divided, as well as an outlet for John's athleticism and his strong competitive spirit.

When John was sixteen, his father died, leaving the family in fairly dire straits. For his part, John was left with emotional issues that remained unresolved to the end of his life. Not too long afterward, he set out on his own. He eventually found his way to the outskirts of London, where he worked in a small grocery store and then at the National Cash Register Company to pay for his living quarters and his lessons with the great Swiss master of school figures, Arnold Gerschwiler.

In 1970, John won the first of six British titles. He worked with a number of gifted coaches in England and America, before landing on the doorstep of Carlo and Christa Fassi in Denver, Colorado. Through the kindness of a sponsor, American businessman Ed Mosler, he was able to afford the intensive work at the Colorado Ice Arena that would make him Olympic champion in 1976. His *Don Quixote* long program* in Innsbruck set the standard of pure artistry for years to come.

After he won the 1976 Worlds in Gothenburg, John set out to truly meld dance and skating through a variety of ground-breaking ventures, most notably his own repertory ensembles of highly trained skaters who applied the basics of the dance class to ice and worked with leading dance choreographers. One of John's great contributions was assembling talented people without thought to their amateur résumés. Well-known and "no-name" skaters alike profited from his work methods and pioneering approach. John's companies performed on Broadway, at the Metropolitan Opera House, and at the Royal Albert Hall. His best-remembered solo tour de force remains Debussy's *L'Après-midi d'un Faune*, inspired by the classic Nijinsky interpretation.

John's final career as a stage actor was cut tragically short by illness and ultimately by his death in 1994 from an AIDS-related heart attack.

---

* Over the years, the ISU has repeatedly revised the nomenclature for free-skating routines. To reduce confusion, we will consistently use the general terms *short program* and *long program*.

✎✎✎✎✎✎

J ohn Curry was the most important historical skater whom I knew well. However, it is both difficult and unpleasant for me to write about him, because he was also the only skater I ever knew personally whom I ultimately disliked.

I first laid eyes on John at the 1972 Olympic Games in Sapporo. He was the solitary skater at the practice session before mine. (He didn't like to practice with other people watching.) I noticed that his figure was lean and trim, in some ways more suitable to classical ballet than to figure skating. On this particular occasion, he wore a long woolen toque with a gigantic pompom on the end.

That hat struck me as a strange fashion statement. At the Olympics, people with influence always scrutinized the talent, especially the newest competitors. I was sure that the pompom toque would raise establishment eyebrows.

It seems ridiculous to add this tidbit as well, but I realized when John performed his long program that his hair was long enough to make a ponytail. In 1972, that was not at all acceptable to skating judges. Perhaps John's obliviousness to establishment mores contributed to his greatness.

John's personal life had already achieved a certain maturity, although the facts were not common knowledge. Even as early as February 1972, when he was just twenty-two years old, I knew him to live intimately with a much older man. That same-sex cohabitation, I thought, bordered on the scandalous. John's homosexuality and the details of his private life are not appropriate literary fodder, except to the extent that his forbidden lifestyle and sexual partners influenced his skating career and his interactions with members of the figure-skating world.

Neither John nor I did well at our first Olympics. I placed ninth, while he finished eleventh. Ondrej Nepela, Sergei Chetverukhin from the U.S.S.R., and Patrick Péra of France were the medalists that year. But at the Calgary Worlds following those Games, we both moved dramatically up the ladder.* It was after Calgary that we both realized, consciously or unconsciously, that we were two hungry competitors, both chasing after the same medals.

My move up the ladder in Calgary was more dramatic than John's. As the eleventh-place finisher in school figures, I won the free-skating competition and catapulted into fifth position. Perhaps in the back of John's mind was the phrase "slow and steady wins the race." At the time I certainly was very much the hare, and John was much more the tortoise.

John and I were different yet the same. Certainly neither of us was the boy next door. Both of us were interested in the fine arts beyond the figure-skating world, and were convinced that skating was more an art than a sport. Both of us laughed at ourselves, yet we were both absolutely convinced about our destinies. Unfortunately, we wanted the same thing, and two people can never win the same Olympic gold medal. (At least, that was the rule until the pairs event at the 2002 Olympics in Salt Lake City, Utah.) Nevertheless, we were genuinely friendly in those early days. We looked forward to seeing one another at the various international exhibitions and competitions.

John embraced classical dance as his number-one influence. All his movements seemed to have been transported from the dance floor to the ice. He was a refined skater with an elegance seldom seen in males, yet, on an emotional level, I found his performances as cold as an iceberg.

I was the antithesis of the classical skater. Unlike John, I was not trained in dance. What I offered, in direct contrast to John, was individuality and originality fueled by passion. During our heydays as amateurs, figure skating was in the throes of athletic and artistic change. John was the prime European exponent of that metamorphosis, and I believe that I was its prime exponent in North America.

Some eighteen months to two years before the 1976 Olympics, I received a telephone call from Carlo Fassi, inviting me to train without

---

* Toller moved up from eleventh place in 1971 to fifth in 1972. John moved up from fourteenth to ninth.

cost. I would receive free lessons, ice time, and even my own car, if I left Toronto and my coach, Ellen Burka, to defect to Colorado. All of us with Olympic dreams were looking for the right vehicle to allow us to realize them, but as tempting as Carlo's offer was, my loyalty remained with Ellen, both as a friend and as a coach. I turned down Carlo's invitation. A month later, I heard that John Curry, my primary competitor, had gone to Denver to train under Carlo and his wife, Christa.

By the time the 1975 Colorado Springs Worlds arrived, John had undergone a disposition makeover. He refused to speak to or acknowledge any of his competitors. Even "good morning" was no longer in his repertoire. As I look back, I realize that this tactic was highly effective and quite devastating to me on a psychological level. I had always thought that competitors were competitors on the ice, but friends could still be friends.

Elva Oglanby cited John's excuse in *Black Ice: The Life and Death of John Curry*:

> Carlo had made me promise that I would avoid my fellow-skaters as much as possible so that I could concentrate fully on my own performance. This particularly bothered Toller, because we had become friends. I had been so impressed by his *Pagliacci* programme in Munich that I had started a correspondence with him, and he had been looking forward to spending time with me. But his flamboyant style and his avant-garde approach had the power to unnerve me – it's difficult to explain why, but for some reason it undermined my confidence and made me doubt my own direction. So I stayed in my own home and spoke to no one except the Fassis.

That situation continued through the Olympics in Innsbruck and beyond.

Because of John's ballet connections, he always wore refined costumes that were understated in an exotic way. For both the short and the long programs, his Olympic costume in Innsbruck was as plain as it could be. He wore a beige, wide-collared, blouse-like shirt under a simple black jumpsuit, with a tiny leather belt encircling his slender waist, a waist that piqued his inordinate vanity.

Like all competitors who are divinely ordained to win gold medals, John sensed that his moment had arrived, and he rode a tidal wave to glory. With his *Don Quixote* long program, he earned fifteen marks of 5.9. (I received five of them, compared to Vladimir Kovalev's one 5.9 from the Soviet judge.)

Standing on that Innsbruck podium, a metal platform topped with strange, round acrylic tubs carpeted in turquoise, John was but six inches higher than I, yet he could have been at the summit of Mount Kilimanjaro. He had achieved, in the most heroic way, what I had failed to accomplish. I don't believe that he congratulated either Vladimir, the silver medalist, or me, in the bronze-medal position.

After his triumph in Innsbruck, John's character underwent a further metamorphosis. Of all the people described in this book, he had the deepest and most multifaceted character. He was the one person within the skating world who was entirely different from the millions of likeable and kind people who existed under the figure-skating umbrella. In his latter years, I don't believe that John enjoyed anyone's company. His least favorite person was himself, and, during his bouts of self-loathing, he punished the members of his inner circle. He flew into rages and sank into depressions, jeopardizing his projects.

After the men's Olympic event concluded, John confided some of his inner torment, in particular the loneliness of his secret homosexual existence, to a young British journalist whom he took for a kindred spirit. The morning after their quiet chat over a bottle of wine in the hotel bar, a newspaper headline screamed what John had worked so hard to hide. He was devastated.

With John's telephone ringing off the hook with calls from other news outlets, Carlo Fassi called a half-hour press conference, so that John could explain the situation in a controlled and dignified manner and perhaps douse some of the raging fires. It was only after the press conference that John was finally able to sit down with his mother to tell her what he had most feared revealing to his own family.

Shock waves coursed through the figure-skating world. For various reasons, Carlo did not want his student to compete at the forthcoming Worlds in Gothenburg, and John reluctantly agreed. Back at home in England, though, he had time for reflection and realized that some unfinished business remained on his agenda. He telephoned Carlo at the pre-Worlds training site and announced that he would arrive the next day. Carlo was horrified, and not without reason. During the weeks off the ice, John had lost his training edge. In Gothenburg, journalists dogged his footsteps and even planted bugs at the practice-rink barrier where John and Carlo worked.

All things considered, I should have won that competition. Going in, I enjoyed a number of advantages over John. In a nutshell, however, once more I did not win. Again John did. Winner and loser, that event marked the end of our amateur careers.

John and I both went on, during the next year, to assemble groups of skaters and create our own shows. For John, it was The Theatre of Skating and then several other ventures. For me, it was Toller Cranston's The Ice Show. After the eventual premature demise of my show (more about that later), with my personal and professional life lying in tattered ribbons around my feet, I decided that my only remaining option was to perform with Holiday on Ice in Europe. Its casts included the dregs of show business, right down to trained bears and skating chimpanzees. Readers of my book *Zero Tollerance* will recall just how strained was my relationship with the monkeys.

One day, while traveling in a frigid train from Dortmund, Germany, to Cologne with Holiday on Ice – how clearly I remember this – I happened to read in *Time* magazine about John's opening at the Metropolitan Opera House. I experienced a flashback to my lonely moment on the Olympic podium in Innsbruck. Years later, John and I were still a million miles apart: geographically, artistically, and financially.

Usually, when competitive skaters have shared common experiences like the Olympic Games or Worlds, there is a common bond that takes hold after the event, once everyone has turned professional. The past is forgotten. That was not at all true of my evolving (or devolving)

relationship with John Curry. I'm convinced that the more often we
ended up on the same bill, the more he came to dislike me and the more
I reciprocated with indifference.

The silly thing is that, no matter what image I aspired to project –
international skating star, multifaceted artist, brainy intellectual, or clothes-
horse – John always made me feel inferior. Our few verbal exchanges
over the years bordered on icy politeness, and no matter what John said
to me, I found his words both painful and intimidating.

John had the remarkable ability to make any skater, world-class
or otherwise, feel that John Curry alone possessed the secret to skating.
He was somehow able to persuade other skaters that his simplest basic
edge was superior to and infinitely more valuable than their triple Axels.

In 1980, John was asked to perform an exhibition at the Olympic
Games in Lake Placid. I'm not certain where I was at the time, but I
remember watching the event on television. It rather shocked me,
because John's skating routine, "After All," contained neither a jump nor
a spin. Renowned dance choreographer Twyla Tharp had choreographed
the number, which was rather long.* At the time, I dismissed the performance as an artistic sham.

Many years later I happened to see that program again on videotape. My jaw dropped. Only then did I realize what a splendidly unique
and original skater John was. It had taken many years for his skating
style to germinate in my mind before I could understand and appreciate it.

As an Olympic gold medalist, John enjoyed substantial box-office
appeal. However, many times when we both skated in the same exhibitions, his bad behavior destroyed the experience for me.

In 1981, Dick Button's Candid Productions, founded in 1980 to
produce figure-skating events for television, sent a cast of skaters
to Beijing, China, where a television crew filmed our individual skating
performances for Chinese audiences, as well as our sightseeing experiences,

---

* Twyla Tharp, one of America's premier choreographers of contemporary dance, created
"After All" in 1976, to Albinoni's *Trumpet Concerto in B flat*. John first performed it
at SuperSkates at Madison Square Garden and in Cambridge, England, with his Theatre
of Skating.

and turned the material into a documentary that appeared on HBO as "International Skating from Peking."

Going to China at that time was a rare privilege. We were one of the first Western contingents (in any art or sport) to do so. All of us found the cultural and historical novelties more than mind-boggling. What could have been one of the greatest experiences of our skating careers was made more memorable, in the most negative way, by John's obnoxious behavior. At least for me, his unpleasantness entirely ruined the trip.

JoJo Starbuck, American pairs champion with Ken Shelley, continued to skate as an individual performer after a splendid Ice Capades career with Ken. During her years as special guest star with John's ice shows, she was his partner. The atmosphere in China at times was so thick (it seems humorous now in retrospect) that, on a particular bus ride to the Great Wall, John used JoJo as his go-between. He refused to address any of the rest of us in person.

On another occasion, at an early version of Dick Button's World Professional Figure Skating Championships in Landover, John and I participated together in a team competition. It was difficult and uncomfortable for me to try to whip up team spirit when John, as a member of my team, obviously didn't want to be there, didn't seem to like any of us, and refused to speak to his fellow competitors. Directly before the competition, although the fact was not publicized, John refused point-blank to wear the assigned team uniform and threatened to flee to the airport. Somehow a deal was struck. John consented to wear *part* of the uniform.

Dick Button, with the most sterling credentials of any male skater, past or present, displayed a personal weakness in such circumstances. Rather than acting with authority, he consistently caved in to every one of John's silly little demands.

A number of Olympic skaters – JoJo Starbuck, Ken Shelley, Peggy Fleming, John, and I – were asked to perform at a special exhibition in La Jolla, California, sometime during the same era. One pleasant surprise awaited me in La Jolla. A former colleague and world medalist whom I had not seen for many years taught figure skating at that ice center. It was such a pleasure to see Julie Lynn Holmes, to catch up on gossip, and to reminisce about our mutual skating experiences.

The pleasure of that reunion quickly evaporated when John informed the club professional, Bruce Hyland, a Canadian and a good friend of mine, that he did not wish to share practice ice with me. He announced to one and all that his demands must be met, because he did not "have to" skate the exhibition otherwise. Bruce replied in a cold and deliberate voice, "Yes, John, you *don't* have to skate here." That was the one and only time I ever heard anyone stand up to John Curry. Both John and I did practice and perform on the same ice, but the acid in my stomach virtually corroded what would have been a pleasant exhibition.

Once, at a professional competition, it seemed that every conversational topic created tension between John and me. The one and only civilized discussion that we held centered on a shared passion. The common denominator that bound us in peace was our extreme admiration for Janet Lynn. When Janet began a run-through of her competitive program, we instantly and compulsively expressed our awe. At the end of Janet's routine, we agreed that figure skating had never produced, and never would produce in the future, an athlete with such sensitivity and quality. John and I then resumed our hostile silence.

In 1984, John made a great splash at the Metropolitan Opera House with a tongue-in-cheek tango number, "Tango Tango," that he skated with JoJo Starbuck. JoJo was a fabulous performer and usually stole the show, but at that time she was experiencing the extreme pain that comes at the end of a failed marriage. She and the famous American football icon Terry Bradshaw were heading toward divorce. JoJo spent much of her practice time sobbing into the telephone, presumably to Bradshaw.

In the middle of an emotional telephone call, a television crew asked JoJo to perform the tango with John for the camera. The second she started the number, her ardent professionalism kicked in. She performed meticulously and passionately. Her metamorphosis from grieving young woman to slick, savvy professional had taken place in seconds. I always remembered that lesson, and it influenced my future professional career.

Some memories are painful, yet they shouldn't be repressed forever. There are lessons to be learned. Elva Oglanby was a housewife from Vancouver, B.C., who became my personal manager and a shareholder in my ice show. I barely survived that shipwreck (as detailed in my book *Zero Tollerance*). Elva then went on to manage Robin Cousins's Electric Ice, which eventually ended like Toller Cranston's The Ice Show.

There was one curious moment during a 1984 Pro Skate event, a professional competition that Elva co-produced with David Spungen. John, Robin, and I were among the performers at Madison Square Garden in New York. My show and Robin's were already history, and Elva had gone on to involve herself in a major way with John Curry's repertory company.

During the intermission of that endless competition (I believe that it went on for four-and-one-half hours), John was given an award that Elva, his manager, had specially created for him. She pronounced him "Skater of the Year." In his acceptance speech, John dedicated the award to his dearest and most loyal friend, Elva Oglanby.

When Robin and I watched that incestuous spectacle together, the public meeting of the mutual admiration society, we shared one of the heartiest laughs of our lives. What situation could be more absurd? We agreed, between chuckles, that it was just a matter of time until John became another of Elva's casualties.

At the end of the run of my Broadway show, I had engaged a lawyer with the encouraging name Stanley Plesent to help me extricate myself from Elva. Although he was unable to do so, in the process he became an Elva Oglanby expert. Irony of all ironies, when John Curry needed legal help to extricate himself from Elva's grasp, he happened by chance to choose the same New York lawyer, Stanley Plesent.

I had tearfully entered Stanley's office to explain the macabre situation in which I found myself. When John, nearly a decade later, entered Stanley's office teary-eyed and dropped the name Elva Oglanby, Stanley nearly fell off his chair. He gasped at John, "Not Elva Oglanby! Surely not the Elva Oglanby who was with Toller Cranston and Robin Cousins?"

I heard that, because of prior contractual arrangements, John was required to give Elva a percentage of his salary for all future skating performances. It is my belief that, when he eventually decided never to perform upon ice again, one of his motivations was to avoid giving Elva one cent of his paycheck.

During the late 1980s, a nasty cloud began to waft over the figure-skating world. That horrible black cloud was the fear of AIDS. Because certain well-known skaters had already fallen victim to the horrible disease, many other major players came under scrutiny. Had the AIDS virus infected them as well?

Rumors began to swirl around John Curry. His initial response was to deny them, in part because he wanted to continue to work in the United States. If his condition were to be discovered, he would be deported. Eventually he would tell the London *Sunday Mail* that he had first heard about the disease in 1986 and even then hadn't fully understood its lethal nature. That may or may not have been the truth. As early as 1985, two of his recent lovers had tested HIV-positive; another had already died. John was diagnosed HIV-positive in December 1987 and developed symptoms of AIDS in 1991.

A number of AIDS benefits took place in the 1990s. Important New York City skaters mounted one of the earliest of those events in the historical New York Armory. Many well-known skaters performed in that show. Once again, John and I locked antlers.

John had always been immensely thin and somewhat frail in appearance, but, at that particular benefit, he did not look at all well. Our one and only conversation took place in the men's dressing room, where our close proximity forced him to say hello. After his terse greeting, I responded, "Well, hello, John. Speaking to me this decade, are you?" That was all that either of us said.

A year or two later, I was invited to skate in a New Year's Day television show in Garmisch-Partenkirchen. Once again John and I bumped into each other. John usually refused to mingle with the other skaters, customarily surrounding himself with a male entourage.

The running order of the show was such that John skated directly before I did. I had been performing a great deal, so my skating ability and physical conditioning were at a high level at the moment. I suspect that John had not been practicing much, and his skating routine contained one solitary single jump.

When John finished his number, he came backstage through the curtain, breathless and close to fainting from exhaustion. Had I known that he was ill from AIDS, I wouldn't have made the remark that I did as I passed him and went out onto the ice to perform my own number. With John gasping for air, I said, "That was a lovely single Axel you did." It was a cruel way of damning him with faint praise. Today I regret having made that comment.

In September 1992, John Curry went home to England, essentially to live out his remaining days as peacefully as possible, then to die of AIDS in the bosom of his family. I never saw him again.

In May 1993, however, Robin Cousins staged an AIDS benefit, Skate for Life, at the National Indoor Arena outside Birmingham, England. Moments before I was announced on the ice, I could not help but be cognizant of the fact that, some fifteen miles away, John lay in a hospital, ailing from one of the periodic complications of his condition. As nervous as I was about performing that evening, I decided to secretly dedicate my performance to him.

The announcer of the evening was a famous British gentleman from the BBC, Alan Weeks. As fellow commentators, we had met many times at the Europeans and the Worlds. When he announced my name to the people of Birmingham, his brief introduction changed my outlook. His said, in essence, "Ladies and gentlemen, it gives me great pleasure to present one of the most important skaters in history, as well as a great star."

For some reason, I suddenly felt that the score had been settled. Whatever anxieties and animosities John had provoked in me were instantly exorcised from my soul. The strange and poetic irony of our lives and careers was that we had suddenly changed places. So many years after the Innsbruck Olympics, I could ask myself who really had won and who had lost. I decided at that moment that I had been the lucky one.

John died on April 15, 1994, in Binton, Warwickshire, at the age of forty-four.

A year later, I received a telephone call from his brother in England, asking me for evidence against Elva Oglanby, who had written John's biography, *Black Ice*.

John's mother, Rita, had heard about the book at the 1995 Worlds in Birmingham and had obtained a pre-publication copy from London publisher Victor Gollancz. She objected to some of its content, especially certain material about John's early family life. Under threat of a lawsuit, Gollancz recalled all the copies that had been distributed. Many had already been shipped to reviewers and others.

Meanwhile, Elva maintained that she and John had planned the book for years and had discussed many episodes of his life with just that intent. She had taken notes and kept a diary. Unfazed, she announced her intention to find an American publisher. That didn't happen. The few extant copies of *Black Ice* became collectors' items. Those who were lucky to obtain photocopies, including my co-author, discovered a large measure of reality, liberally seasoned with petty inaccuracies and self-serving truths.

In an interview with the *Manchester Guardian*, I netted front-page headlines with a particularly snappy remark: "I never regretted losing the Olympic gold medal, but I did regret meeting Elva Oglanby."

John was truly a unique contributor to the art of figure skating. To paraphrase the lyrics of Frank Sinatra's song, he did it his way. I can imagine him floating around heaven (accompanied by classical harp music) with all the other skating angels who have left us.

Of all the male skaters I have known during nearly five decades of life in figure skating, no one is more important than John Curry. Yet it took me thirty years to recognize that simple truth.

Publicity Photo, 1996

CHAPTER 6

BEATRIX SCHUBA

⁊⁊

The Queen of Compulsories

B eatrix (Trixi) Schuba, born in Austria in 1950, became the world's foremost practitioner of compulsory figures, under the tutelage of Jutta Seyfert (later Müller) in East Germany. That was a very great advantage, because figures were still heavily weighted in determining an event's outcome. Skaters performed six compulsory figures over a period of two days.

After winning two world titles and the 1972 Olympics in Sapporo, Trixi signed with Ice Follies. In 1974, she joined International Holiday on Ice as the company celebrated its twenty-fifth European anniversary.

⁊⁊⁊⁊⁊⁊

F or every skater, the first world championship in his or her career is memorable, for better or worse. Not unlike our first sexual experience, its details, impressions, emotions, and disappointments etch themselves indelibly in our memories.

53

My first Worlds event was especially memorable for me for many reasons, the least of which was my poor performance both in school figures and free skating. It took place in 1970 in the provincial city of Ljubljana, a city that existed under a Communist pall. My trip to Ljubljana was my introduction to Communism, and I recall that palpable anxiety and nervousness permeated the atmosphere. We from the West fancied ourselves valiant white knights, competing at an outpost of what Ronald Reagan would later call the Evil Empire.

As a new generation of skaters marches into the twenty-first century, the old ways of world championships fade from memory, but it is worth recalling that, as recently as 1970, the school figures accounted for 50 percent of the final points that accumulated to determine championship medals. And in Yugoslavia – it horrified me at the time – we practiced our school figures on outdoor ice rinks. During those intense sessions, we combated rain, hail, and snow. We were forced either to adapt to the conditions or simply disregard them.

By that time in skating history, we North Americans had been spoiled. We wouldn't have considered practicing school figures out of doors in our home countries. We were hothouse flowers, artificially conditioned to the luxury of heated indoor rinks. Therefore we were at a huge disadvantage at competitions where the facilities were less hospitable.

Fortunately for me and for my fellow North American competitors, the actual compulsory-figure event took place indoors in a normal arena that may even have boasted a primitive heating system. I remember walking into the rink on the morning of the women's figures, one day before the men's event, and hanging over the boards to observe some figures that had already been laid down.

One particular figure stood out so dramatically that I remember remarking to my teammate David McGillivray, the Canadian champion, in a nervous and excited voice, "Who the hell did that?" The "who the hell" was Austrian champion Trixi Schuba. Remembering that tracing so many years later, I still stand in awe of it.

School figures are judged upon many criteria, all complicated, vague, and subjective. However, one did not need to be a judge to recognize that the capabilities of the person who had executed that figure were utterly beyond those of any other skater in the competition.

That bracket-change-bracket figure – a large figure eight with an outward-facing turn at the top of each lobe, executed on one foot, then retraced twice on that foot and three times on the other – was two times larger than anybody else's. Its perfect circles betrayed no evidence of tracing. They appeared to have been etched in one single, unwavering line. While mere mortals obviously had executed the other figures that stood beside it on the ice, the superhuman Schuba figure seemed to have been inscribed by a gigantic mechanical compass.

After the women's competition, I was introduced to the young lady who had traced those extraordinary designs. Trixi was a large woman, whose figure was both tall and bulky – just one hair away from chubby. She was blonde, fair-skinned, and intelligent of face, with a friendly, natural smile. It was obvious to me that she exhibited neither overweening ego nor artistic temperament. It's fair to say that Trixi would have been a suitable television spokesperson for dairy products. That's how wholesome she was.

School figures, so necessary and important to a skater's career, inspired acute attacks of nerves in most of us, males in particular. Unlike free skating, that human geometry on ice punished rather than rewarded aggression and courage. Brilliant free skating and the brilliant execution of school figures required antithetical emotional states.

My coach, Ellen Burka, often humiliated me by at least implying that my ineptitude at school figures was the result of a lack of intelligence. It was the general consensus among great coaches that only "intelligent" skaters could perform good figures. If this were true, Trixi Schuba was a veritable skating Einstein. In truth, Trixi was intelligent enough, but certainly no genius.

Decades later, I developed the convenient theory that no truly intelligent person, male or female, would spend five to seven hours daily just going around in circles on the ice. I now believe – and it makes me feel much better – that the great skaters of figures in the world were basically stupid – and if not stupid, then chronically dull.

One other thing was true: the body type requisite for brilliant free skating was the opposite of the body type necessary to a superior school-figure skater.

In the ladies' free-skating competition that followed the compulsory-figure event, there was one outstanding performer, Gabriele Seyfert of East Germany. Gaby, the ten-time East German champion, had won the 1969 world title in Colorado Springs. In free skating, she was in a class by herself, not unlike Katarina Witt – who, incidentally, was taught by Gaby's mother, Jutta Müller.

If Gaby Seyfert had been given the compulsory-figure marks that she deserved in Ljubljana, she would have had no hope of repeating as a gold medalist. However, heavy political support from the Communist judging bloc held her up in the standings. Conversely, if Trixi, although she did win the school-figure event, had been given accurately high marks, she would hardly have needed to free skate in the finals at all. At 50 percent, her compulsory-figure marks would have mathematically secured her victory.

Trixi was not altogether a dud as a free skater. It was clear, notwithstanding her rather painfully lethargic, labored, inartistic, and dull performances, that she possessed authentic talent for jumping. Trixi placed second overall and won the silver medal.

Gaby, who placed first and won again, demonstrated extraordinary athleticism not dissimilar to Tonya Harding's. Unlike Tonya, however, Gaby possessed a star's personality and infinite charisma on the ice.

American promoters lusted to sign Gaby for ice shows and television commercials. However, when the International Skating Union (ISU) tour of top world medalists ended in London, a personal escort whisked Gaby to the plane bound for East Berlin. That was the end of her amateur career, the end of what might have been her professional career, and the end of a life of international travel. The East German government, worried about defection, held her within its national borders, virtually under house arrest, and Gaby wasn't heard from again for some time. She told me years later that she was kept in East Germany until she was past her prime, and performing opportunities were no longer available.

In the cruelest twist of irony, her mother/coach was apparently complicit in that arrangement.

With Gaby Seyfert's forced retirement, Trixi Schuba's major career obstacle vanished, with time to spare before the 1972 Olympic Games in Sapporo. That posed an enormous problem for the figure-skating establishment. There was no doubt that, as a school-figure skater, Trixi was in a class by herself. But because of the archaic scoring system, she prevented great free skaters from winning world medals. She was a lovely young woman, but an exceedingly unpopular choice for Olympic champion.

The judges in Sapporo were hamstrung by the system. Nobody could think of a workable way to get Trixi out of the equation. At the new Mikaho Skating Rink, Trixi executed even more brilliant school figures than in previous years. I remember seeing the finished products etched like the finest Belgian lace on an azure background. The ice had been colored South Pacific blue, great for Trixi but bad for other skaters – and a veritable catastrophe for me. On the blue background, a judge or spectator could see in clear relief every single tracing with all its imperfections.

Both Canadian Karen Magnussen and American Janet Lynn skated rings around Trixi in the free-skating event at the Makomanai Arena. Janet won, performing to Beethoven's "Leonora Overture" from *Fidelio*. One of the judges awarded Janet a perfect 6.0. It was all to no avail.

Attired in a matronly dark-blue dress, Trixi handily won the Olympics with a ploddingly boring program of mostly single jumps. Because of her lead in the figures, she placed first overall on every judge's card. Even a seventh-place finish in the long-program event wasn't enough to pull her down to second place.

It was clear that the global popularity and the very future of figure skating were in jeopardy. It was also clear that the marking system had to change. The weight of the free-skating portion of the competition had to increase.

Of course, the system could not be changed overnight. Trixi built up a lead of 130.8 after the compulsory-figure event at the 1972 Worlds in Calgary, Alberta. That was enough to compensate for a sluggish free skate and her missed double jumps: Lutz and Salchow. Trixi squeaked out her

second world title, to the great disappointment of the Canadian crowd
that supported Karen Magnussen.

Trixi, who understood better than anybody exactly why she was the
Olympic and world champion, seemed to view the situation with a dry
sense of humor. At the Worlds exhibitions in the Stampede Corral, she
performed her famous back loop for a warmly appreciative audience. I
don't believe that anyone had ever before offered a compulsory figure
in exhibition.

The world tour that year traveled throughout North America, appearing in a new city every night. It was exhausting for most of the cast, but
Trixi had only to perform her figure eights, accepting the audience's
respect with grace and getting off the ice as quickly as possible to make
way for the great free skaters.

Trixi Schuba is an extremely important skater in the history of the
sport, not because she contributed to the art of figure skating, but
because by fairly exploiting the rules she made change inevitable.

Winning an Olympic gold medal, no matter how it is done, is a
colossal achievement, one that deserves remembrance and respect. The
skating world at large may have forgotten Trixi, but I have not. If the
scoring system and competition format had not been altered for the 1973
season, and incrementally over the years,[*] the one-of-a-kind Trixi Schuba
could still be a serious contender today.

---

[*] Beginning with the 1972–73 season, figures counted 40 percent and the short program,
worth 20 percent, made its first appearance. In 1975, figures were downgraded again to 30
percent, then altogether banished from international competition after the 1990 Worlds.

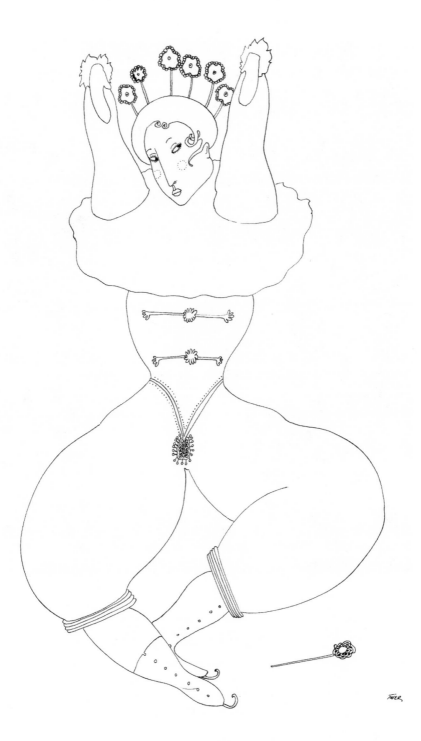

Champions on Ice, Binghampton, New York, 1997

CHAPTER 7

DOROTHY HAMILL

✒

Eyes Wide Shut

D orothy Hamill was born in Chicago, Illinois, on July 26, 1956, but soon moved with her family (parents Carol and Chalmers, brother Sandy, and sister Marcia) to Riverside, Connecticut. She first skated at age eight, on Binny Park Pond in Old Greenwich, wearing hand-me-down skate boots padded with socks to make them fit. Eager to learn to skate backwards, Dorothy convinced her parents to enroll her in weekly group lessons in Rye, New York.

The summer that Dorothy turned ten, she attended skating school at Lake Placid, where she studied with the great Czech coach Otto Gold. There she began to learn compulsory figures, pass United States Figure Skating Association (USFSA) tests, and develop her free-skating moves. Somehow she also became convinced that she was an inartistic skater. She concluded that she should emulate John Misha Petkevich rather than Peggy Fleming.

The following summer, fortune shone on Dorothy again, in the person of Gustave (Gus) Lussi, the father of modern figure skating, a genius at teaching centered spins and solid jumping technique. Throughout her amateur career, Dorothy repeatedly returned to Lussi's tutelage.

Just before winning the 1969 U.S. novice title, Dorothy began training with Sonya and Peter Dunfield, spending summers at the Toronto Cricket Club and winters at the new Sky Rink in New York City. At her first senior U.S. Nationals, she placed second to Janet Lynn in the long program and fifth overall. She was then selected to compete in an international event in Sapporo.

Julie Lynn Holmes's teacher, Carlo Fassi, served as the team coach, taking Dorothy under his wing. By the end of the Sapporo competition, he had expressed interest in working with her full-time.

Dorothy moved in with the Fassi family in Tulsa, Oklahoma. Later they all relocated to Lake Placid, while Carlo waited for the 1972 completion of the Colorado Ice Arena (CIA) in Denver, the rink at which he would serve as one of three limited partners and as manager of the figure-skating program.

Carlo prepared Dorothy for the Olympics, honing her weak school figures. When he realized that she could barely see her tracings, he shipped her home to be fitted for her trademark large-framed eyeglasses.

In the summer, Carlo routinely sent Dorothy back to work at the Cricket Club, this time with Ellen Burka, former Dutch champion, who taught Dorothy the importance of edges, stroking, posture, and musicality.

Just before the 1976 Innsbruck Olympics, Carlo accompanied John Curry to the Europeans at Geneva. Dorothy, abandoned to fend for herself, went back to New York for a last-minute tune-up and pep talk from coach Peter Burrows.

Through her collaborations with world-class teachers, Dorothy ultimately won three U.S. championships, one world title, and the 1976 Olympic gold medal.

As a new professional skater, Dorothy signed a three-year contract with Ice Capades. She starred in television specials, made commercial endorsements, won half a dozen world professional titles, and toured extensively with theater and arena shows like Festival on Ice, The Nutcracker: A Fantasy on Ice, and the Tom Collins Tour of World and Olympic Champions.

In 1982, Dorothy embarked on a short-lived marriage to Dean Paul Martin, son of singer Dean Martin. They divorced after less than two years. Later she married Dr. Kenneth Forsythe, a former Olympic skier for Canada and an orthopedist and sports-injury specialist whom she had encountered in Palm Desert, California, on the golf course and tennis courts. In the late summer of 1989, the couple's daughter, Alexandra, arrived.

In March 1993, Dorothy, Ken, and businessman Ben Tisdale took over the bankrupt Ice Capades. The moribund show had been playing to what a journalist called "tragically small crowds." Dorothy Hamill International retooled the production for a more sophisticated audience. Frozen in Time . . . Cinderella on Ice was an impressive show with high production values. Dorothy served as its producer and director and as the star of one of the two touring companies.

By February 1995, however, Dorothy was forced to sell Ice Capades. The following March, she declared personal bankruptcy, blaming her estranged husband for fiscal mismanagement. She filed for divorce in November 1996.

One of Dorothy's most rewarding collaborations was with John Curry, and later with Curry protégés Tim Murphy and Nathan Birch of the Next Ice Age repertory company. Today she lives in Baltimore, Maryland, where she continues to perform with the ensemble.

ᘒᘓᘒᘓᘒᘓ

D orothy Hamill features prominently in some of my earliest figure-skating memories. During the summer of 1968, I enrolled at the famous training center in Lake Placid, a mecca for skaters from all over the world, many of whom would eventually become champions.

I had been unable to secure a place on the Canadian World Figure Skating Team, and it was becoming painfully obvious to one and all that I probably never would. In the eyes of some observers, I was a has-been at the age of sixteen. It was a pivotal point in my skating career, time to do or die, a period of my life that I described in detail in my book *When Hell Freezes Over, Should I Bring My Skates?*

During that summer, I met Dorothy for the first time. She was a full skating generation younger, so she practiced on the juvenile and intermediate sessions while I trained with my fellow seniors. I found many opportunities to observe her, however, because she seemed to be everywhere, perennially underfoot, like a darling little black spaniel puppy who endeared herself to everyone.

A tiny hurricane swirled around Dorothy, while she remained outwardly tranquil and unaffected, comfortable in the safe eye of the storm. As I look back now, that hurricane metaphor continued to apply – through her amateur glory days, her professional stardom, and two failed marriages. She epitomized precocity with a capital *P*. In her world, she was always the star. Keeping up with her activities was one of the main spectator sports, even in that summer of 1968 in Lake Placid.

World-famous coach Gus Lussi trained Dorothy, in particular in the fine art of spinning, a hallmark of her future years. Had I studied her analytically, I would have detected an Olympic future for the talented young skater.

Dorothy came from a normal, middle-class Connecticut family. Her doting parents seemed to shower all their attentions on her. In my own bleak situation, devoid of parental financial assistance, I began to believe that Lake Placid, summer or winter, was more suited to vacationing than to serious training. No matter the time of day or night, the ice was too crowded for full program run-throughs. When I eventually listened to my inner voice and crept off to Toronto, the tutelage of martinet Ellen Burka taught me in a most painful way what real training was. I learned the agony of full run-throughs.

The Cricket Club was also a major training center of the time, a watering hole for international skaters. Two important teachers from New York, Sonya and Peter Dunfield, came to Toronto the next summer, accompanied by a bevy of talented skaters. Once again, Dorothy and I crossed paths.

She was still very much a novice skater, but I remember being impressed by one particular incident. At the end of the summer's training, there was traditionally a free-skating event that attracted top talent from both the United States and Canada. Dorothy was due to compete on Friday afternoon. On Thursday, she learned how to perform a double Axel. The next day she won the competition, executing two double Axels as though she had been doing them all her life.

Another phenomenal young lady placed second that year. Lynn Nightingale from Ottawa, Ontario, Dorothy's archrival for the next decade, will go down in history, along with Dorothy, as one of the great female jumpers. For what it's worth, Lynn displayed far more natural jumping talent than Dorothy.

Because Dorothy was American and I was Canadian, we generally saw one another only when we appeared in the same events. We next met at the Jimmy Fund cancer benefit at Harvard, where she performed with me and with many other skaters whose careers were on the move.

The Dorothy Hamill whom I encountered in Cambridge was no longer a child. She was a leggy, trim thoroughbred of a young woman, who had matured dramatically. Although she was not yet a world and Olympic competitor, those opportunities seemed to be within her reach. Janet Lynn was the premier female skater at those exhibitions, but everyone became well aware of Dorothy's promise.

After the 1973 season, Janet Lynn retired from amateur skating, and Dorothy easily filled her spot as America's number-one female figure skater. By then, Dorothy had left the Dunfields to train under the stewardship of world-famous coach and skating politician Carlo Fassi, the teacher of three Olympic gold medalists: Peggy Fleming, Robin Cousins, and John Curry.

A dramatic event transpired at the 1974 Munich Worlds. Directly before Dorothy was to skate her long program, German champion Gerti Schanderl preceded her with a primitive-yet-dazzling display of airborne athleticism. As Dorothy removed her skate guards and headed for her spot at center ice, the German audience erupted like an angry Argentinean soccer mob, furious with Gerti's modest marks.

Dorothy, who thought that the crowd's boos and catcalls were directed at her, did not know what to do. She elected to leave the ice and burst into tears in the arms of her coach. Like spectators at the Roman

Coliseum, the audience quickly changed its tone. Realizing that they had sent Dorothy inappropriate and unkind signals, the Schanderl partisans gave the American a thunderous ovation when she ventured near the entrance to the ice to retrieve her skate guards. Encouraged, Dorothy skated out to perform her number.

Fortune had smiled upon Dorothy in the guise of trauma. Her tears had been cathartic. The audience's boos, followed by hearty applause, had exorcised all her nervousness. She went out and skated fabulously, virtually without error, and took home a silver medal. Christine Errath of East Germany won the gold.

In 1975, Colorado Springs hosted the Worlds. Dorothy skated brilliantly again, but lost to an American skater who represented the Netherlands, Dianne de Leeuw. My own showing in Colorado Springs was disappointing. I placed fourth in spite of winning the free-skating gold medal for the second time in my career.

The winter leading up to the 1976 Innsbruck Olympics was a quiet time for many serious competitors. Dorothy came to Toronto to train with my coach, Ellen Burka, who selected Dorothy's free-skating music, short and long, and choreographed her routines.

One week before the U.S. Nationals, Dorothy left Toronto and returned to Carlo Fassi. It had been quite brilliant of Carlo to use Ellen as Dorothy's boot-camp sergeant. When a big competition came around, of course he accompanied Dorothy to the event and accepted all the credit. That was an extremely bitter pill for Ellen to swallow. Dorothy won the 1976 U.S. Nationals and became a major contender for Olympic gold in Innsbruck.

Figure skating then was far more political than it is today, because judges were able to play nasty tricks when they marked the arcane school figures, which were performed away from public scrutiny. Dianne de Leeuw, reigning European and Worlds champion, was Dorothy's number-one rival in Innsbruck. Dorothy was the superior free skater, but Dianne's school figures were of higher quality.

When Dianne executed a good first figure, the U.S. judge held up a mediocre mark. That signaled to her European colleagues that America did not want de Leeuw to become the Olympic champion. Dianne's house of cards began to fall.

Once the free skating had taken place, it was clear that Dorothy deserved the gold medal that she received. Americans who watched the event on television will remember her simple green dress and her naive charm. An ABC "Up-Close-and-Personal" segment revealed the fascinating and empathy-generating news that the champion often vomited with nerves before performing. Dorothy further endeared herself to the public by squinting nearsightedly to see her marks on the scoreboard. It was all quite heartwarming, and Dorothy played her ingenue role to the hilt.

As far as I know, Dorothy's amateur career was a fairy tale, free of any setbacks or tragedies that might have impeded her from achieving her golden destiny. My own career simultaneously spiraled downward in a bronze haze. I was going down, and Dorothy was going up. We were passing like two elevators bound for opposite levels. At least that's what I thought.

Dorothy next entered the 1976 Worlds in Gothenburg, winning her one and only world title. Although she was still a teenager, her life was about to change dramatically: from black to white, from the anonymity of the Cricket Club and the CIA to the glare of the spotlight. She became professional and signed with a top Hollywood agent, Jerry Weintraub, who represented John Denver and Neil Diamond.

Some Olympic medals, even if they're golden, are commercially worthless. Others, particularly within U.S. borders, are worth their weight in gold. Dorothy's gold medal was priceless. She was a beautiful young American girl with a million-dollar smile, practicing a premier sport that had widespread entertainment value. The American ice shows hungered for a major Olympic star, and Dorothy was their ticket to ride. Her contract with Ice Capades included many perks and a fabulous weekly salary. She had hit pay dirt.

I remember watching Dorothy's much-publicized professional debut on Ice Capades' opening night. If the Pope had skated, he wouldn't have received more publicity than Dorothy did. Her debut was unimpressive, however, from a skater's viewpoint. The Olympic champion fell upon her golden derrière.

The people around Dorothy, as they always had, coddled and protected her. They told her that, in spite of the fall, she had been fabulous, just fabulous. Thus she began her long glide down the slope to Fantasyland. She entered stardom's glass bubble. Glitter, fame, and wealth became her prison.

Generally speaking, men in ice shows did not earn as much as the featured women. However, I, too, skating in Europe, earned a healthy salary at the time. The main difference between Dorothy and me was that she was an entertainer and I was an artist.

I had little contact with Dorothy during those early years after the Olympics. I knew, however, that as the principal Ice Capades star, she had become a major celebrity and was living *la vie en rose*. All those in the employ of Ice Capades would surely have accommodated her every whim. Limousines, suites in first-class hotels, fabulous food, and an entourage of journalists would have contributed to her acceptance of fantasy as reality. Yes, she was a high-priced star, but her reality wasn't real – not in the way that most people experience life.

Like Sonja Henie, Dorothy made a practice of traveling with a splendid array of valuable jewelry: diamonds, rubies, and pearls. Once, during her Ice Capades days, she made the national news when a thief entered her San Francisco hotel suite and made off with her jewelry. She was convinced that it had been an in-house job, probably perpetrated by the chambermaid, but the facts were never established. The net worth of the jewels ran to hundreds of thousands of dollars. I believe that Dorothy's insurance company declined to reimburse her for her loss. Like so many privately owned valuables, the jewels had been too expensive to insure.

Dorothy married a young man who was accustomed to movie stars and the lifestyles of the rich and famous. I first met Dean Paul Martin, son of the American singer and actor Dean Martin, at one of Dick Button's Landover competitions. Dean Paul was young, blond, handsome, and athletic. He topped his slick, charismatic Hollywood persona with a healthy dollop of American charm. In my mind, he possessed star quality, yet he was not a star. Tragically for his own ego, he was the son of a real-life movie star and the husband of America's sweetheart. After less than two years, the marriage dissolved.

Dorothy later told me that the breakup had come to her like a bolt from the blue. One day Dean Paul had returned to their Los Angeles residence and had simply announced his intention to seek a divorce. I'm certainly no expert on Dorothy Hamill's personal life, but if that is indeed what happened, then Dorothy must not have grasped the true status of her marriage. This is not a criticism, merely an observation.

When people become stars in any media, it is extremely difficult for them to keep their feet squarely on the ground. Few within their circles treat them normally. Their heady, intoxicating situations are divorced from the real world. Dorothy could not have prevented her descent into fantasy, for the simple reason that she would have been completely unaware of it.

In the professional competitions produced by Candid Productions, there were many important skaters, among them world and Olympic champions. And then there was Dorothy Hamill. She didn't ride on the chartered bus with her old skating friends, preferring to be chauffeured in enormous limousines. She engendered envy among her peers by demanding and receiving a hefty appearance fee above and beyond the $25,000 winner's pot.

Dorothy certainly profited from great leverage. The host broadcaster, NBC-TV, insisted that Dorothy be among the competitors. No Dorothy, no television show. Besides, Dorothy's phenomenally aggressive agent of the moment, Michael Rosenberg, negotiated fat contracts.

Judges who, it seemed to me, possessed no real understanding of the art of figure skating evaluated Dorothy's professional performances over the years. At a pro competition in Paris, I challenged one of the judges, a former world champion, to explain the first-place marks she had given Dorothy. The second-place finisher was a former world champion from Switzerland, Denise Biellmann, whose technical program had contained every triple jump in the book. Dorothy had offered a solitary double flip. The judge vehemently defended her marks, stating that Dorothy's superior edges had outweighed her obvious lack of difficult jumps. Granting

Dorothy superior edges, any serious person with skating knowledge would know that remark was preposterous.

Dorothy's many professional victories were based less on her skating skills than on her reputation. I must note that she was a fine skater with splendid qualities and great charisma, but charisma is a poor substitute for jumping skill. Shortly after the 1976 Olympics, Dorothy shelved her double Axel altogether. The double Axel is an important competitive jump, especially for women.

Once, prior to a Landover World Professional Figure Skating event, Dorothy was asked to perform a small portion of her number under spotlights for a promotional television commercial. Michael Rosenberg turned to me and said, "Look at her out there. She is the epitome of magic – just like you, Toller." I said nothing. Later I told a fellow competitor that the difference between my magic and Dorothy's was that my magic jumped and hers didn't. Once again, her reality was built on falsehoods. None of her janissaries told her the truth.

Ellen Burka pointed out to me that in one of Dorothy's television specials, a single Axel had been electronically altered to appear to be a double. Even a jump could be artificial.

To her great credit, Dorothy did hone her star quality to a fine degree. In all the years that I knew her, I never heard a harsh or critical word slip from her lips. Dorothy was essentially an East Coast woman. She was always impeccably dressed and made up. Her taste in clothes was understated, the epitome of refinement, like the preferences of a blue-blooded private-school girl. She became the perennial, quintessential American ideal, right down to the wedge hairstyle that millions of young American women copied.

That is why Dorothy received an outpouring of public sympathy when her ex-husband, Dean Paul Martin, was killed in an airplane crash. Apparently he had piloted his private plane into a mountain, whether by accident or with suicidal intentions. My own assumption was that he had taken his own life.

During the ensuing years, Dorothy remarried. That was probably her greatest mistake and worst misfortune. Her new husband was a Canadian doctor, Ken Forsythe, who had received his medical education at Mexico's Guadalajara University, which, incidentally, is neither Harvard nor Cornell. He was an orthopedist without a practice, and he struck me as a Svengali figure in Dorothy's life. In fact, it seemed to all Dorothy's friends that Ken wielded undue influence over her career.

Dorothy eventually abandoned Michael Rosenberg, then fell out publicly with International Management Group, her new agency. In October 1991, she would file a legal complaint against IMG, and the matter ended in messy litigation. Ken Forsythe became Dorothy's newest agent.

In 1988, Canadian champion Brian Pockar asked Dorothy, along with many other renowned skaters, to perform in the closing ceremonies that he had been hired to choreograph for the Olympic Games in his native Calgary. At the beginning of those Games, Dorothy and I met at a public reception. She happened to mention that Ken had just given her a stunning black mink coat, presenting himself with a fur coat as well. In essence, her husband had demonstrated his largesse and affection, but his generosity had been directly linked to Dorothy's own bank account.

The organizers of the closing ceremonies sequestered all the special performers, including world-famous skaters and popular singer k.d. lang, in a holding area. We then entered the outdoor stadium through a heavily guarded subterranean passage. The performances were broadcast live worldwide. When our moment came, we skaters made our way onto the ice surface. More than a few eyebrows arched when Ken Forsythe ran down the corridor, despite the admonitions of the security guards, and threw himself in front of one of the television cameras, in a blatant act of self-promotion. Either Dorothy was unaware of the gaffe or did not understand the negative impact that such an audacious and inappropriate act exerted on all her fellow skaters.

Despite the rocky beginning, something wonderful happened at the end of those closing ceremonies that any spectator or performer who was there will remember for the rest of his or her life. The entire Calgary audience descended onto the stage and the stadium ice surface. It was a benevolent riot: innocent, enthusiastic, and emotional. For the star skaters and VIPs, the situation presented a major problem: how to safely extricate ourselves from the confusion. Vans arrived, and I happened to wind up in the same vehicle as Dorothy, Ken, the Protopopovs, and Karen Magnussen.

The fabulous success of the 1988 Olympics was due largely to the one thousand volunteers who had helped with various organizational functions. One particular volunteer, who had been invaluable to the VIPs, knocked on the window of our van and begged to hitch a ride. Ken Forsythe stunned the other occupants of the van by forbidding the driver to open his door to the volunteer (whom we all knew well). Ken stated, "We cannot have people like that traveling with people like us." We then rode to Dorothy and Ken's hotel, the Westin, in frozen silence. None of us knew what to say or do, yet we were all appalled by Ken's rudeness. Dorothy did not react.

Dorothy was the only important void in the cast of stars at the 1992 AIDS benefit Skate the Dream in Toronto's Varsity Arena. She had agreed to participate, and right up until the last minute, creator and co-producer Brian Orser expected her to appear. He even arranged a private plane to fly her to and from Toronto. The day before the show, with all arrangements set, Dorothy sent a telegram apologizing for her inability to perform. Brian was livid.

However legitimate her excuse may have been, Dorothy was unable to open her eyes to the magnitude of the event and to the importance of demonstrating solidarity with figure skating's royal family. World and Olympic champions gave of themselves freely, without remuneration, for a cause that had been espoused by our colleague and friend Robert McCall before his death from AIDS. I'm certain that, as she floated, cushioned, in her giant isolation chamber, Dorothy was never challenged face to face about her decision to cancel the appearance.

During my second-to-last year with Stars on Ice, I observed Dorothy practically on a daily basis. Before the days when the Stars on Ice cast flew by private plane, we traveled from city to city, from show to show, in a private bus that was specially equipped with sleeping bunks and even a private lounge in the rear. Although no one spelled out the rules for me, the private lounge seemed to belong exclusively to Dorothy, to her baby daughter, Alexandra, and to Alexandra's nanny. Yes, there was great rapport among all of us in the cast, including Dorothy. Yet she existed in a world apart that was simultaneously close to and removed from the rest of us. She was friendly and charming but never particularly personal.

I was once invited to skate in a Christmas exhibition in Palm Desert. It was, in essence, "Dorothy Hamill and Friends." I arrived without luggage at the beginning of the first night's performance. Because of snowstorms and the consequent delays, I had spent eleven hours in transit. Ken Forsythe advised me that, either I would skate the show in street clothes or I would not be paid. I chose to wait for my music and costumes, and I performed the following day. In due time, I was paid for one show, not two.

In the lobby near our dressing rooms, there was an enormous bouquet of exotic plants and flowers, all of them somehow furry, prickly, or fuzzy. The card, ostentatiously displayed, was imprinted, "Good luck on opening night, Dorothy. Love, Ken." Once again, Ken had attempted to overwhelm us with a show of generosity. I found the juxtaposition of those costly flowers and my own underpaid situation quite ironic.

Near the end of the Hamill-Forsythe marriage, there were a number of notable financial imbroglios.

Ice Capades and similar shows were gigantic extravaganzas that made fortunes in the 1950s, 1960s, and 1970s. Then that particular entertainment concept ceased to make sense to potential customers, so the carrying costs of such shows became too great to bear. The original Ice Capades company declared bankruptcy. Yet, with the aid of a wealthy skating fan from Alaska, Dorothy bought and resurrected the company and renamed it Dorothy Hamill's Ice Capades. With her husband as the general manager, Dorothy created a new show. Her intentions were unassailable.

The show's solitary theme was the fairy tale *Cinderella*. Certain classic fairy tales, familiar through the generations, unfortunately have been replaced in the hearts and minds of today's youth by American cultural icons like the Smurfs, the Simpsons, and worse. From all reports, the show was quite good, set to an original score composed by Michael Conway Baker and performed by a strong ensemble cast. Yet it was doomed to fail miserably. The writing was on the wall. Dorothy, as the premier star and owner, seemed to wear blinders. The show abruptly closed after a year, drowning in a sea of red ink.

The *coup de grâce*, I imagine, was Dorothy and Ken's failed investment in the Dorothy Hamill Skating Centres, including the rink at the Clackamas Town Center in suburban Portland, Oregon, where Tonya Harding infamously skated.

So Dorothy's idyllic career, with so many emotional highs, ground to a halt. She declared personal bankruptcy in March 1996 and won an acrimonious divorce from Ken Forsythe.

At the risk of being seen to pile on, I offer one further cautionary anecdote. After an amateur career ends, there is often an estrangement between champion and coach. Certainly the great mover, shaker, and dealmaker Carlo Fassi lusted after a portion of Dorothy's future fortunes. I do not know the details of their relationship, but their personal and professional rift became common knowledge.

When Carlo died at the 1997 Worlds in Lausanne, his friends and colleagues celebrated his life at a memorial service in the Olympic Museum. Both Peggy Fleming and Robin Cousins spoke with great emotion. At a scholarship benefit performance five months later, given in Carlo's honor in Lake Arrowhead, California, where he had taught, Dorothy once again estranged herself from her fellow skaters. She and she alone demanded a performance fee. Failing to receive it, she declined to perform a routine. Robin, Peggy, Caryn Kadavy, Lisa-Marie Allen, Paul Wylie, and several other great skaters did perform. Dorothy narrated part of the show. That wasn't the same.

Rather than passing judgment in relating these anecdotes, I hope to illustrate something that happens to so many big stars within their private orbits. They are prevented from living in the real world by the bastion of sycophants that surrounds them. I know this because I was a player in a similar scenario. Just before the blade fell on the executioner's block, I opened my eyes and escaped. Where Dorothy is concerned, I am reminded of the Stanley Kubrick film title *Eyes Wide Shut*.

On the positive side of the ledger, Dorothy's adoring American fans have never flagged in their loyalty. Her star has twinkled above the skating world for several decades. She has given more pleasure and love to the American public than practically any other skater I can name.

Dorothy may not be as rich today as she once was. She may not live in the same luxury. But I suspect that her life as a single mother is far more honest than her previous existence under the spotlight's glare.

Dorothy's career is far from over. She continues to perform, make television commercials, and preside at various functions, ever the American heroine.

Recent publicity photo

CHAPTER 8

ROBIN COUSINS

✍

The Greatest Song-and-Dance Man

R obin Cousins was born in Bristol, England, on August 17, 1957, the third son of a professional soccer prospect and a long-distance swimmer. As a child, he loved both dance and figure skating. He was a particular devotee of televised song and dance and Gene Kelly movies. Fred and Jo Cousins supported Robin and his elder brothers, Nick and Martin, warmly and equally in all that they endeavored.

At the age of fifteen, Robin moved away from home and from the Bristol ice rink to live on his own in London, where the renowned Gladys Hogg coached him at the Queens Ice Skating Club in Queensway, Kensington. Miss Hogg sternly supervised his ascent to ninth in the world, third in Europe. However, England offered little ice time, even to a national champion.

In 1977, following the second of several bouts of knee surgery, Robin moved to Denver, where Carlo and Christa Fassi prepared him to win the men's gold medal at the 1980 Olympics in Lake Placid. During his amateur career, Robin earned five British championships, one European title, three world medals, and three world free-skating titles.

Turning professional after the 1980 Worlds, Robin began a second skating career that lasted longer and brought him more acclaim than the first. He won numerous pro skating titles and headlined Holiday on Ice in Europe.

In 1983, Robin formed his own repertory company and created the stage show Electric Ice, an ensemble production based on the Vangelis score for the film *Chariots of Fire* and Mike Oldfield's "Tubular Bells" from *The Exorcist*. Electric Ice played London's West End before opening in Robin's hometown and touring other British cities. Robin's second stage show, Ice Majesty, offered a more varied repertoire.

Robin choreographed his own solo work. His best-loved routines include "Satan Takes a Holiday," "Blue Serenade," "12th Street Rag," "Busy Being Blue," "Music of the Night," "Satan's Li'l Lamb," "Pie Jesu," and programs set to Rachmaninoff's Piano Concerto No. 2 and Addinsell's *Warsaw Concerto*. A gifted interpreter of any genre, Robin was most lavishly rewarded for pieces with a light, song-and-dance feel.

Ultimately Robin choreographed prolifically for stage, screen, large-scale ice shows, and gymnastics events, as well as for many well-known individual performers, including Denise Biellmann, Barbara Underhill and Paul Martini, Brian Orser, Rosalynn Sumners, Nicole Bobek, Lu Chen, Elizabeth Manley, and Lucinda Ruh.

Adapting to the theatrical boards, Robin appeared as Munkustrap in a touring company of *Cats* and as Dr. Frank N Furter in the West End's *Rocky Horror Show*.

With former ice dancer Nicky Slater, Robin created a production company, Adventure! on Ice, that brought innovative programming like Improv-Ice, a competition featuring improvisation, to American television. Today, Cousins Entertainment Ltd. mounts events on and off the ice in the United States and Europe. Robin's new position as creative director of Holiday on Ice has brought him full circle as an ice professional.

ぐるぐるぐる

R obin Cousins and I, if I may write immodestly (and not for the first time), were two of the three great male skaters of the Golden Age of Figure Skating, a period of prolific experimentation and growth that spanned a decade beginning in the early 1970s. The third member of the triumvirate was John Curry. Together we were the three Cs. Each of us changed the sport of figure skating, but with radically different approaches and temperaments. Robin and I were not really head-to-head competitors during our amateur days, but we were keenly aware of each other without revealing that fact.

The first time that I laid eyes on Robin, at the 1974 Skate Canada international competition in Kitchener, Ontario, a harpoon of fear pierced my body. I sensed a rare talent and genius within him that bespoke a great destiny, a destiny that might threaten my own. I knew that I was looking upon a gravely dangerous potential competitor, armed with technical skill and obvious artistic promise.

The same palpable fear had accosted me in 1970 the first time I saw Terry Kubicka skate, at an ice carnival in southern California. Terry went on to become an American champion, but Robin was destined to be an Olympic gold medalist. His future (he must have been all of sixteen at the time) was already transparently clear to me. Nevertheless, the great star that I was, already the three-time champion of Canada, I pretended that I didn't notice him at all.

At the 1976 Innsbruck Olympics, I fought – and lost – a dramatic battle for the gold medal against British champion John Curry. My coach, Ellen Burka, visited me in my dressing-room cubicle (each competitor was assigned his own private cell) prior to my long program and announced to me that Robin Cousins had skated fabulously but hadn't received the marks that he deserved. If Ellen was trying to pump me up for my own performance, that news flash didn't help my ego. I took solace in the fact that, at least at this competition, the bias implicit in international skating politics would protect me against the younger and less experienced Robin Cousins. That particular type of political advantage no longer exists in figure skating (witness Tara Lipinski's gold-medal triumph in 1998 at her first – and only – Olympics).

Probably one of my cardinal sins or tactical errors (there were so many) was that I was sincerely friendly to and interested in all my fellow competitors. Robin was to be a great friend and colleague for the rest of my skating career. We eventually performed on the same bill at almost every important exhibition in the world.

Although I was truly a full skating generation ahead of Robin, I once managed to sneak away from a three-month Parisian engagement with Holiday on Ice in order to fly to London to perform with him in a charity exhibition in Solihull, England. Robin had just won the men's Olympic title, so the charity exhibition served the additional purpose of celebrating his victory and his British homecoming.

JoJo Starbuck and Ken Shelley were the only other professional skaters on the bill, but the program also featured an up-and-coming British amateur ice-dance team who were talented and quick of foot. Their names were Jayne Torvill and Christopher Dean, but when Robin introduced them to me, he referred to them collectively as "Happy Feet."

I recall being sensitive to how I treated Robin at that event, and I was even more sensitive to how he treated me. Now that he had become the skate god of 1980, I wasn't at all sure that the balance of power hadn't changed. Perhaps I was now expected to kiss the hem of his robe. Hem kissing wasn't my forte. As I soon learned, the balance of power had indeed changed dramatically, but Robin had remained basically the same person whom I had always known – a mixed blessing.

JoJo Starbuck and I confessed to one another that we felt like cast-off Christmas decorations beside the new Olympic gold medalist, but we managed to skate with a certain nobility.

I confess to being outwardly thrilled, but secretly consumed with jealousy, upon hearing about Robin's many illustrious post-Olympic well-wishers. *Billets doux* from movie stars had arrived upon his doorstep. Michael Jackson and Paul and Linda McCartney fit into the scenario somehow, and I believe that Carol Connors and Billy Preston had sent Robin the score of their pop hit "With You I'm Born Again." With the latter revelation, I was surprised when the warm smile didn't fall off my face and splinter onto the floor. Such was my unselfish joy.

Robin is historically important and a great Olympic champion. For the record, however, in my opinion his free-skating performance in Lake Placid did not merit the gold medal, at least from a technical standpoint. I watched the event on television backstage at Holiday on Ice in Paris.

Robin skated his long program first in the last flight. In those days, few skaters performed the entire repertoire of triple jumps: loop, toe loop, flip, Salchow, Lutz, and Axel. Robin didn't attempt either a triple flip or a triple Lutz, and he two-footed his triple loop. The front-runner, Jan Hoffmann of East Germany, countered with a flawless, yet wooden, performance that included both a triple Lutz and a triple flip, rendered with robotic precision.

Apart from Robin's superior artistry, however, this particular Olympic competition turned somewhat on the Machiavellian machinations of Robin's Italian-American coach, Carlo Fassi, who was at the height of his political influence. I'm personally convinced that Fassi had sewn up the competition for Robin before a blade touched the ice, though this is pure conjecture, and no one will ever know the truth now that Carlo is no longer with us. The men's competition preceded the women's, and I will stake my life on my belief that East German Anett Pötzsch's victory over American Linda Fratianne was meant to compensate East Germany for Hoffmann's loss.[*]

However, providence and destiny are stronger forces than the athletic velocity of triple jumps. The best and most deserving skater did win the correct medal at Lake Placid. Robin went on to a glorious and multi-faceted professional career. Jan, following the 1980 Worlds in Dortmund, evaporated from the ranks of active skaters and became one of the great unknowns. Today he is a physician and an international skating judge.

In the early 1980s, promoters like Elva Oglanby, Pro Skate impresario, and Dick Button, progenitor of the World Professional Figure Skating Championships, created an entirely new phenomenon in the

---

[*] This persistent and widely held view cannot be proven, and an analysis of the behavior of specific judges largely debunks it.

entertainment world. The concept consisted of little more than a series of professional skating competitions, not unlike the pro tennis circuit. The idea was perceived as radically new and potentially dangerous, simply because such competitions could theoretically place skaters in an international pecking order. It all seems so ridiculous now, but certain people (notably Peggy Fleming, John Curry, and Dorothy Hamill) truly believed that if a lower-seeded skater beat someone who was higher up the ladder of stardom, the latter's career would vanish on the spot. That perception, which many serious skaters embraced, was a myth created by twisted imaginations.

My first professional competition – and Robin's first as well – possessed some amusing attributes. It was held in one of the world's great skating cities, Montreal, in one of the great temples to hockey and the Ice Capades, the Forum. At the time, I was headlining the Ice Capades at the Colisée in Quebec City. The last day of my run was a Sunday. We had two matinees, but no evening performance. With a private jet waiting on the runway to whisk me off from Quebec to Montreal, I asked in my most diplomatic manner if I could skate both shows but miss the second finale.

Dick Foster, one of the owners of Ice Capades, happened to be in attendance that afternoon. With a demonic smile that would have frightened the Cheshire cat, he replied, "Absolutely not!"

I dozed on the jet in preparation for the evening's technical program, due to start half an hour after my Montreal landing. I did enjoy the surprise that my late arrival created. Everyone, including Robin, had been certain that I had bolted from the competitive lineup.

I was more than warmed up as a result of the two matinees, so, while all the competitive water bugs tore around the ice for six minutes of warm-up, I elected to sit on the boards and chat with friends. I later discovered that my nonchalance had exerted a frightening psychological effect on my competitors.

My performance that evening did not lack fire and brimstone, but I do recall that I committed a technical error. I believe that I finished a convincing third, with the artistic event still to come. Robin won the technical segment handily.

The artistic event the next evening played to a sold-out house. Because Robin was the reigning and recently crowned Olympic champion, most onlookers presumed that he would win hands down. However, as an old show-dog, I knew that a deep reservoir of performing experience should never be underestimated. Although my performance was just about as good as it could be, there were other, more potent, reasons for my astounding near-perfect marks.

First, I'd been doing the identical number in Ice Capades twelve times a week. Second, and arguably more significant, every one of the nine judges was a devoted childhood friend or colleague of mine. One judge, Thom Hayim, my friend of longest standing, managed to pull out a mark of 11.0 when the highest allowed was 10.0. The Montreal audience took it all in good fun and truly understood the competition as a form of entertainment, nothing more. Robin and Carlo, however, instantly lost their sense of humor.

This recollection may seem to be more about me than about Robin, but I mention the Montreal event simply because I take great satisfaction in knowing that I soundly trounced Robin in the first professional competition of his career. Unfortunately I must hasten to add that, although I truly outskated Robin on several occasions over the next decade, that triumph in Montreal would be my one and only victory. Robin went on to earn more than a dozen professional titles.

Robin's background, like my own, was middle-class. He grew up in a duplex on the outskirts of Bristol, an inland port on the River Avon. The Cousinses and the Cranstons were on an economic par, although I believe that my parents were more intellectual than Robin's.

Robin's fundamental nature never changed, no matter how high he climbed on the ladder of fame, wealth, and status. That fact baffled me, because I had left my own suburban character – fittingly, I thought – in the suburbs. This observation is not meant as a criticism. Robin and I had different styles and approaches. I once attended a Hollywood party wearing a white silk Russian peasant shirt, white shantung knee-length bloomers, and a full-length wolf coat that trailed on the ground behind me. I was on a star trip. Robin was not.

Robin quickly became an aristocrat of another sort within the circles of great skating champions. That truth was self-evident every single time he performed on the ice. His impact derived from noble carriage, impeccable lines, fluidity, height, hang time, and exceptional musicality.

Such nobility and grandeur, however, were not evident in the dressing room. I remember a particular SuperSkates exhibition at Madison Square Garden in New York City. I arrived in the men's dressing room to find Robin Cousins, Olympic champion, sitting cross-legged on a bench, sewing sequins onto his costume. That made an interesting contrast to the image of another Olympic champion, Scott Hamilton, who was at that moment just down the hall in a large private dressing room, with two bodyguards on alert.

I often suspected that Robin suffered from a slight sense of insecurity, which struck me as strange. With the huge talent and skating credentials that he possessed, he was guaranteed to be a big fish in any pond.

When insecurity crept into his psyche, he sometimes embellished the truth.

In the manner of John Curry but in an entirely different style, Robin had formed an ensemble company and had created and headlined his own theatrical ice shows. They were great artistic successes. Nonetheless, like my own show and those of John Curry, they sometimes had run into financial and logistical difficulties.

At the 1985 SuperSkates exhibition in New York, Robin told me that he had just come back from a fabulous, brilliant, out-of-this-world run with his own company of skaters in Kuala Lumpur, Malaysia. I was suitably impressed and quite envious until I heard an entirely contradictory report from Robin's friend and production partner, Brian Klavano. Brian revealed that, in the far reaches of hot and humid Kuala Lumpur, Ice Majesty had played to sparse audiences on a melting ice surface laid over a basketball floor. The run had ended in total economic disaster.

I cite this particular recollection simply because I believed then that the royal family of skaters would consistently maintain a high level of honesty among peers. Even among good friends of many years, Robin was sensitive about how others perceived him. Of course, every great skater has had his share of weaknesses and strengths.

Through the countless times that I saw Robin perform, there was a disturbing consistency of quality – disturbing, that is, to my own ego. Robin is unique in my skating memory for never having given a poor performance. With his height, posture, control, and spring, his signature moves were sensational: the slide spiral, the delayed Axel, agile footwork, and inventive spins that rotated in both directions.

Some of the truly great skaters over the years acquired an acute sense of self. That is to say they knew exactly what they had to give and how they could best sell it to their public. Robin had several equals in this department, but nobody was ever his superior. His truest métier was light song and dance *à la* Gene Kelly, exemplified in quick, happy numbers like "Satan Takes a Holiday." Yet he could also weave a lyrical spell.

Despite the quality and artistry of Robin's style, I don't feel that his skating was fundamentally original – not like Gary Beacom's, to cite the best example. Robin was one of the great interpreters. Beyond that, his style was a mirror image of himself and his middle-class British background, an expression of his early love for song and dance.

Robin was one of the very few skating entertainers who wielded a double-edged sword of talent. To his great credit, he was just as at home on-stage in London's West End as a singer, dancer, and actor as he was in the Olympic ice arena.

I judged Robin many times in professional competitions. One performance in Toronto was particularly memorable for me. Robin's technical ability by the early- to mid-1990s had melted down to a double Axel and a back flip (due primarily to bad knees), in direct contrast to the technical fireworks of Paul Wylie and even Brian Orser.

The 1948 Olympic champion from Canada, Barbara Ann Scott King, sat beside me, made her technical evaluation of Robin's performance, and presented a perfect mark of 10.0. I discreetly castigated her, informing her that there was a huge difference between a triple Axel, flawlessly executed, and a double Axel. She admitted that she had blown it. Her marks were too high. Brian Orser placed third in the technical program. He was so furious with the scoring that he almost left the competition before the awards ceremony.

Robin's technical performance was an interesting study in the true art of skating. As a judge, although I didn't agree with Barbara Ann's marks, I knew exactly what had happened to her. Robin had the unique ability to make every jump, spin, and movement, however simple, seem better in quality than everyone else's. The authentic magic of his skating always wove a hypnotic spell over judges and audiences alike. Few were immune to his charms.

Within Robin's extensive fan club, I place myself at the very top of the heap. He is simply a unique property in skating history.

"Bolero," Torvill and Dean: The World Tour, 1986

CHAPTER 9

JAYNE TORVILL

AND CHRISTOPHER DEAN

❧

The Height of English Style

J ayne Torvill and Christopher Dean were both born in Nottingham,
England: Jayne on October 7, 1957, and Chris on July 27, 1958
(the same month and day as Peggy Fleming). Chris was ten when he
received Christmas skates, which he used to learn to ice dance. They
were a gift from his stepmother. His biological mother had left the family,
for reasons he never knew, when Chris was just six. He didn't see her
again for nine years.

Jayne grew up in a simple council house in suburban Nottingham,
surrounded by a close family. She first took to the ice at age eight during
a school outing, wearing ugly brown rental boots. She then began training as a singles skater.

Everyone learned to ice dance in those days, especially in England,
and the public sessions included dance intervals. Chris stuck with
dance, while Jayne went on to pairs skating. In 1972, Jayne and her
partner, Michael Hutchinson, finished second in British Senior Pairs,
while Chris and his partner, Sandra Elson, became champions in British
Primary Dance.

After four years together, Chris and Sandra parted ways. Jayne had lost her partner too and had returned to singles skating. Their parents and Chris's coach, Janet Sawbridge, cooked up the new pairing, and Chris and Jayne thought the idea was a good one. Both rather shy and diffident, they never made a commitment to work together for a specific length of time. However, weeks stretched to months, which stretched to years, and then decades.

Jayne had a job as a clerk with the Norwich Union Insurance Company. Chris was a Nottingham police cadet. For many years, their training hours were set to accommodate those jobs that paid the bills.

In 1978, Janet Sawbridge had a baby and quit teaching, so Chris and Jayne convinced the great coach Betty Callaway to take them on as students. Under Betty, they immediately began doing off-ice work with a dance instructor. When they won their first British title, they took short, unpaid leaves from their jobs to train briefly in Hungary.

All those new experiences proved beneficial. Over the next few years, Chris and Jayne moved up from eleventh in the world to eighth and then to fourth. During the summer of 1980, Betty was invited to teach at the German national training center in Oberstdorf, West Germany. Chris and Jayne's brief taste of that facility whet their appetites, and they would spend months and even years there in the future. At the end of their first summer in Oberstdorf, they quit their civilian jobs permanently, went in search of financial support, and made full-time commitments to skating.

As a result, Chris and Jayne won Worlds each of the next four years and took the gold medal home from the 1984 Olympics.

There were three separate events in international ice-dance competition: three compulsory dances; the Original Set Pattern dance (OSP), with one prescribed rhythm; and the free dance, equivalent to the long program in other disciplines. Among Torvill and Dean's most popular programs were the "Summertime" blues OSP and their "Mack and Mabel" free dance (1982); their rock 'n' roll OSP and "Barnum" free dance (1983); and "The Cape Dance" paso doble OSP (to "Capriccio Espagnol" by Rimsky-Korsakov) followed by their "Bolero" free dance to music by Ravel (1984).

In 1985, Jayne and Chris's company, composed of fifteen professional skaters, opened in Torvill and Dean: The World Tour at the Sydney Entertainment Center and eventually played dates in New Zealand, England, Canada, and the United States.

Chris and Jayne, both married to other partners, have retired from performing.

℘ℶ℘ℶ℘ℶ

S cott Hamilton and I share at least one sentiment in common: we both abjure ice dance in its present-day incarnation. *Abjure* (which means to strongly reject) is too diplomatic a verb. *Detest*, at least for me, is far more precise. The reasons for my abhorrence are quite complicated. Yet no matter how one defines and understands ice dance, today it is 90 degrees away from sport and a full 180 degrees from art.

Why has competitive ice dance become a monstrous artificial hybrid, performed in costumes that exceed bad taste and in makeup and hairstyles that hide lines and impede movement? Because the old dogs in the ISU have never been able to figure out what ice dancing really is and how it should be judged.

Richard Harris, star of the Broadway musical *Camelot*, opened that production by singing the title song that described the kingdom's golden days. Ice dance also enjoyed a period when sport and art merged, creativity reigned, and performers imbued their routines with sincere emotion. A prime exponent of those qualities was the British ice-dance team of Jayne Torvill and Christopher Dean.

Great Britain can claim only five winter Olympic gold medals,[*] compared to thirteen each for the old Soviet Union and the United States, eight for the new Russia, and seven each for Austria and Germany (including East Germany). That makes it all the more surprising that,

---

[*] Besides the three individuals or teams mentioned here, two women won gold medals: Madge Syers in London in 1908 and Jeanette Altwegg in Oslo in 1952.

between 1976 and 1984, England was the spawning ground for three gold medals: John Curry's, Robin Cousins's, and Jayne Torvill and Christopher Dean's. What's more, those particular champions were uniquely important to the history of figure skating.

The first time that I ever saw Jayne and Christopher skate was at a benefit performance directly after the 1980 Lake Placid Olympics. The event, which I mentioned in connection with Robin Cousins, took place in Solihull, England. Their personalities and costuming made no vivid impression upon me, but I do remember their skating performance. The alacrity of their steps indicated that this young couple would enjoy an extremely bright future.

Great talents can spring from just about anywhere. Jayne and Christopher rose like meteors to skating heights that few have ever experienced, and they did so from humble beginnings.

At the 1982 Europeans in Lyon, France, I recall being pushed aside in the press room by British journalist Alexandra Stevenson, who was rushing to see the great Torvill and Dean perform their OSP, the "Summertime" blues. At the time, I had all but forgotten the couple.

That ice-dance competition, unlike today's events, was jammed with spectators. The arena was a beehive, with people hanging over the boards. The Torvill and Dean phenomenon was already in full throttle. Their OSP thrilled the audience. Three judges awarded perfect 6.0 artistic marks, which soon came to be the standard for that couple.

Ludmila Pakhomova and Alexander Gorshkov had turned ice dance into a legitimate art form, but over the years, with future practitioners, their fine Russian art had somehow metamorphosed into a silly cartoon of the original. Christopher and Jayne's style contrasted markedly to the overly melodramatic, artificial Soviet style of their day. Torvill and Dean offered sincere virtuosity. They gave us skating, not false drama.

In contrast to Pakhomova, who had drawn all the attention away from Gorshkov, Christopher Dean, as the male partner, was more fascinating than Jayne Torvill. Jayne was nothing less than the perfect foil for her creative, athletic, and egotistical male counterpart. She complemented him in every way, while remaining in his creative shadow. Her real genius was in not detracting from Christopher's spotlight role, yet she was able to keep up with him in every respect.

Over many years of interviewing Torvill and Dean, participating with them in some competitions, and watching them compete in others, I cannot truthfully say that Jayne and I ever had a serious conversation, although I spoke with Christopher many times. Just as he took the dominant role in partnering Jayne, he also served as their mouthpiece. I suspect that Jayne was painfully shy.

There was genuine synergy between the two, yet never a hint of the sort of sensual or romantic energy that many of the teams who preceded them, or competed against them, exuded. Like Paul and Isabelle Duchesnay, a brother-and-sister team, Christopher and Jayne skated together in a purely platonic relationship, whatever the public liked to imagine and whatever fantasies the press liked to encourage.

Christopher and Jayne's free dance at Lyon netted them their second of three European titles. Many memorable free dances would follow, but the Lyon choreography, adapted to Jerry Herman's *Mack and Mabel*, came as a breath of fresh artistic air after years of suffocation from Soviet melodrama. Torvill and Dean reinvented ice dance and popularized it on the global stage. During their amateur years, ice dance became the most interesting event at figure-skating competitions.

At the 1984 Olympics in Sarajevo, Yugoslavia, Torvill and Dean's win was the most significant and convincing among the four skating disciplines. They stunned the world and rendered the audience spellbound with their most famous and artistically important number, "Bolero." They sustained enormous pressure in doing so, because everyone presumed they would win.

Their popularity was at such a level of fanaticism in Great Britain that Princess Anne attended their free-dance performance, but I was somehow able to resist the enchantment and view their skating objectively. Neither the OSP nor the free dance at Sarajevo was flawless. I thought about the story of the emperor's new clothes, when I realized that spectators and judges alike had lost their ability to see what was obvious to me. Although Torvill and Dean were very good at those

Olympics, they achieved true greatness during many other performances of the same material.

Silver medalists Natalia Bestemianova and Andrei Bukin, at least on a technical level, gave the great performance of the evening. However, the Torvill and Dean victory was a foregone conclusion.

When anyone treads upon virgin creative territory, they may break the rules, or at least bend them. Christopher and Jayne possessed sufficient technical ability to do so with impunity. One controversy hinged on the fact that "Bolero" was based on a single rhythm, contrary to the ISU requirement that ice dancers perform programs containing rhythmic variety. Any judge who was aware of the violation chose simply to rationalize or disregard it.

The second British team after Jayne and Christopher was the duo of Karen Barber and Nicky Slater. Because Britain had now become the dominant force in ice dance, Karen and Nicky were perceived as more proficient than they actually were. Once Torvill and Dean retired, Barber and Slater lost their mystique and came to be viewed as grade-B ice dancers. They competed for one more season. Then Karen joined Christopher and Jayne in their professional show.

As professionals, Christopher and Jayne were as creative as they ever had been as amateurs. They mounted, rehearsed, and performed their first touring show in Australia, a clever strategy. Australia, colonial cousin of Great Britain, had never seen skaters of such quality. It was an untapped market.

Christopher and Jayne hired Canadian skater Gary Beacom as a principal male performer. Before departing for Australia, Gary telephoned me, and we discussed his professional strategy. I have always felt avuncular sensibilities toward other skaters. I told Gary that, in the event that he got into trouble or felt lonely, he was to phone me collect from Australia at any time of the day or night. Over the next few months, he called me several times in a vulnerable emotional state. Working under Christopher Dean, it seemed, was living hell.

A new production, Torvill & Dean and the Russian All-Stars, toured England several years after the first, with Robin Cousins billed as a special guest star. His designated raison d'être was to fatten the home-country box office. However, his charismatic performances were conveniently cut from the filmed version of the show.

In 1977, dance choreographer Ron Harris took me to see a New York production that he had worked on: Liza Minnelli's *Liza with a Z*. It was causing a sensation at the time. While we watched the performance, Ron told me a number of things about Liza that struck me as peculiar. Probably due to insecurity, she never permitted a blonde or true brunette to share the stage with her. By decree, every female cast member had mousy-brown hair. The men were either Asian or black. Caucasian-American Prince Charmings were not allowed.

According to Ron, Liza once heard deafening applause for somebody else's performance between two of her own ten solos. She had the culprit fired instantly. Nobody would steal applause from Liza twice.

So it was with Christopher Dean. Scott Williams, an American hunk, always brought down the house in the Torvill and Dean show that I attended in Toronto. Scott told me that Christopher therefore placed him first after the opening number, ensuring much more tempered applause than Scott would have received later in the running order. What Liza Minnelli and Christopher Dean failed to understand, whether due to insecurity or the massiveness of their egos, was that the more varied and fabulous the supporting cast, the better the star is appreciated in the long run. Yet Christopher was not at all happy sharing his ice surface with other males who exhibited virtuosity.

Christopher and Jayne's first tour did land-office business, with sellout crowds for weeks and even months. Their show, the first of its kind, was unusual, because most of the stars were ice dancers – Kelly Johnson, Marianne van Bommel, Wayne Deweyert, Petra Born, Rainer Schonborn, Salome Brunner, Jonathan Thomas, Barry Hagan – with a token representation of pairs and singles skaters. The latter, like Gary Beacom, were chosen for their individuality and their entertainment value, not for their amateur credentials.

The tour owed its success to the fact that, while they were amateurs, Jayne and Chris had captured the imagination of a global public. Their

market awaited. It didn't have to be developed from scratch. No ice-
dance couple before or since has had the box-office clout to create a
similar production.

Torvill and Dean's market was not at all the high-end, sophisticated,
ballet-going crowd, but rather the tea-and-crumpet matinee set. Especially
in those days, British skating crowds were heavily skewed toward middle-
aged and elderly women.

One thing that I could never accept was the fact that Jayne and
Christopher, but Jayne to a greater degree, failed to stretch their legs
and point their toes. That was the one flaw that prevented them from
truly becoming dancers on the ice. It made me think of them as
entertainers rather than modern dancers. I have never heard anyone
corroborate my observation, but I interpreted their lack of stretch as a
lack of refinement.

In addition to their touring shows, Christopher and Jayne mounted
a number of television specials. A typical example, "Fire and Ice," was
filmed in Germany over a period of many weeks at enormous cost to the
producers. However high Christopher and Jayne's artistic integrity (and
indeed it was very high), the results were often television specials that
were too esoteric to be commercially successful. I perceived two major
creative flaws in the various specials that I watched. First, I found that a
whole hour of ice dance, without significant complementary singles and
pair numbers, became boring. Second, if Christopher's acting ability was
minimal, Jayne's was nonexistent. They were Olympic gold medalists in
ice dance, not all-around artists.

In December 1984, at the height of the Torvill and Dean mania, Dick
Button invited them to skate at his big professional competition in
Landover. Like Dorothy Hamill and the Protopopovs in their heydays,
Christopher and Jayne were treated as superstars and given preferential
consideration. I performed on the same bill with them at their first pro
competition, and I felt that their program was less a competitive routine
and more a special exhibition by guest artists. Christopher and Jayne
were *hors concours*, not part of the rank and file.

While we minor stars took the bus from the hotel to the arena, a limousine chauffeured Torvill and Dean. I mention this only because other

skaters of the past had been given the same royal treatment, but sooner or later their stardust had lost its twinkle. Then they were forced to ride the bus like the rest of us. I realized with amusement that it was only a matter of time before that base fate overtook Christopher and Jayne.

On that first occasion in Landover, Christopher and Jayne performed a number lifted right from Torvill and Dean: The World Tour – Graeme Murphy's pas de deux from *Song of India*, to music by Rimsky-Korsakov. Although I always admired and understood Torvill and Dean's performances, I was rarely emotionally caught up in them. *Song of India* was the exception to that rule. It was a genuine work of art. Every judge awarded it a perfect 10.0.

The following December at Landover, Christopher and Jayne presented another number extracted from their show: "Venus, the Bringer of Peace," from Gustav Holst's *The Planets*. It featured an enormous red ball that swung like a pendulum, to and fro, above the ice surface. I was wearing two hats on that occasion, as I often did: competitor and CBC commentator. During my commentary, I voiced the opinion that, when skaters arrived with mechanical props, they set a dangerous precedent.

American skating champions Judy Blumberg and Michael Seibert were the only other participants in the dance event. Although no judge or spectator would have considered bucking the Torvill and Dean mystique, I boldly informed the Canadian television audience that the Blumberg and Seibert number, performed to Malcolm McLaren's *Rock Madam Butterfly*, was superior by far to Jayne and Chris's offering. Although Torvill and Dean had sincerely created their program in the name of art, I found it ridiculous.

Over the years, in fact, I found Torvill and Dean's choreographic success rather hit-or-miss, compared to the consistent mystical excellence of Pakhomova and Gorshkov. However, few people with discerning eyes were able to see through their legend and objectively evaluate their choices.

In the wake of huge success, Christopher began to choreograph works for Paul and Isabelle Duchesnay, whose amateur career in Canada had spun its wheels for quite some time before they moved to represent France. Thanks to Christopher Dean, the team began an aggressive climb up the international competitive ladder. Christopher can legitimately claim 95 percent of the credit for the choreographic content of the Duchesnays' important amateur free dances.

However, Christopher may have received more than his fair share of credit for originality. A small, dark cloud came to float above his head when a number of people, including Isabelle herself, noticed that certain attributes of several of the Duchesnay programs were conspicuously similar to compositions from the dance world, notably Christopher Bruce's *Ghost Dances*. Christopher Dean came to be painted in some circles as derivative.

During the time when Christopher choreographed for the Duchesnays in Oberstdorf, he and Isabelle fell in love. I have always been a huge Duchesnay fan, and I was deeply sensitive to the creative battle that they fought. It was not unlike my own. I received an invitation to Isabelle's May 1991 marriage to Christopher. Many skating luminaries attended those festivities, but for some reason, I secretly decided to pass on the wedding and attend the divorce.

When the marriage broke up after two years, Isabelle asked me why members of the figure-skating world hadn't warned her about what she was getting into. That was a telling question. When a young woman falls in love and decides to get married, surely she should know exactly whom she is marrying, but Isabelle was painfully naive.

Christopher was an extraordinarily successful skater and choreographer with a complex character. I sensed that Isabelle, because of her love for her husband, subconsciously wanted him to live in a box with the lid tightly shut. As a creative artist, Christopher could never have lived in anyone's box, even his own.

One of the motivations that drove him, something that Isabelle could not understand, was his need to return to Olympic-eligible competition. Isabelle and Paul were still preparing for the 1992 Games, even as Christopher began to contemplate (if subconsciously) his own return in 1994.

Torvill and Dean reinstated as amateurs, determined to add another gold medal to their belts. What happened to them at the 1994 Lillehammer Olympics was complicated but interesting. Unbeknownst to Christopher and Jayne, they were no longer in a position to break the rules of ice dance and win. The number that they concocted for their free dance, "Let's Face the Music and Dance," was a great disappointment to me. They played creative Russian roulette and lost quite spectacularly to the Russian team of Oksana Grishuk and Evgeny Platov.

Christopher had forgotten, or compromised, the reasons for their former successes. He and Jayne had heretofore offered the skating world something new and different each year. In Lillehammer, they presented merely a compilation of greatest hits: every successful trick that they had ever performed, strung into a predictable and irregular choreographic necklace. There was no novelty. Their bronze medal came as a shock to the skating world, but it was a far greater shock to Christopher's ego. In Christopher and Jayne's defence, their Olympic free dance garnered the best audience response of the competition and was probably the most entertaining performance.

As I watched the television coverage from Lillehammer, one particular interview struck me as absurd. American Jill Trenary, the 1990 world ladies' champion and later the second Mrs. Christopher Dean, sputtered and spewed into the microphone about the grave injustice that the judges had perpetrated upon Christopher and Jayne. Their bronze medal, she felt, was a travesty, especially since the audience had preferred them to the first- and second-place couples.

Jill Trenary is by no means an ice-dance expert, and she failed to acknowledge that the crowd had reacted with such boisterous enthusiasm to entertaining but illegal moves.

In 1984, when they rode their wave to victory, Torvill and Dean had been on the cutting edge, creating, changing, and molding a new form of ice dance. The rules be damned! By 1994, the ISU had cleared the chessboard many times. There was a new game, with new players, in an entirely new ice-dance era. The old magic didn't work on the judges who controlled the sport's future.

After I outlived my performing career, I began to judge the Landover professional competitions in which I had formerly competed. The last event that I judged occurred in December 1995. The ice-dance segment featured Torvill and Dean, as well as Russians Maia Usova and Alexander Zhulin, Finns Susanna Rahkamo and Petri Kokko, and the 1992 Olympic

champions from Russia, Marina Klimova and Sergei Ponomarenko. The
Torvill and Dean myth was still thick in the air, and their success was a
foregone conclusion among the other judges on the panel.

Torvill and Dean's artistic program showcased a comedic element.
Chris played a lovesick, bespectacled nerd. Femme fatale Jayne rejected
the nerd's romantic advances, all this to Paul Simon tunes. I found the
number weak in skating skill, slow, and totally without humor. All
the other judges but one (who voted 9.9) awarded perfect 10.0s. I
gave the great skating legends the insulting mark of 9.4, because I just
hadn't bought their routine. In a tidal wave of disapproval, the audience
booed me vociferously. Undaunted, I jumped out of my seat, extended
my arms like a conquering hero, and bowed to my detractors.

When I sat back down, the judges to my right and left whispered to
me in unison, "I wish that I had had the guts to do what you just did." I
turned to each (one a former American bronze medalist in ice dance, the
other the Canadian coach of Olympic ice-dance bronze medalists) and
told them, "But you didn't, and I have been left to hang out to dry."

My choice that evening was the married team of Klimova and
Ponomarenko. Although they were overly melodramatic, as Russians
usually are, they skated harder, stronger, and faster than Torvill and Dean.
In any case, the high and low marks were thrown out. Torvill and Dean
tied Klimova and Ponomarenko in artistic scores and won the overall
competition with higher technical marks. For whatever reason – and I can
think of quite a few – I was never again asked to judge at Landover.

A judging panel comprised of people with major talent, impressive
credentials, and ample intelligence should be allowed to entertain legitimately diverse opinions. I found it personally insulting that, with my
credentials, I could not call the shots as I saw them. Over the years, as
the dust settled, I decided that, even if I were asked to judge the event
once again, I would have no interest in wasting my time.

When last I saw Torvill and Dean perform, their tour was playing
Toronto's Maple Leaf Gardens. I knew practically every member of their
cast and had coached a number of them. Before the show began, I headed
backstage with the intention of wishing all my friends, including Jayne and
Chris, good luck. The arena guard told me firmly that "fans" could not go

backstage, but that the cast would receive autograph-seekers after the show. That was my very first dismissal – ever – at any event, in any arena.

I watched several performances, then fled the building. The problem for me was that Jayne and Chris were simply not the skaters they had been when they won the 1984 Olympics. Their latest show was just an inferior rerun of performances that I had seen in the past. I left under cover of darkness, unobserved, and opted not to stick around to solicit autographs. Perhaps my earlier rejection had caused me to feel a bit jaundiced.

Torvill and Dean will go down in history as one of the greatest ice-dance teams of all time. They brought refreshing conceptual innovations to the sport, popularizing the medium as never before – and certainly as never since.

To quote an ancient Chinese saying, "No feast lasts forever." But Torvill and Dean's feast included a larger share of legitimate glory than any other diners at skating's great banquet table had ever before received.

Hamilton, Ontario, 1986

CHAPTER 10

S COTT H AMILTON

✐

American Skate God for Life

S cott Hamilton's early life was thoroughly chronicled by ABC's "Up-Close-and-Personal" crews, because it contained a number of potent human-interest elements. It began biologically on August 28, 1958, then started in earnest six weeks later when Dorothy and Ernie Hamilton adopted a baby boy in Toledo, Ohio, and brought him home to Bowling Green, where Ernie taught at the university. Dorothy was a teacher too.

Foreshadowing a lifetime pattern, Scott was scrawny and mischievously active, climbing out of his crib at six months of age. When he was three, his parents noticed that he was often ill and didn't seem to grow, no matter how much he ate. He spent several years visiting doctors, enduring tests, adhering to a rigid diet, and eventually putting up with a feeding tube.

In 1967, Dr. Henry Schwachman, a distinguished Harvard Medical School professor, ruled out some of the more dire diagnoses and suggested Scott resume a normal life. One of the activities that Scott craved was ice skating with his elder sister, Sue. As it turned out, skating filled

103

the doctor's prescription, for Scott's condition began to improve. In early 1968, he began regular figure-skating lessons. By the end of the year, his health problems had all but vanished, and he was infatuated with the ice.

When Scott's progression stalled at the novice level, his parents sent him to Rockton, Illinois, to train at the Wagon Wheel Ice Palace with distinguished French pairs champion Pierre Brunet, and later with Mary Ludington and Evy Scotvold. Scott was thirteen when he left home to stay in the rollicking Wagon Wheel dormitory and skate with the likes of Janet Lynn and Gordie McKellen.

The 1976 U.S. Nationals coincided with a watershed in Scott's life. His mother had recently announced that she had been stricken by breast cancer and that the family's finances were unable to bear further skating costs. Then, the day before Scott performed what he thought would be his last long program to win the junior title, his mother told him that benefactors Helen and Frank McLoraine had come forward to finance his training.

Only afterward did the other shoe drop. The agreement meant that Scott would henceforth train with Carlo and Christa Fassi at the Colorado Ice Arena in Denver. His departure from Mary Ludington and his friends at the Wagon Wheel was bittersweet.

In the inspirational international CIA environment, Scott progressed alongside Robin Cousins and many other foreign national champions. His mother's death in the spring of 1977 drove him to improve his work ethic and train harder than ever. In 1978, he won the U.S. bronze medal, but slipped a place the following year after Carlo took on Scott's chief rival, Scott Cramer.

That drove Hamilton to make a coaching change. He and Don Laws of Philadelphia had worked together periodically in the past and had shared a good rapport. He went to work with Laws, who enjoyed the confidence of Scott's sponsors. Don took Scott to four national and four world titles and ultimately the 1984 Olympic gold medal. After his victory, the student saluted his mentor with a moving tribute to "The Wind Beneath My Wings."

Scott had wanted figure skating to enjoy the same athletic status as gymnastics. He had hoped to make the sport seem more legitimate as a male pursuit. To that end, he had adopted streamlined, masculine costumes that evoked other winter pursuits, like speed skating and bob-sledding, and he had assiduously avoided effeminate themes.

As a new professional in 1984, Scott continued to develop his dis-tinctive style, one that was well seasoned with self-deprecating humor. He performed with Ice Capades for two seasons. Then, in 1986, he began headlining the fledgling Stars on Ice (originally called Scott Hamilton's America Tour), the company whose name eventually became synony-mous with his own. Scott played many characters over the years: Cuban Pete; a self-absorbed lounge lizard; a clown; the Barber of Seville; a sixty-four-year-old man; Don Quixote; and a hippie confronting baldness – art imitating life.

Through many performances and professional competitions, Scott entered into American lore. Never was his impact greater, though, than when he went public with details of his personal fight against testicular cancer and launched a campaign to support treatment and cure for others. Scott's return to professional skating in the fall of 1997 was one of the most inspirational moments in the sport's history.

ℒℭℒℭℒℭ

Scott Hamilton was by far the most complex and multifaceted skater of the latter part of the twentieth century. People in the figure-skating world who thought they knew him well probably did not. His charismatic, humorous, slick personality often hid the person behind the mask. This is an observation, not a criticism. It is simply my view that what one saw on the exterior in no way revealed Scott's inner self.

My first encounter with young Scott Hamilton took place in Philadelphia, where I was performing as a special guest star with Ice Capades. Scott was the reigning American men's champion. His coach, Donald Laws, an old friend of mine, had brought him to see the show.

Whenever an important person from the skating world is in the audi-ence, the performers push themselves to their physical limits, trying to impress and please. At the end of the show, Scott came backstage. He was very polite, but made absolutely no comment about either the show or my performance (which I recall had been better than average). From that day until this moment, I have never been at all sure what Scott thought about me – or about anyone else, for that matter.

The 1984 Olympics in Sarajevo represented the seminal event in Scott's life. It was clear to the American contingent that Scott was a major contender for gold. Outside the rink one day, I bumped into Scott, Donald Laws, and Scott's choreographer, Ricky Harris. They were all turned out in full sartorial splendor, sporting identical American team uniforms – except that Ricky dripped with costume jewelry. It dangled from every conceivable body part, coordinating perfectly with each hue of her U.S. ski suit. As the days went by, Ricky's getup became ever more creative.

Scott performed competently in the compulsory-figure event. Whether his figures were really the best that day is questionable, but he won – the first time he had done so at the world level. Jean-Christophe Simond of France placed second, followed by Rudi Cerne of East Germany. Brian Orser, Scott's major free-skating rival, lay buried in seventh place at the end of the day. In retrospect, that sad fact would determine the final outcome.

Scott woke up on the morning of the short-program event with a head cold. His performance that evening was tense and wobbly. He made an error in his camel-change-camel spin and performed an easier combination jump, double loop/triple toe loop, than Brian Orser's triple Lutz/double loop. Brian finished in first, Scott in second, but Scott was still first overall.

The long-program competition, and in fact the entire Sarajevo Olympics, seemed to me to be a custom-made ABC-TV production. America was going to have an Olympic champion, no matter what it took.

In pairs, Kitty and Peter Carruthers had already finished a *surprising* second. Later in the Games, Rosalynn Sumners would finish a *disappointing* second – which proves that how a placement is viewed depends on prior expectations. Ice dancers Judy Blumberg and Michael Seibert would soon narrowly miss out on the bronze medal. It was all up to Scott, and he felt the pressure of expectations.

His long program truly paled in the light of some dazzling free skates, notably Brian Orser's. Scott popped his triple flip into a single and doubled the triple Salchow. Somehow, though, his marks put him second to Brian, and he eked out the supreme trophy.

At the exhibition gala, Scott skated directly before popular ice-dance champions Jayne Torvill and Christopher Dean. After Scott's performance, I noticed that Christopher put his arm around Scott in what I interpreted as a gesture of consolation. Christopher and Jayne seemed to recognize that Scott was slightly embarrassed by his sub-par Olympic performance.

Ottawa hosted the Worlds that year. Most people in the know speculated that the establishment was set to compensate Brian Orser for his Olympic loss. Scott, a true competitor and a fighter, walked determinedly into the Canadian lion's den, knowing that he was marked to be defeated by the hometown hero. That defeat did not occur.

Scott won his last and most legitimate world title at Ottawa, while Brian placed second. It was time for Scott to abandon the amateur world.

Team Hamilton, including Donald Laws and Ricky Harris, had good reason to expect that Scott's gold medal would result in piles of green in everyone's bank account. However, Scott soon terminated both professional relationships.

Where Donald was concerned, it was true that he had brought Scott to the Olympic level. But as the coach of a professional Scott Hamilton, he would have become a babysitter for a pupil who didn't need one. Scott was ready to fly solo.

Ricky Harris, an ex-chorus girl from dance shows, had tried her best to elevate Scott's pedestrian choreography and style. Her results had been little more than mediocre, so Scott did not become Ricky's ticket to fame and fortune.

Ricky, oddly enough, lives with her husband, a hairdresser, in the same small Mexican town, San Miguel de Allende, that I call home. She told me one day that Scott had promised to give her a big, shiny Cadillac if he happened to win the 1984 Olympics. She is still waiting for that car to appear at her cobblestone curb.

As a new professional skater, Scott faced several handicaps. With a diminutive physique and an extremely slender body, even by his own admission he was a far cry from Prince Charming. He didn't fit the champion stereotype. Various companies wondered how to market this unusual young man. Second, his victory had not been the clear-cut triumph of a Mark Spitz or a Mary Lou Retton. His gender was a third handicap. Ice queens were in high demand and handsomely rewarded. Ice kings were practically a dime a dozen.

In the early years of his professional career, while Scott performed with Ice Capades, major endorsements and television specials eluded him. Like me, he signed a contract with International Management Group (IMG). I suspect that the international conglomerate was stymied at first, unsure what to do with its new client.

When Scott lost his Ice Capades job, IMG turned a negative into a huge positive by creating a little touring show starring Scott as the principal performer, and including other skaters from the IMG stable. I was a charter member of Scott Hamilton's America Tour. In the second season, I became a charter member of its new incarnation, Stars on Ice.

The little show at first played minor markets and stayed away from major buildings that hosted Ice Capades or Disney on Ice. Then it grew and grew and grew. Over a comparatively short period of time, Stars on Ice became a huge entertainment vehicle and a cash cow.

During those years, I saw Scott on a daily basis and observed him at close range. The skaters in the cast were extremely friendly with one another, and it is accurate to say, at least for me, that there were virtually no social wrinkles within our little company. We thought of our cast as a family.

However, as friendly as Scott and I were, he never invited me out for a cup of coffee and certainly never invited me to his home in Denver. This is not a complaint. It simply illustrates that Scott maintained a professional skating existence that rarely merged with his personal life.

In his professional persona, Scott possessed the unique ability to suck energy from audiences and use it to his own advantage. It seemed to me that he was never happier nor more vitally alive than when he stood under the spotlights, beaming a wide grin to the audience and accepting their love and adoration. That veritable titan under the spotlights, however, had a quiet private presence. Sometimes he was barely noticeable in large groups of people.

One of the many facets of Scott's talent was his intelligence. It did not take him long after turning professional to understand exactly what he possessed that he could sell to an audience in order to reach his commercial potential. In his most memorable performances (of which there were countless examples), his comedic sense was supported by extraordinary athleticism that included a substantial arsenal of brilliant jumps and spins. Scott was able to endear himself to audiences, to have them eating from his hand, all the while poking fun at himself.

Scott took great care of himself and continued to train religiously and hone his skating techniques, even when he was not specifically involved in a skating engagement. I performed with Scott probably hundreds of times in many different shows and on several continents. His professional skills, whether skating, acting, or commentating, improved and became more refined over the years. That was no accident. Scott embraced his professional career with the same ardor and discipline that had produced his amateur triumphs.

Scott did not possess a great reservoir of creativity, but he had the intelligence to select a choreographer, Sarah Kawahara, who understood what Scott had to sell and, conversely, what tools he lacked. Through collaboration with Sarah, Scott became an entertainer of such magnitude that, for me, his contributions to entertainment were no less important than Fred Astaire's or Charlie Chaplin's. Scott, against all odds, became a giant.

I believe that it was at Christmastime of 1993 that I performed with Scott in a series of holiday exhibitions in Vail, Colorado. Each evening I crept out of the dressing room to watch two of the performances, something that I normally didn't do. At that moment I couldn't imagine two better skaters than Scott Hamilton and Paul Wylie. Paul was no less the genius, with his passionate, classical approach. In fact, I thought that he was the better rounded of the two. He excelled equally at every aspect of the sport: athleticism, artistic line, and passion. Scott, however, was more multidimensional, with a greater range in his repertoire. I don't remember Paul ever performing comedic numbers, while Scott could range from slapstick comedy to the solemnity of numbers like "The Battle Hymn of the Republic."

In November 1994, at the Gold Championship, a remarkable competition that Dick Button mounted in Edmonton, Alberta, Scott competed for the astounding sum of U.S.$200,000. His rivals were both Olympic gold medalists: Brian Boitano and Viktor Petrenko.[*] I flew in from Mexico to judge the competition, which also included a field of three women.

Scott was always highly competitive, but for this particular competition he had apparently trained fanatically and honed his skills and physical conditioning to their highest levels. In what was probably his greatest skating triumph ever, Scott beat the American virtuoso, Brian Boitano, in the technical program. At intermission, Brian's long-time coach, Linda Leaver, engaged me in conversation. She could not understand why Scott had received higher marks than Brian, when Brian had executed a triple Axel and Scott had not.

I asked Linda to please sit down while I explained my marks. I told her that it was quite true that Brian had skated magnificently to "Carousel Waltz" and had, in fact, executed a fine triple Axel. However, I had given Scott higher marks, as had the other judges on the panel (seven perfect 6.0s for style), because Scott's performance to big-band standards had been brilliantly multifaceted. It had been marked by superior footwork, superior spins, superior musicality, and flawless technical finesse, all wrapped into a package that had towered over Brian's in personality, humor, and dramatic nuance.

Scott maintained his edge in the artistic phase of the competition, skating to Aerosmith's "Walk This Way."

Brian, however brilliantly he has performed over the years, is a splendid but one-dimensional athlete. Scott, on the other hand, has shown himself to be so uniquely multidimensional in his choice of routines over the years that, as an entertainer, he has realized his full artistic and

---

[*] In his autobiography, *Landing It*, Scott notes that he was invited to compete only after 1994 Olympic gold medalist Alexei Urmanov pulled out of the event.

physical potential. There is no other skater in history whom I could describe in those terms.

After the competition, with Scott in receipt of the princely sum of $200,000, some of the other judges and I went out for dinner in a neighborhood restaurant. Lo and behold, there were Scott and his entourage, dining at the same place. I summoned Scott to my table and demanded point-blank that he pay for the dinners of all the judges who had helped him to win his $200,000. He pleasantly agreed to my proposal, and I dropped our check on his plate as I left the restaurant. That was the only time that Scott ever treated me to a meal, and I enjoyed it thoroughly.

Almost exactly a year later, Scott performed poorly at the same Gold Championship event. However, his third-place finish soon paled in the light of the events of November 20, 1995. With the Stars on Ice cast gathered in Lake Placid for tenth-season rehearsals, pairs skater Sergei Grinkov collapsed onto the ice and died, leaving behind a devastated young widow, Ekaterina Gordeeva, and their beautiful three-year-old daughter, Daria.

What could have felled a twenty-eight-year-old athlete, apparently in prime condition? The doctor who performed the autopsy found that Sergei's heart was enlarged and diseased, and that two of his coronary arteries were almost fully occluded. He also learned from Katia that Sergei had suffered from untreated chronic hypertension. The irregular rhythm that caused the fatal event had been triggered by a silent heart attack within the past twenty-four hours, doctors determined. No doubt the predisposition had been congenital. Sergei's father had also had an enlarged heart, and had died of heart failure in his fifties.

Scott took Sergei's death very hard. He had lost one of his closest friends. Scott and Paul Wylie flew all the way to Moscow at their own expense to attend Sergei's November 25 funeral at the Red Army Club arena. I admired their loyalty. During the next year in particular, Scott made it his business to do anything for Katia and Daria that he could. They were like his own family.

Scott was always a popular guy within the figure-skating world. He had some very special ties with skaters, but none of his closest friends was a male Olympic gold medalist, with the single exception of Sergei. Perhaps Scott just did not share common interests with Robin Cousins, Viktor Petrenko, and others. Or perhaps his competitive nature got in the way.

In March 1997, not much more than a year after Sergei's death, Scott experienced a second major personal setback. During a tour of Stars on Ice, he discovered that he had testicular cancer. The outlook for recovery was in doubt, and the entire skating world, indeed the entire American public, prayed for the restoration of his good health. Scott's rehabilitation from surgery and chemotherapy must have been very difficult. It took him many months to fully recuperate.

In December of the same year, my professional career was winding down when IMG mounted a televised tribute show for me at Varsity Arena in downtown Toronto. Scott was still very weak as a result of his illness, but he agreed to come and skate for me that evening. We had a brief conversation before the show. I asked him about the psychological pain that he had surely experienced along with the physical pain caused by the cancer. How had he felt about the possibility of prematurely terminating his professional career? How had he reacted to confronting the impermanence of life?

Scott gave me a sage and profound answer. He told me that what had happened to him had been marked by many positive aspects. With respect to his career, his personal life, and his scale of values, it had probably been more a positive than a negative experience.

That response deeply impressed me. It explained why Scott was such a phenomenal champion and celebrity. Everything I knew about Scott came together in my mind and made perfect sense.

In October 1997, many important skaters honored Scott by participating in a televised special filmed at the Great Western Forum in Los Angeles. The event was a fundraiser for the Cleveland Clinic's new Taussig Cancer Center. Although I was not invited to perform, I would have loved to have been part of that celebration.

I haven't had the occasion to speak to Scott in person since the evening of my own tribute in Toronto, but I recently enjoyed his television commentary from the 2002 Olympics.

Scott and I began our careers as commentators at about the same time. Whereas I had been around the block a few times, Scott started out as little more than a wet-behind-the-ears Olympian. Demonstrating his appealing candor, he later remarked in an interview, "When I went to CBS, everybody was telling me that I had to be more like a news guy or be concise or do this or do that. My first live calls were in Tokyo at the [1985] world championships, and they *stank*."

Someone took Scott out for a beer and suggested that he relax, act natural, and say whatever was on his mind. That worked up to a point. His smoothness and his vocabulary have dramatically improved throughout the intervening years.

It was interesting to me as a television viewer, no longer a commentator myself, to listen to Scott's enthusiastic, knowledgeable, and precise analysis of the skating events in Salt Lake City. He demonstrated a unique style of commentary and analysis, and I felt strangely aligned with him. The essence of what he said was exactly what I myself believed and would have said on the air if I had been given the chance.

It's just a hunch, but I suspect that Scott, co-commentating with former Canadian pairs skater Sandra Bezic, precipitated the International Olympic Committee's (IOC) decision to award second gold medals in the pairs event to Jamie Salé and David Pelletier.

If so, that's just another example of Scott's influence on skating. Kurt Browning got it right when he remarked in 1994, "Scott Hamilton is skate god for life, and that is no joke."

"Hell," Torvill and Dean: The World Tour, 1986

CHAPTER 11

GARY BEACOM

%Ó

Rebel with a Cause

G ary Beacom was born on February 23, 1960, in Calgary. His parents, Bruce, a Canadian, and Sylvia, an American, skated at the Royal Glenora Club in Edmonton, where Gary took lessons beginning at age seven.

By the time he reached his teens, Gary was attending high school and skating in Toronto. Just before his seventeenth birthday, he won the 1977 Junior Men's national title.

Gary earned a degree in physics and philosophy at the University of Toronto while skating competitively at the championship level. By the time of the 1984 Olympics, he was acting as his own coach – out of a wish for independence as well as a lack of time and money for formal lessons. Besides, he felt that by then he had learned everything that coaches could teach him.

Gary took an analytical approach to school figures. That is why he was particularly incensed when judges demonstrated political bias or outright incompetence. His highest overall finish was tenth at the 1984 Worlds.

Although Gary intended to continue to compete through 1988, a clash of wills with the Canadian Figure Skating Association (CFSA) at the 1984 Skate Canada competition persuaded him to turn professional virtually on the spot. Several months later he joined the Torvill and Dean tour, which gave him public exposure and the chance to explore technique and choreography at their highest levels. His performance as the devil in the "Hell" production number was particularly well received.

When the Torvill and Dean tour closed, Gary created a one-man show, Hard Edge, then went on to work with the Ice Theatre of New York. In 1988, he was invited to serve as artistic director of the weekly ice shows in Sun Valley, Idaho. He and his partner, Gia Guddat, invented non-traditional routines like "I Think I'm Losing My Marbles" that intrigued audiences across North America. Many of Gary's deep-edged rubber-band-man moves seemed to defy the very laws of physics that he had studied.

Gary toured with Brian Boitano and Katarina Witt in Skating and in Skating '92, and took part for many years in Stars on Ice and Tom Collins' Tour of World and Olympic Champions.

While living in America, Gary espoused a philosophy of tax evasion allegedly based on constitutional grounds. In 1996, he ran afoul of the Idaho Tax Commission. The state of Idaho, unimpressed by his arguments, demanded payment of back taxes plus legal fees.

In 1997, the U.S. Internal Revenue Service got into the act, indicting Gary on three counts of failure to file returns and pay federal taxes. He represented himself in court, lost the case, and was sentenced to pay back taxes plus fines and to serve a twenty-one-month jail term in Pennsylvania's Allenwood Low Security Correctional Institute.

A math and grammar GED (General Equivalency Diploma) tutor while incarcerated, Gary was released for good behavior after eighteen months, then taken into Immigration and Naturalization Service custody pending the finalization of deportation proceedings. On August 7, 2000, he was released in Fort Erie, Ontario, and prohibited from re-entering the United States without government permission.

Today Gary, no longer with Gia Guddat, lives with his wife, a former Ice Capades skater, in Vancouver, B.C. He is involved with the Canadian

Ice Dance Theatre, carving out a new niche for himself in the skating world. Gary plans to publish several treatises that he wrote while imprisoned.

愛愛愛愛

W ithout a doubt, Canadian eccentric Gary Beacom wove the strangest texture into the great tapestry of skating. The spawning tank of the Toronto Cricket Club produced, in Gary, one of its most exotic specimens. His skating vocabulary was unlike anything that had ever existed, as though given life through Immaculate Conception. I can identify no influence that stamped itself upon his personal style. The reverse is not true, however. Gary's style exerted a considerable influence upon a number of skaters who followed him, notably Allen Schramm and Laurent Tobel.

My memory of Gary goes back to his youth. In the early 1970s, he was a tiny waif. Unlike some of the great skaters (young Dorothy Hamill and Robin Cousins come to mind), he evidenced no precocious talent that I could discern. How wrong I was.

Gary was a thoroughly introspective youth from a middle-class background. He seemed neither artistic nor athletic nor unusual. The two great pillars of skating creativity at the time when Gary trained at the Cricket Club were my coach, Ellen Burka, and an equally creative spirit, the legendary Osborne Colson.

But Gary chose Sheldon Galbraith as his coach. It is difficult for me to extol Sheldon's virtues. He taught a former adversary of mine, one-time Canadian champion David McGillivray. Sheldon was therefore a declared enemy of my camp, and we were barely civil to one another. His dry, technical approach represented the antithesis of absolutely every artistic ideal that Ellen and I believed in and strove for. There couldn't have been a more unsuitable catalyst, in my opinion, to trigger whatever unique innate talents Gary possessed.

Gary first impressed me at the 1980 Canadian Figure Skating Championships (Canadians) in Kitchener, the very competition where Brian Orser's skating first caught my eye. Having grown dramatically, he cut a tall, slim, imposing figure on the ice, and I discovered that the "untalented" child had become a rather competent young man. His truly unique approach to skating, one that ultimately horrified and flabbergasted the figure-skating world, was not yet evident.

Nonetheless, his iconoclastic ways, both on and off the ice, flew in the face of the Canadian establishment, in direct contrast to Brian Orser's polite compliance. From all reports, Gary outskated Brian at the 1984 Canadians in Regina, Saskatchewan. He probably should have won the Canadian title. He did not.

At the 1984 Olympic Games in Sarajevo, Gary competed as Canada's second-placed male, obscured by Brian's looming shadow. I learned that Gary had arrived at the competition without a coach. Particularly at the Olympic level, coaching oneself was as eccentric as it was suicidal. Gary had petitioned the CFSA to accredit his girlfriend, Gia Guddat, as his official coach. His request was denied, but he brought Gia along anyhow to keep him company.

One extraordinary incident occurred during the compulsory-figure event. After executing a good, but not great, back loop-change-loop (a seventh-test serpentine loop), Gary waited on the ice as if to intimidate the judges into giving him high marks. If that was his intent, the strategy failed. The marks were not at all encouraging, and Gary made international news and even a mention in *Time* magazine by violently kicking the boards and cussing profusely. The judging panel did not outwardly react to that unaccustomed assault upon its authority.

It occurred to me that, if I had known during my own amateur career that such irreverent behavior could garner publicity in *Time*, I certainly would have done the same thing myself.

During the free-skating event, it became transparently clear to everyone in the arena that Gary Beacom had developed into a wildly eccentric skater, one with a unique, self-invented style. During my commentary, I referred to him as a mad genius, and I meant it. His novelty and originality were qualities to be admired and taken seriously.

The Canadian judge, a Calgarian and former Canadian champion, Margaret Berezowski (née Crossland), was anything but an aggressive and demonstrative woman. Besides, she was preoccupied with trying to help

Brian Orser win a gold medal. With Machiavellian diplomacy before the event began, I encouraged Berezowski to put her neck on the chopping block and make a stand, albeit a solitary one. I felt that she should award Gary a serious artistic mark for his long program. To her credit, she gave him a 5.7.

Although Gary had skated reasonably well, he was placed eleventh in the long-program event, eleventh overall, respectable within that illustrious group of male skaters, but not as high a placement as he deserved.

The referee is an official on the judging panel who, rather than awarding marks, polices the event and theoretically ensures justice and fair play. The referee for the men's event in Sarajevo was a Canadian, Donald Gilchrist. In the wings was a long-time skating enemy of mine, an Italian named Sonia Bianchetti, who wielded enormous power within the ISU. Gilchrist's reluctance to buck Bianchetti and advocate for the two Canadian men created an abscess of resentment within me that has not yet healed. I blame his weakness for Brian's silver medal and Gary's relatively low placement.

Less than a year later, without fanfare, Gary simply quit amateur skating and turned professional. When I heard of his defection from the amateur world, I was sad. Rare talents require special treatment. If only Canada, and particularly David Dore, director general of the CFSA, had been more sensitive to Gary, Gary might have altered the history of skating in a more positive and emphatic way.

As a new professional, Gary found himself in a difficult position. He possessed unique talent but not a titled résumé, so he was obliged to launch his career from one of the ladder's middle rungs. He became one of the few skaters in history to mount his own one-man show. He starred himself and no one else. I found that egocentric but admirable.

Although other professional opportunities came along, like many renegades within the skating world Gary won few professional competitions. Both of his first-place finishes occurred in 1989. He did become a great crowd-pleaser, however. He was a consummate professional, who knew how to work the audience better than anyone else, milking it for as much applause as possible. In that department, he was a champion of Olympic proportions.

Gary made one particularly astute move. He settled in Sun Valley, Idaho, a popular figure-skating mecca, with his girlfriend and skating partner, Gia Guddat. Together they produced weekly ice shows, taught skating, and performed highly unusual and entertaining routines.

Gary's attraction to Sun Valley certainly had something to do with the progressive mind and choreography of his resident mentor, Frank Nowosad, who had already settled there. Frank was a peculiar breed of skating coach, an intellectual and an elitist. He was convinced that he was the one person in the world who possessed superior figure-skating knowledge. Such hubris certainly must have infected and influenced his unusual pupil.

Though Gary wasn't a championship title holder, Tom Collins gave him one of his biggest breaks when he signed him to a multi-year contract to skate on the Tour of World and Olympic Champions with many of the sport's amateur and professional titans. Through those performances, Gary earned a great deal of money and cemented his status as a legend.

Gary's revolutionary skating vocabulary paralleled Oscar Wilde's intellectual witticisms. Wilde's formula for cleverness was to make a statement that he then entirely contradicted in the very next phrase. Similarly, Gary's formula was to take a standard move and perform it backwards or upside down. For example, instead of walking forward on his toe picks, Gary would walk forward on the heels of his skate blades. If a traditional move were to be performed on a forward outside edge, he would present the same movement on a backward inside edge.

Gary was not renowned for his jumping ability, so there were few standard jumps in his programs. Moreover, the type of boots that he wore, and the mechanical ways in which he altered the blades, made conventional jumping difficult or impossible. However, Gary used outrageous flamboyance and his lack of inhibition, all in the name of art, to make up for any technical deficiencies.

The gradual metamorphosis of Gary's personality and style produced some peculiar effects. He began innocently enough by skating wearing dark glasses. Next he affixed skates to his hands and performed on all fours. He also began appearing completely covered in a hooded black body-stocking.

The sublime became the ridiculous when Gary appeared at the opening of Ottawa's new coliseum. He strapped a small propeller to his back and allowed it to propel him across the ice at a snail's pace. As far as I recall, he did no actual stroking. Fifteen minutes of that particular spectacle lulled the twenty-thousand-member audience into an excruciating state of boredom. Brian Orser and I watched from backstage without any amusement, searching in vain for a long hook with which to pull Gary off the ice. Our second thought was to locate a straitjacket.

At times Gary's eccentricity manifested itself in peculiar street clothing. He often sported loose, tie-dyed hippie shirts. Skating boots minus the blades became his shoes. My theory about eccentrics is that they should be taken seriously only if their eccentricities are unconscious. Although I have always thought of myself as Gary's friend, I have invoked my rule and ceased to take him seriously.

In 1997, for what was supposed to be, and wasn't, my final professional performance, at Varsity Arena in Toronto, I invited a collection of great skaters and personal friends to perform with me. Gary was part of that group. He skated magnificently in classic Beacom form, even though he was involved at the time in an internationally prominent lawsuit. His contention was that, by law, he did not owe U.S. income tax. Backstage I whispered into the ears of some of the other skaters that, although most people thought that they were there to see *my* final performance, the real swan song would be Gary Beacom's.

In a chat with Gary, I counseled him not to return to the United States, since I feared that he would go straight to jail. He dismissed my advice. Two weeks later, in an American courthouse, Gary was sentenced to prison.

Barbara Tuchman, an important American historian, wrote a book entitled *The March of Folly: From Troy to Vietnam*, in which she cited numerous examples of humans who have marched consciously and willfully to their own ends. Had she lived long enough, she might have been inclined to add a chapter about Gary Beacom.

Gary, again like Oscar Wilde, had the chance to save himself and escape to the protection of friends. He chose, instead, to go to jail. That is just what I would have expected of him.

When the INS released Gary in the millennial year, the skating world, like the era, had changed. Tom Collins had sold his tour to a conglomerate. Gary's fame and consequent opportunities had largely disappeared.

After Gary's release from prison, his peers and skating colleagues failed to immediately embrace the prodigal son. They bandied about a proposal to mount a charity show to help him get back on his feet, but they gave the idea no serious thought. Many taxpaying skaters were still outraged by his refusal to pay what he owed. Others, although more sympathetic, claimed to be deterred by their fear of an IRS audit.

Any spectator or skating fan who was lucky enough to experience his art will long remember the glory of Gary Beacom in his heyday. Still, I have always felt that one of the golden rules of life is that each individual must play to the best of his ability whatever cards are dealt to him. Destiny dealt Gary a wondrous set of cards. I regret that he didn't play them very wisely. Instead, he gambled with his destiny, right down to the last card in his hand. Jokers were wild.

At their farewell show, Toronto, 1998

CHAPTER 12

BARBARA UNDERHILL

AND PAUL MARTINI

✂

Sweet Synchronicity

P aul Martini was born on November 2, 1960, in Woodbridge, Ontario. Barbara Underhill was born on June 24, 1963, in Oshawa. They became Underhill and Martini when Barb was just fourteen and Paul seventeen. He eventually grew to be a six-footer, while his partner stopped at five feet. That made them a perfect pair in the Soviet style of tiny-and-tall partnering. Barb and Paul won their first of five national titles in Thunder Bay, Ontario, in 1979.

It was when Canadian choreographer Sandra Bezic got into the act that the drawbacks of being tiny-and-tall flew out the window, and a distinctive style emerged. The pair's coach, Louis Stong, contacted Sandra in 1979 and asked her to help him prepare the team for the 1980 Olympics. Sandra found that Barb and Paul could do all the pairs tricks but lacked line. None of the traditional choreographic logic worked for them.

It took Sandra a long time, by her admission, to figure out a solution, but in the end it was her "method skating" approach that clicked. Every movement had to spring from an emotional motivation. The movements, linked together, told a story. For Underhill and Martini, at least on the ice, it was a love story, sometimes chaste and sometimes steamy.

Barb and Paul capped their amateur career with a world title in Ottawa in 1984, one of the most memorable moments in sport. But their greatest successes were yet to come, especially at the World Professional Figure Skating Championships in Landover.

Some of Barb and Paul's best-loved hits were "Meditation" from *Thaïs*, "Starlight Express," "An American Anthem" from *East of Eden*, "Les Misérables," "When a Man Loves a Woman," "It Had to Be You," and "Unchained Melody." They bowed out of the performing arena with a televised special, "One Last Time," filmed on May 26, 1998.

Paul and his wife, Liz, are the parents of two children, Kate and Robert. Barb and her husband, Rick, also have a daughter, Samantha, and two sons, Matthew and Scott. Barb devotes considerable time to the Stephanie Gaetz KeepSafe Foundation, which raises money to promote childhood safety awareness, while Paul commentates for the CBC and serves as president of iskater.com.

ᏋᏛᏋᏛᏋᏛ

I n the early 1980s, at the time of the rise in the amateur ranks of pairs skaters Barbara Underhill and Paul Martini, I was virtually cut off from personal contact with prominent Canadian skaters because of my commitments to touring shows and theatrical ice productions.

When I was introduced to Barbara in the Cricket Club lobby after a late-night practice, I probably started with the perfunctory "How do you do. Nice to meet you." Then I asked, "So, who are you, and what do you do?"

Those weren't the right questions to ask. Barbara and her partner, Paul, were the reigning Canadian pairs champions. Their careers were on the ascent. In essence, I was embarrassingly oblivious of the Canadian skating hierarchy. That faux pas was, in part, intentional. Having ended my amateur career on a sour note at the 1976 Olympics and Worlds, I was bitter, and I had purposely estranged myself from the figure-skating world.

I don't precisely recall first meeting Paul. From time to time, I saw the team practice at the Cricket Club, but their home training center was the Granite Club, fifteen minutes away. When I did observe their training sessions, I wasn't terribly impressed. I thought that they were quite good, nothing more. Canadian pairs, however excellent, invariably display weaknesses in individual skating, at least to one degree or another. Usually solo jumps are the problem. Underhill and Martini were subject to that Canadian curse.

I have no subsequent memory of the team until the 1984 Olympics in Sarajevo. One afternoon I strolled to the Zetra Arena with friend and colleague Sandra Bezic, who had won a number of Canadian pairs championships with her brother, Val. Sandra, as Underhill and Martini's co-coach and choreographer, expressed the belief that they were prime candidates for Olympic gold. That fantastic suggestion left me speechless. I listened to Sandra without expressing an opinion.

During their practice, I watched Barbara and Paul strut their stuff. My overall opinion remained "quite good." It is true that, biased commentator that I was, I was infinitely more partial to Russian teams than to North American duos.

Barbara and Paul's Olympic short program was a cruel confirmation of everything that I had suspected. In one of the most egregious two-minute disasters in the history of pairs skating, Barbara lost her edge and slid into Paul, bringing him down with her. At one point in the program, it seemed to me, they simply lay on the ice, but in a criminal display of political bias, Canadian judge David Dore had the effrontery to award the flawed performance second place overall. The majority of judges placed the team sixth.

I recall reasonably accurately my CBC commentary. I believe that I said, "Normally it is the Soviet bloc of judges that is conspicuously political in its evaluation of skaters. However, in this case, the guilty party is the Canadian judge, David Dore." I wanted to mention his Ottawa address, hoping that he would receive hate mail. Fortunately for Mr. Dore, and even more fortunately for me, I did not have his address at my fingertips.

Barbara and Paul performed their long program in a somewhat strained and nervous state. Barbara singled the first side-by-side double Salchow in their routine. Paul singled the second. Then Barbara lost her edge again while attempting to land a throw double Axel. The Soviets, Elena Valova and Oleg Vasiliev, won the gold medal with a convincing and unbeatable display of virtuosity, but the highlight of the evening was the silver-medal performance of American brother-and-sister team Peter and Kitty Carruthers.

U.S. skaters traditionally raise the quality of their performances in direct proportion to the number of American fans in the audience. There was a sizable American contingent in Sarajevo. Perhaps they even out-numbered the Yugoslavians. Peter and Kitty surprised me, however, since I hadn't taken them seriously. I'm certain that they surprised even themselves. Such is the drama of sport.

Peter and Kitty announced their retirement from the amateur world almost immediately and appeared shortly thereafter on *Hollywood Squares*. Peter subsequently told me that it was the perfect moment to retire, because they felt that they had reached the height of their physical abilities and would probably never attain that level again.

Barbara and Paul, in their abject states of shock and depression, must also have performed a postmortem and considered an early retirement. However, as it is often noted, the darkest moments of night come before the dawn. In Barbara and Paul's bleak night, brilliant sunlight lay ahead.

Prior to the Olympics, Barbara had acquired a new pair of skate boots that simply never worked for her. That experience is devastating. From one day to the next, one's skating ability seems to fly out the window. After the Olympics, Barbara had the idea of changing back to her old, comfortable skates. I can only imagine that she felt like a blind person receiving the gift of sight. She regained her old confidence and security.

Fortunately, Barbara and Paul had registered to compete at the 1984 Worlds at Ottawa. Their short program there was excellent, but their long program was sublime.

In all great skating performances, technique becomes secondary to emotional content. Barbara and Paul were so sure-footed that the outcome took on an aura of inevitability. With each successful element, the audience grew more excited. A minute before the end of the routine, the spectators began to stand, clap, shout, and stamp their feet. It seemed as though the roof of the Civic Centre was about to fly off into space. That flawless, inspired program ended in a thundering crescendo. Every member of the crowd had become an honorary Canadian.

Perhaps the torture that Barbara and Paul had experienced at the Olympic Games enhanced their euphoria in Ottawa. A day after the pairs event, people milling on the Civic Centre's upper concourse saw Barbara bouncing up and down out of sheer exhilaration, like Michael Jordan's basketball.

As owners of a bona fide world gold medal, Barbara and Paul could rightfully anticipate a brilliant professional career. That is why, I am ashamed to confess, I did something rather base and unworthy. There was to be an exhibition in Anchorage, Alaska, that included Underhill and Martini. Although I was invited, and although I made the commitment to perform, the thought of kissing the hems of the robes of the newly crowned world champions – citizens of my native Canada – humiliated and appalled me. I found the suggestion of kowtowing to the rather brash young Paul Martini particularly repugnant. On the feeblest of excuses, I squeaked out of the engagement.

That exhibition in Alaska took on historic overtones when Dorothy Hamill, seemingly on a whim, eloped with her current boyfriend, Ken Forsythe. It is apparent in hindsight that Barbara and Paul were at the start of all things positive, while Dorothy was beginning her descent into a private hell.

In 1984, the two major agencies that handled skaters were International Management Group (IMG), an international sports management agency with offices worldwide, and Michael Rosenberg's Marco Entertainment. Both companies were interested in signing Underhill and Martini, who now possessed gilt-edged credentials.

Although IMG was a full symphony orchestra and Rosenberg was a one-man band, Barbara and Paul elected to sign with Michael, perhaps because the IMG stables were becoming overcrowded. Besides, when it came to contract negotiations, Rosenberg was viewed as a benevolent pit-bull terrier.

For a number of years, I didn't see much of Barbara and Paul. As principal performers with Ice Capades, they were well compensated, but the company imposed such a heavy performing schedule that virtually no employee had time to venture off into supplementary freelance work.

The big shows like Ice Capades, Holiday on Ice, and Ice Follies were old-Hollywood dinosaurs, but the professional experience they provided was invaluable. When Barbara and Paul completed their contractual obligations, they emerged as splendid professionals. It was then that I began to see them more often at joint skating performances, though we had a somewhat distant rapport. For chronological and social reasons, we just didn't move in the same orbit.

In time, Barbara and Paul defected from the Rosenberg camp. Rather than sign with a new agency, Paul began negotiating their skating contracts, eliminating the agent's fee.

At that point, IMG hired Barbara and Paul as special guest stars with Stars on Ice. I was highly apprehensive about performing in the same show with them, because I was convinced for some reason that they didn't particularly like me. Even more painful, I feared that they didn't take me seriously as a skater.

Paul Martini was a tall, muscular, country-boy sort of fellow with a somewhat brash manner, fueled by what I initially considered a primitive sense of humor. Frankly, I had always felt intimidated by Paul, probably for the same reasons that he may have felt intimidated by me. On one point we could at least agree: we did not come from the same planet, and we certainly did not speak the same language.

On my first road trip together with Paul, we were slated to gather at Toronto's Lester B. Pearson International Airport, so that the Canadian Stars on Ice contingent could fly to some distant destination to rendezvous with the American members. To assuage my somewhat fragile ego, I dressed to the nines when I traveled. If strangers didn't know me, then my clothes certainly communicated to them that they should. Paul's philosophy was the extreme antithesis of mine. He sported jeans, a plaid shirt, and sneakers.

When I saw Paul in the distance, my pace quickened, and I puffed myself up like the grand star that I had convinced myself I was. I was prepared for what I presumed would be a frosty hello.

Paul acknowledged me and then flabbergasted me by asking, in perfect Boy Scout style, if he could help me with my suitcases. This so affected me that I almost collapsed on the floor. That one gesture changed everything. I saw Paul in an entirely new light. I began to realize that he was a nice guy, well brought up, funny, and sage. That day marked the beginning of the admiration and respect for Paul that continues to grow in me to this day.

Barbara and Paul's first number in Stars on Ice preceded mine, so I enjoyed the great luxury of watching them skate, taking inspiration from their performance. That seemed to exert a positive effect on my own efforts. Either positive or negative energy tends to yield more of the same.

After I was dismissed from Stars on Ice, the company gave me a farewell dinner. I swear that I truly didn't know at the time that it was my Last Supper, but I took the hint when I received notes from well-wishers congratulating me on my retirement. Although IMG escorted me out into the pasture to graze, I continued to skate seriously for another twelve years, and I made more comebacks than Marlene Dietrich.

The World Pro event in Landover was the biggest and most important professional competition of the season, and so it remains today (although the venue now is a new arena in downtown Washington, D.C.). After many years of competing there, I was asked by Dick Button to serve as a judge, and I had the chance, as a professional spectator, to observe Underhill and Martini's virtuosity. As a pair, they were not physically well matched. Barbara was tiny and skated with an extremely deep knee bend. Paul was tall and lacked the soft knees in his skating that were so apparent in Barbara's. There were probably other incongruities, both physical and mental. One could discuss a host of reasons why this pair was not a classic textbook match.

That didn't matter. What they achieved, consistently and without flaw, was technical and emotional magic, unmatched by any other couple on the ice. Sandra Bezic spoke about Barbara and Paul at their induction

into the Canadian Figure Skating Hall of Fame, expressing the nature of
their magic far better than I could have explained it myself. Paul, according to Sandra, was the living fantasy of all the women in the audience.
They could thrill vicariously to Barbara's performance by putting themselves in her place. There have been other splendid pairs in skating
history, but Barbara and Paul will be remembered forever for their sensual
maturity and their unique synchronicity.

One day in May 1993, Barbara experienced a senseless tragedy in
her private life. Her eight-month-old twin daughters, Stephanie and
Samantha, were wriggling around on the floor of the family room.
Somehow Stephanie, who couldn't even crawl properly yet, crept out the
kitchen door, across the patio, and into the swimming pool, where she
drowned. After that devastating experience, Barbara withdrew for a time
from the skating world. No one could blame her.

Eventually, Barbara regained her desire to skate. In Landover in
December 1993, she returned to the ice with "Yesterday," an emotional
number dedicated to Stephanie's memory. The period that followed her
return saw the culmination of all the team's experiences and gifts.

At my retirement tribute show, Barbara and Paul were the last performers to skate. Everyone was splendid that night, but they were the
cherries on the sundae.

Some months afterward, while in Mexico, I watched a video of
Barbara and Paul's own tribute, performed and filmed at Maple Leaf
Gardens. Their final performance, "Not a Day Goes By," exemplified the
ultimate in pairs skating. It exerted a profound psychological effect on
me. I knew that I would never skate again, because no skater could ever
top their performance. If the ultimate had been accomplished, any
further attempts would be redundant.

Thank you, Barbara and Paul, for everything that you gave to the art
and sport of skating.

At home in Aylmer, Quebec, 1997

CHAPTER 13

ISABELLE AND
PAUL DUCHESNAY

⁊⁊

The Ice-Dance Jungle

H enri Duchesnay was an engineer with the Canadian Armed Forces, attached to NATO and stationed in Metz, France. Liliane, who worked on the army base, was a young French widow and mother of a son, Gaston. Henri and Liliane were married on Bastille Day 1960. On July 31, just over a year later, Paul arrived.

Henri brought his young family home to Canada. They settled on the air-force base in Saint-Jean d'Iberville, Quebec, south of Montreal, where Isabelle was born on December 18, 1963. In 1968, the Duchesnays moved to Aylmer, Quebec, just across the Ottawa River from the Canadian capital.

Paul, like most Canadian boys, played hockey – first on a frozen puddle and then on the rink that was built in the center of Aylmer when he was twelve. Isabelle tried figure skating as an after-school activity. Paul was coaxed to try it too, and he and his sister became a pairs team. That lasted until Isabelle fainted during a one-armed lift and fell to the ice, a dead weight, fracturing her skull and collarbone. Henri announced that his children would henceforth do ice dancing or nothing.

The Canadian Figure Skating Association (CFSA) wanted Paul and Isabelle to train with Bernard Ford at the National Ice Dance Centre near Toronto. With the Duchesnays, however, family and school were more important than skating. They balked and continued to train at the Minto Skating Centre in Ottawa. In retrospect, perhaps that early decision was the start of their troubles with the Canadian figure-skating hierarchy.

In the spring of 1982, the CFSA sent Paul and Isabelle to a seminar in Oberstdorf, prior to the Saint-Gervais Grand Prix and the Oberstdorf Nebelhorn Trophy events, and there they trained that summer with Martin Skotnicky. Once things went permanently sour with the CFSA, the Skotnicky-Oberstdorf connection became their future.

Paul retained his French passport even after he became a Canadian citizen. Isabelle derived French citizenship from her mother. When the two failed to make the 1984 Canadian Olympic team and were told outright that Karyn and Rod Garossino from Calgary would stand a better chance in four years of being selected for the Calgary Olympics, they accepted an invitation to represent France. The transfer date had passed for the year, so they competed for Canada for one more season.

The French federation allowed the Duchesnays to continue to train in Oberstdorf, where Christopher Dean choreographed the free dances that sent them to the top of the ice-dance world, stirring up emotions and controversies all along the way. In 1986, Paul and Isabelle were twelfth in the world; ninth in 1987; sixth in 1988 (with Dean's "Savage Rites"); third in 1989 (with "Eleanor's Dream"); second in 1990 (with "Missing"); and gold medalists in 1991 (with "Missing II").*

In the spring of 1990, Jayne Torvill announced her engagement to Phil Christensen. During the summer of the same year, in what may have been a related development, Christopher Dean proposed to Isabelle Duchesnay. Chris and Isabelle were married a year later during a ceremony that the press portrayed as a royal wedding. The bride wore a

---

* After 1986, the Garossinos never beat the Duchesnays in world and Olympic competition. They finished tenth at the Worlds in 1985; ninth in 1986; tenth in 1987; eleventh in 1988; and eighth in 1989. Additionally, Karyn and Rod placed twelfth at the 1988 Olympics, compared to Isabelle and Paul's eighth-place finish.

$10,000 Nina Ricci gown. The marriage was arguably the worst event that could have befallen either partner. They were temperamentally unsuited to one other, and they entertained vastly different views on what constituted a harmonious relationship.

A succession of injuries, as well as a family tragedy, marred the 1991–92 Olympic year. Isabelle and Paul's half-brother, Gaston, although he had never smoked, died a painful death from lung cancer. To make matters worse, Chris insisted that the Duchesnays perform their Olympic free dance to "West Side Story," a musical selection that he planned to use in his next tour with Jayne. According to Paul and Isabelle, Chris told them that, if they refused his choice, he wouldn't do their choreography.

Compared to routines of past seasons, "West Side Story" seemed hackneyed and trite. Moreover, Isabelle performed it with bronchitis. Lacking their customary passion, and outskated by the Russians, the Duchesnays took silver medals and bad memories home from Albertville, France.

By 1993, Isabelle's marriage lay in shreds. Her professional career was having its ups and downs as well. It all came to a screeching halt on June 22, 1995, when Paul suffered a broken disc. A year later, he was beginning to feel sound when a near-fatal rollerblading accident sent him to the hospital for major reconstructive surgery. The final turn of the screw came in February 1997, during a "pizza lift." Paul aggravated his earlier back injury and faced the choice of continuing to skate while risking permanent paralysis or finding something else to do with his life.

Paul moved to Florida with his parents to start a family business far away from Canadian ice. Isabelle tried her hand at commentary and film work and continued to recuperate from the physical and mental duress of the 1990s.

⚜⚜⚜

W ell before we met, Isabelle Duchesnay decided that she hated me. (She confessed those sentiments many years after the fact.) Commentating on the Junior Worlds performance of Isabelle and her brother Paul while they still competed for Canada, I had apparently remarked that, although their performance was better than mediocre, their talent and potential were far greater. I, who forget nothing, have no recollection of that mild criticism, yet Isabelle claimed that my remark festered for years in her mind.

There is no team in the history of figure skating for whom I feel a greater affinity. As Canadian ice dancers, Paul and Isabelle concluded that, because of the attitudes of David Dore and ISU members Joyce Hisey and Barbara Graham, their international skating future was doomed. During my own career, I waged war with similar CFSA factions. In my day, David Dore was not yet director general, but he was able to influence my chances for selection to international teams. Fortunately, Joyce Hisey was qualified to judge only ice dancing, not men's singles, but it was she whom I believe blocked, for more than twenty years, my honorary lifetime membership in the Cricket Club.

Paul, Isabelle, and I had valid reasons for feeling that our own federation discriminated against us. We were all somehow unable to convince the establishment of our talents and our potential. The Canadian powers-that-be were eventually forced to recognize me because of my success abroad. The Duchesnays, on the other hand, made the audacious decision to leave Canada and represent France. The Canadian power structure, specifically David Dore and Joyce Hisey, had to swallow some unpleasant medicine when Isabelle and Paul achieved phenomenal renown all over the world as representatives of France.

I don't know why the CFSA was unable to detect the Duchesnays' unique talent. As a CBC commentator, I was entirely in their court. I made a point of referring to the injustices that beset them as often as I could for the benefit of the Canadian viewing audience. I'm certain that my caustic remarks brought further resentment down upon Paul and Isabelle's heads and probably provoked full-blown loathing for me. I didn't care.

At the 1987 Worlds in Cincinnati, British coach Betty Callaway, the former teacher of Jayne Torvill and Christopher Dean, made a point of telling me to watch the Duchesnays. Their number had excited the European public, she said, and they certainly had a chance to do well at the Worlds.

During the years since my commentary on their Junior Worlds routine, Paul and Isabelle had matured dramatically. Although the Spanish number they presented in Cincinnati (to "Spanish Dance for Guitar and Orchestra," "Concierto de Aranjuez," and "Malagueña") was somewhat fascinating, it hardly rendered me speechless. The medium of ice dance is about a man and a woman performing together while romantic frissons pass between them. In that respect, the Duchesnays were at a disadvantage. As brother and sister, they were obliged to avoid incestuous gestures and overtones.

The ice dancers were generally trite and silly in 1987, with the exception of Russians Natalia Annenko and Genrikh Sretenski, who offered a divine program to Tchaikovsky's *Romeo and Juliet*. They were blond and gorgeous to begin with, and someone had costumed them divinely in a soft shade of apple-blossom pink. The music, the floating clothes, the physical beauty of the partners, their Russian technique, and their spiritual passion combined to create a special moment in skating history – all for naught, because the politically motivated judges were interested only in "protocol judging," i.e., conforming to preordained outcomes. For all their beauty, excellence, and magic, Annenko and Sretenski finished fourth across the board.

The turning point in Paul and Isabelle's amateur career occurred at the 1988 Europeans in Prague, Czechoslovakia. Sometimes only an audience can discern and appreciate a revolutionary approach to skating. The judges may have neither the eyes nor the inclination to perceive and acknowledge innovation. Isabelle and Paul's "jungle dance," skated to "Savage Rites," flew in the face of every traditional free dance. The Duchesnays wore what looked like tattered brown animal skins. Their music was composed of tribal drumbeats. Such intensity, passion, and conviction had never before been seen in competitive skating.

Following the conclusion of the number, pandemonium erupted. Czechoslovakia was still very much under Soviet influence. I sensed that the Czechs' reaction to the Duchesnays paralleled and expressed their necessarily repressed political reaction against the Soviet presence. Perhaps the routine had helped to ignite anew their beliefs about freedom, self-expression, and individuality that had lain dormant since the Soviet takeover.

The Polish judge, ignoring the audience reaction, awarded the Duchesnays a 4.8. The Russian judge, more astute, begrudgingly pulled out a 5.7 and a 5.8. It was the Polish judge who required a police escort to leave the building.

I interviewed the Duchesnays after that performance and found them rather tongue-tied and fabulously naive. Even they could not quite grasp the magnitude of what had just happened because of them.

At the 1988 Calgary Olympics, ice-dance tickets were among the most prized. The Duchesnays, thanks to Christopher Dean's choreography, performed the most memorable OSP, "Valentine's Tango." It was an interesting study, both intellectually and artistically. I openly admit that I know nothing about the technical peculiarities of ice dance, yet I pride myself on knowing everything about good, honest skating. For me, Paul and Isabelle's performance captured the essence of how a tango should be performed. The choreographic sum was greater than its parts.

Nonetheless, the marks were low. At the Olympics, many judges operate according to personal agendas. They try their best to help their own skaters win medals. I felt that the marks that Canadian judge Ann Shaw gave to Paul and Isabelle were particularly insulting. Ann was trying desperately, and ultimately without success, to push the Canadian team of Tracy Wilson and Robert McCall into second place. Tracy and Rob finished third across the board.

For their free dance, Paul and Isabelle once again skated to "Savage Rites," and it was certainly one of the more sensational performances at those Olympics. In spite of fanatic support from the crowd of eighteen thousand, the Canadian judge once again posted one of the lowest marks on the panel: a shameful 5.2. The Duchesnays' composition marks ran from 5.1 to 5.7, while their presentation marks spanned the gap from 5.3 to 5.8. They ended the Olympics in eighth place.

After the event, I spoke to the American ice-dance judge, Nancy Meiss. Her 5.8 had been Paul and Isabelle's highest mark. Nancy told me that she had felt no qualms about giving such a high score. With no serious American contenders, she had been free to call it as she saw it.

I particularly remember Nancy's final comment: "I gave them a 5.8 because I thought that they were totally fabulous." That remark summed up the sentiments of 99.9 percent of the spectators in Calgary. I optimistically believed that Russian domination of ice dance had started to ebb away. The Duchesnays' star was on the rise.

During the next several years, thanks in large part to Christopher Dean, the Duchesnays produced some of the most mystifying and truly interesting ice-dance performances of all time. Their team, which included trainer Martin Skotnicky, played creative Russian roulette. They pushed ice dance to such heights that it became far and away the most popular event at international skating competitions.

Whenever I had the privilege of commentating about one of Paul and Isabelle's performances, I made a point of remaining silent throughout the routine. I started my analysis only after they had finished skating. Their programs were too fascinating for viewers to put up with a commentator's droning.

At the 1990 Europeans in Leningrad, wearing the simplest, least-pretentious costumes (a little red dress for Isabelle and a pair of black pants and a torn red shirt for Paul), the Duchesnays caused another revolution by skating a program called "Missing" to haunting Chilean pan flutes. The music, from English choreographer Christopher Bruce's ballet *Ghost Dances*, commemorated the "disappeared" who had vanished after the overthrow of Salvador Allende.

The citizens of Leningrad reacted with fervor similar to that expressed in Prague. The applause was so deafening that it forced the Duchesnays to return to the ice to acknowledge their supporters. I burst out laughing on live television, because the situation was not only dramatic but also a trifle absurd. Isabelle displayed body language that reminded me of Eva Peron receiving her public.

Marina Klimova and Sergei Ponomarenko won the competition, performing to "My Fair Lady," while their fellow Russians, Maia Usova and Alexander Zhulin, finished second, but neither couple received the standing ovation that their countrymen had accorded the Duchesnays. The great ice dancer Andrei Minenkov (former partner of Irina Moiseeva) remarked, "Their performance was so beautiful, I couldn't tell you what struck me the most. It was like a painting that moves you to ecstasy without even distinguishing the colors. Just stunning."

Perhaps the most fabulous of all the Duchesnays' numbers was one that never saw the light of a world championship. At the 1991 Europeans in Sofia, they presented "Reflections," set to a piano piece called "Ocean Waves" from the album *Winter into Spring* by George Winston. Creatively and artistically, it was their most outrageous program – so outrageous, according to the establishment, that if they elected to perform the same number at the Worlds, they would be slaughtered. The fact that Isabelle and Paul fell unceremoniously in their final pose probably didn't improve the critics' opinions.

The number was so avant-garde that Paul and Isabelle, who resembled one another to a remarkable degree, wore identical costumes and acted as one man and his mirror image. They were photographed for a striking double-page spread in *Life* magazine – a singular honor.

At the 1991 Munich Worlds a month later, everyone expected to see "Reflections." Instead, Paul and Isabelle assumed the ending pose of "Missing." Familiar music began to play. With their free dance "Missing II," the Duchesnays finally won their one and only world title. I found the program very good, but not as memorable as some of their earlier routines.

By 1992, the Duchesnays were as famous as the Eiffel Tower, and they were determined to win the Olympic gold medal in Albertville. For the record, the Russian team of Marina Klimova and Sergei Ponomarenko was just too strong to be beaten – by anyone. The Duchesnays, whether due to injury, family concerns, time constraints, or all three, were unable to compete at the Europeans that led up to the Olympics. I interpreted that as a major setback for them.

In addition, the routines that they skated were far and away my least favorite. Judges placed their original dance, a polka to "The Lonely Goatherd" from *The Sound of Music*, second in a five-four split for first place. One of the five judges who preferred the Russian team was the Canadian, Bill McLachlan.

The pedestrian free-dance musical choice, "West Side Story," paled in comparison to "Savage Rites" and "Missing." Isabelle played the Maria role, while Paul played her brother, Bernardo, in a routine that had been tamed to fit the stringent rules of ice dance.

In an interview that was televised coast to coast, I mentioned that the Duchesnays' big mistake at the Olympics had been to try to win the gold medal by playing it safe. Isabelle happened to hear my remark and refused to speak to me for a number of weeks while we toured Canada with Stars on Ice.

Isabelle, almost like a dominatrix, ruled the roost and called the shots. However, she was among the most sensitive and fragile people I have ever known, and she was subject to extreme depression and terrifying nervous bouts. During important competitions, Paul became the anchor of their ship.

After the Olympics, Isabelle and Paul retired from the amateur world and never competed again, even as professionals. Isabelle told me that the money they might have won didn't justify the unbearable emotional pain that she experienced just *thinking* about competition.

I performed with the Duchesnays once in an exhibition in Reno, Nevada. The production was televised as a Christmas special starring Kristi Yamaguchi. During the practice session, always a rather casual event among friends, I tried to begin a conversation with Isabelle. When she did not speak to me, I asked why. She explained that, when she and Paul practiced together, it was all work. There was no room for social chit-chat. I truly admired her artistic dedication, unlike any other I had witnessed.

After her marriage to Christopher Dean fell apart, Isabelle suffered a nervous breakdown, and she and Paul returned to Aylmer to live with their parents. Eventually Isabelle was well enough to join Paul in their own French touring show. As world stars and French heroes, they were huge box-office draws. I'm certain that the show did well for a period of time. However, as with many such shows, the promoter absconded with the profits and it all fell apart.

At a certain point, Paul, Isabelle, and I decided to work together to create a new program for their upcoming Tom Collins tour. That never happened, primarily because Paul's back gave out.

Soon after their retirement, I told Martha, my co-author, that Isabelle and Paul were looking for a collaborator to help them write an autobiography. I even arranged for Martha to stay with my brother's family outside Ottawa while she conducted preliminary interviews in Aylmer. After two trips from western New York State to Aylmer, dozens of tapes, and at least a thousand hours of work, Martha found an eager publisher for the book. Expecting that Isabelle and Paul would be equally eager, she contacted them and waited. Many weeks later, the editor assigned to the project still hadn't heard from the Duchesnays.

It turned out that Isabelle had completely lost her nerve. She didn't want to write a book that didn't air all her grievances, but she was afraid of potential repercussions, in particular from Christopher Dean. Paul was never one to buck his sister when she was in a foul mood, so Martha received neither a cent nor a thank you.

When I think today about the Duchesnays, I believe that the public enjoyed their fabulous career, however short, more than Paul and Isabelle themselves did. Pain and emotional turbulence prevented them from savoring the heights they achieved. That is a shame, because they were among the most fascinating creative artists in the history of ice dance.

After the Duchesnays left the scene, ice dance declined dramatically. Today it has become low-level schlock. Its future is in jeopardy. This mystical art will be salvaged only if skaters like Paul and Isabelle carry the creative torch and illuminate the minds and passions of future ice-dance couples.

World Champion, Cincinnati, Ohio, 1987

CHAPTER 14

BRIAN ORSER

⁂

The Silver-Plated Golden Boy

B rian Orser arrived on December 18, 1961, to complete Joanne and Harl "Butch" Orser's close-knit small-town family of seven that already included siblings Janice, Bob, Mike, and Mary Kay. When Brian was four, Butch was offered the opportunity to manage, and eventually own, the Coca-Cola bottling plant in Penetanguishene, Ontario, so the family moved from Belleville north to Midland, Penetanguishene's twin, and later to Penetanguishene.

The Orser children attended Catholic school and participated in many sports, including recreational figure skating. Brian loved skating for the sensations of speed, lift, and abandon that it offered, although the instruction available in Ontario cottage country was rudimentary.

That was until twenty-one-year-old Doug Leigh arrived. At a local carnival, Donald Jackson had seen Brian skate and had recommended to Joanne that her son take private lessons. She scheduled a fifteen-minute session with Leigh, the young coach based in Orillia who taught one day a week in Midland. Thus began their decades-long association.

Brian first attracted the attention of the CFSA when he won the pre-novice free-skating event at the 1974 Central Ontario Sectionals. The association sent him to a summer seminar that gave the twelve-year-old his first exposure to skating on a national scale

After a period of setbacks marked by three leg fractures in a year and a half, Brian began to make steady technical progress. At the 1978 Canadians, he attempted but missed the triple Axel, a jump that no one had ever successfully completed in competition. A month later, Canadian Vern Taylor made history at the Worlds in Ottawa with the first officially certified triple Axel.

Triple Axels numbers two, three, and four belonged to Brian. He would virtually own the move until 1982. He consequently became known as Mr. Triple Axel, landing the first triple-Axel combination and performing the first two-triple-Axel program.

In 1979, the CFSA pressured Brian to leave coach Leigh and move to one of the established training centers. The letter detailing that plan infuriated Brian and Doug and encouraged them to dig in and stand their ground in Orillia, where Brian lived by then and trained full-time.

In his first season as a senior, Brian finished fourth at the 1980 Canadians in Kitchener. By the next year, he was on the top step of the podium, where he remained for eight consecutive years.

It was at a summer seminar in 1981 that Brian met Uschi Keszler, the German-American teacher and choreographer who henceforth influenced the course of his career and the development of his personal skating style.

Although Brian won the first of two Olympic silver medals in 1984, the culmination of his work with Uschi came with the brilliant "Sing Sing Sing" short program that he performed in 1987 at the Worlds in Cincinnati, Ohio. He defeated defending champion Brian Boitano, winning his only world gold medal and his third of four world freestyle titles (for the highest finish in the short and long programs combined).

All that remained was the legendary "Battle of the Brians" at the Calgary Olympics the following year, followed by a distinguished and varied professional career that continues to this day.

Brian was a long-time featured performer with Stars on Ice. He headlined three television specials, won an Emmy for his role in *Carmen on*

Ice with Katarina Witt and Brian Boitano, and skated in countless shows and professional competitions.

ᘓᘐᘓᘐᘓᘐ

I can't just promenade down memory lane when I think of Brian Orser. That journey is more like a marathon on the Trans-Canada Highway. I've seen so much. I've heard so much. I know so much.

Let me begin at the beginning of a brilliant skater's remarkable career. Brian first prowled into my mind at the Canadians in Kitchener in early 1980. In those days, young Brian seemed to me rather faceless and bodiless. He projected no charisma and was almost anorectically thin. Since I had not previously seen him skate, I anticipated his senior men's performance with reserve.

My precise memory of Brian's Kitchener performance has long since evaporated. The three qualities that I do recall are his phenomenal ability to leap and rotate; a lack of personality that made him seem almost wooden; and the poisonous pea-green suit that enveloped him without a touch of elegance.

Throughout Brian's career, no matter with whom he worked (coach or choreographer, some less than brilliant), the sterling genius of his technical talent shone. That virtuosity remains to this day, while Brian's showmanship, personality, and attire have improved exponentially over the years.

One skating season after the Kitchener event, the Worlds took place in Hartford, Connecticut. During Brian's long program, broadcast across Canada, he executed a perfect triple Axel. At the time, that feat embodied shocking virtuosity. Brian nonetheless received what, in my opinion, was a modest set of marks that in no way reflected his technical superiority. He finished sixth.

In those early days, I saw Brian as a timid but diligent workhorse, consistently dependable and humble about his talent. Team Canada, including coach Doug Leigh and his entourage, was probably satisfied with the top-ten finish. I was also delighted with Brian's sixth-place results, but not at all for the same reasons. My contentment was based on the fact that young Mr. Orser had not medaled at the event, so he was not yet treading upon my reputation as Canada's premier male skater.

Brian was the son of Butch and Joanne Orser, a couple who lived over time in several provincial Ontario towns north of Toronto. I surmise that Brian was brought up in a middle-class environment, although Butch Orser was not a poor man by any standard. I mention this because Brian, as a budding young skater, enjoyed the best of everything, as far as I could tell. Unlike myself during those early years of development, thanks to his parents, he wanted for little or nothing.

Brian eventually trained in Orillia, Ontario, a dot on the map. Training in a small town was both positive and negative. The positive aspect was that serious training was uninterrupted. There were no distractions whatsoever. On the negative side of the ledger, such a sleepy town offered few of the external cultural influences that are so necessary to the sculpting of a great talent like Brian's. During his amateur career, he hovered in the chasm between the blue-collar approach and truly stylish skating.

Brian was the first of a group of major male ice stars to spring, one after the other, from Canadian rinks. He enjoyed an unusually long amateur career, winning the Canadian men's title eight years in a row, for which I was grateful, even though Brian surpassed my own six national titles. As his amateur reign continued, I was delighted that I wasn't forced to share or cede my position in the professional ranks.

The CFSA and its judges, unlike our American neighbors, have never been comfortable with two Canadian skaters of international brilliance competing at the same time. Better to choose one clear-cut representative. There were certainly other skaters who offered Brian fair competition, but the judges propped up Brian when necessary. Although he was ultimately in a class by himself, there were questionable performances at three separate Canadian championships.

The greatest injustice occurred in 1982 in Brandon, Manitoba, where Brian Pockar of Calgary totally eclipsed Brian Orser, in my opinion. Pockar went on to win the bronze medal that year at the Worlds in Copenhagen, Denmark.

Although I didn't witness the second flawed performance, fellow professionals and skating peers who viewed the 1984 Canadians in Regina, Saskatchewan, insisted that the senior men's title that year should have belonged to Gary Beacom.

The third storm cloud of doubt that hung over Brian concerned his win at the 1988 Canadians in Victoria, B.C., where some felt that Kurt Browning outskated the champion. Kurt subsequently became a four-time world gold medalist.

The point of this reminiscence is, at least in part, self-serving. If, on those three occasions, Brian had placed second, my record of six wins would still be the Canadian benchmark. As far as Canadian officials were concerned, however, the question was, How could they send their second-ranking male to win a world title? The premier candidate, in their eyes, had to be the reigning Canadian champion.

As for international competition, Brian became epoxy-glued to the second-place spot. His teammate Robert McCall, 1988 Olympic bronze medalist in ice dance with Tracy Wilson, enjoyed joking, "Heigh-ho, Silver. Go, Brian, go!" (a humorous reference to the Lone Ranger's horse).

As the CBC's head skating commentator, I was part of a large contingent sent to Sarajevo for the 1984 Olympics. Although attending the Olympic Games, particularly on the inside track, is certainly a rare privilege, those particular Games, with regard to all sports, struck me as dull in every way – with the exception of a few sterling achievements, among them Brian Orser's. He delivered one of the great performances of his career.

The Olympics are a poker game. Often the competitors themselves are the least significant players. Like greyhounds running mindlessly around a track, they chase the mechanical rabbit. The real heavyweights, the people with all the cards, are the members of the IOC and the CEOs of the various international television networks.

At Sarajevo, it seemed to me, the American network ABC controlled the city, the Games, and practically everything else. In fact, ABC went so far as to have a hotel built to accommodate its multitudes of technicians and officials. I well remember the many nights I spent in that Holiday Inn, gambling my brains out with fellow commentators in order to assuage the boredom of those endless Games. In the post-Milosovic era, that Holiday Inn is a pile of rubble.

The men's competition began with the school-figure event. American champion Scott Hamilton won with convincing marks. Brian finished that event in seventh place, outside of the top three but still close enough, with a lot of luck and wildly jumbled ordinals, to win the gold medal. As a commentator and interested spectator, I joined many others to pore over the tracings on the ice surface. The Orser figures, it seemed to me, were similar in quality to Hamilton's. The one big difference was that Scott was American, and the American television network craved a home-grown champion.

The men's short-program event took place in the afternoon and was marked by many exceptional performances. Sometimes, as if by osmosis, bad performances, spewing negative energy, produce more performances of the same poor quality. In this case, the reverse seemed to occur. An exception was Scott Hamilton's timid and lackluster performance.

Brian's short program followed Scott's. He skated with flawless and terrifying virtuosity, wearing a peculiar shade of sunset-cantaloupe-yellow for his *Cats* routine. To this day, I have never seen another skater wear that color on the ice. In a live interview after Brian's first-place finish, I referred to the originality of his costume. Brian was so polite that his responses to all my questions began with "Yes, sir" or "No, sir." His vulnerability and naive charm touched me. Had I performed that god-like short program, I would surely have behaved with arrogance.

In the mid-1980s, while still working for the CBC, I conceived and hosted a television program that focused on the great skating perform-ances of the decade. There were many to choose among, but the long program that Brian skated at Sarajevo, to music from the Biblical film *King of Kings*, was an obvious choice.

Precise details of truly magical events are often impossible to recall. What one remembers is the electrifying emotional effect. Brian's long free skate in Yugoslavia seemed to be fueled by reckless and irreverent genius. By the highest historical skating standards, it was flawless. To this day, it holds its own as an example of timeless excellence.

The same could not be said of the long program offered by soon-to-be-crowned Olympic gold medalist Scott Hamilton. ABC's champion gave another brittle and weak performance, containing just three triple jumps – in contrast to Brian's six. Although the judges ranked Scott second after Brian, the Canadian's lower figures placement had already sealed his fate. That monstrous injustice ranks for me among the gravest ever perpetrated upon a competitive skater. Once again, "Silver" had to pretend to be content with second place.

Brian's global superiority as a free skater was well known. Sooner or later the silver streak that haunted him so stubbornly was bound to turn to gold. However, the golden moment was more distant than anyone could have foreseen.

In the 1986 men's event at the Worlds in Geneva, no one was a true favorite, although Brian's track record certainly stood him in good stead. Alexander Fadeev, the 1985 world champion, was expected to be a factor in the mix. So was the gifted Czech, Jozef Sabovcik. Act I of the long rivalry between Brian Orser and American heavyweight Brian Boitano was about to take place as well.

Often, when there is no clear favorite, certain competitors are uncomfortable throwing down the gauntlet. Ultimately – and I could write a book on this topic (perhaps I already have) – losing brilliantly can be far more comfortable than winning. It was Brian Boitano who tossed down the gauntlet, and perhaps an entire suit of chain mail as well. He pulverized his competition.

Otherwise the men's long-program event was particularly poor that year, and Brian Orser's contribution was no exception. I watched it on German television while appearing with Holiday on Ice. Upon my return to Canada for a post-Worlds engagement, I happened to meet the returning Canadian team at Toronto's Lester B. Pearson International Airport.

Brian Orser wasn't among the group, having been invited to perform on the ISU Tour of Champions. However, Doug Leigh, sporting a fire-engine-red ski jacket emblazoned with crests, pins, and the words *Canadian Team*, saw me on the concourse but did not say hello. Instead he greeted me with a whiff of bitterness, couched in upbeat jive, saying simply, "Well, we blew it again." That was *all* he said. I don't know what I had expected, but I found the remark so peculiarly negative that I never forgot it. At least for that moment, silver ingots were sewn into Brian's pockets.

Because of my passion for historical minutiae, I would like to mention one further incident before leaving the subject of Geneva. A friend of mine, the Soviet international judge Tatiana Danilenko, astounded the audience and the entire figure-skating world by pushing her favorite skater, Alexander Fedeev, with the flabbergasting mark of 5.9 for a program so fraught with mistakes that it wouldn't have won the Eastern Canadian Men's Juvenile title. As a result, Valentin Piseev of the Soviet federation banned Danilenko forever from the judging ranks.* The high mark notwithstanding, she at least had placed Fadeev second. The Austrian judge had actually placed him first.

The loss of Tatiana Danilenko's services certainly did not pose a problem for the Soviets, who had many other judges ready to attend the next year's championship, follow the same instructions, and perpetrate the same political act. If Fadeev had skated well, Danilenko would not have suffered. The fact that he did not almost destroyed her judging career.

By 1987, Brian Orser had accumulated three world silver medals. His luck was bound to change sooner or later, and it did in Cincinnati. I was the commentator at the Worlds for CBC Television, which had signed a four-year contract to broadcast the event, supplanting long-time broadcaster CTV.

Winning a world title is a task that can be accomplished only through discipline, courage, and a fortunate destiny. Brian presented a supremely adequate long program, wearing a refined shade of grayish teal blue that I found to border on dull. I do not begrudge Brian his win in Cincinnati. By winning, he dethroned the reigning world champion, Brian Boitano, in Brian's own backyard. That was no mean accomplishment.

---

* The suspension was not permanent. Tatiana Danilenko was recently spotted judging the ladies' event at the 2002 Olympic Games in Salt Lake City.

Ted Reynolds, my CBC colleague, announced Brian's win on the Canadian airwaves. He delivered his announcement at the end of the evening's programming, remarking to the public that Toller Cranston could not speak, because he felt too emotional about Orser's win. True enough, emotional frissons surged through my body, but they were not quite the frissons that Ted presumed they were. The reason why Brian's win had silenced me on the spot was that, with a new Canadian world champion, I was forced down the ladder several rungs. Perhaps that sounds a bit mean and self-absorbed, but it is the truth.

The Calgary Olympics loomed, and Brian approached them as the reigning world champion and Olympic silver medalist. Those facts, coupled with the Canadian venue, would cement his fate (his countrymen thought). Brian's fellow Canadians expected him to win gold. Human strategies rarely work out so neatly.

Skate Canada, an important preliminary international competition, was held at the very Calgary Saddledome that would host the Olympics less than four months hence. In a show of brazen courage, Brian Boitano entered that competition, knowing that he ventured into the lion's den. Orser was the heavy favorite.

From all reports, Boitano outskated Orser in the decisive long-program event. However, Orser won on all but two judges' cards, and Canadians accepted the outcome as foreshadowing. Orser would bring home the Olympic gold medal that he and Canada so richly deserved. It was a *fait accompli*.

Two words in the English language seem equally odious to me: *if* and *assume*. Strike *if* from your vocabulary and never, ever assume. Orser flew home from Skate Canada on a wave of confidence, fueled by his ever-expanding entourage. Boitano returned to San Francisco with not only a silver medal, but also a cold blue flame ignited deep within him. The next time that Boitano met Orser in competition, things would be different. Boitano would counter Orser's confidence with his own deadly ambition.

The 1988 Canadians took place in Victoria. Orser's poor performance raised eyebrows. Perhaps grabbing that Olympic gold medal would not be as easy as his countrymen might have supposed. When a skater performs a set program poorly, it is like a potter discovering cracks in a ceramic bowl after it has been fired.

In the months leading up to the Olympics, more and more people entered Brian's service in order to ensure, without question, that he would win. That is a potentially dangerous situation, one that conjures up images of a favorite childhood story of mine, *Thidwick the Big-Hearted Moose* by Dr. Seuss.

Thidwick had remarkably accommodating antlers. One by one, other animals came to perch within them, taking up residence and encumbering Thidwick to an impossible degree. But Thidwick was too kind to evict his guests, so he nearly starved to death for lack of grazing mobility.

Team Orser seemed to grow and grow and grow. There were physical trainers, choreographers, medical specialists, sports psychologists, costume designers, biographers, mothers, fathers, lovers, friends, and even a rolfer. (Rolfing is a form of deep massage, purported to relieve physical and emotional tension.) It seemed to many of us that the members of Team Orser wanted the gold medal more than Brian did.

I can only surmise that Brian felt tense. I can only surmise that a little voice of doubt from within occasionally protested against the certainties of everyone around him. Meanwhile, somewhere in a suburban rink in the San Francisco area, the other Brian trained diligently with his long-time coach, Linda Leaver. Together those two composed a lean-and-mean Team Boitano.

Anybody who experienced the Calgary Olympics will remember those Games as among the most magical and exciting in recent memory. Even the weather cooperated to enhance the international crowd's enjoyment. Throughout the Games, one of Calgary's famous chinook winds blew gently, warming the freezing temperatures to an almost subtropical degree. I recall that, while sporting my CBC snowsuit, I pined for a pair of Bermuda shorts. Indeed, many of the Olympic competitors, specifically the Jamaican bobsled team, wore the briefest of briefs as they strolled through the venues. The warmth of the weather was eclipsed only by the molten energy of one thousand Calgary volunteers.

Although I had access to every venue for the duration of the Games, I do not recall ever having a conversation with Canada's silver-plated golden boy. Each Olympics provides minor melodramas that distract and entertain. The Battle of the Brians, as reported in the media, offered pure entertainment. Equally amusing was the daily Canadian reportage that faithfully described the activities and emotional states of Butch and Joanne, Brian Orser's devoted parents.

Olympic competitors usually take pleasure in being sequestered in apartments in the Olympic Village, protected from the palpable frenzy of the fans and press corps. More importantly, they become infected with positive energy, seemingly by osmosis. Brian Boitano, accompanied by teammates Christopher Bowman and Paul Wylie, stayed in an apartment in the village, embracing the Olympic spirit. Brian Orser, however, as Canada's most special and valued Olympic hopeful, was relegated with other members of Team Orser to a private residence called Canada House.

The men's short-program event took place in the old Stampede Corral, the rink in which I won the 1972 world free-skating title. That old barn of a building did not seem as big in 1988 as the one that loomed so large in my memory.

The three world champions, Fadeev, Boitano, and Orser, entered the event in one-two-three order after the figures. A number of other fabulous skaters competed that day, skaters who, years later, would carve magnificent destinies for themselves: Viktor Petrenko, Christopher Bowman, Paul Wylie, and Kurt Browning.

As the competition progressed, one nearly flawless performance followed another. Every stunning achievement provoked a standing ovation. Canadian audiences are truly the most appreciative and generous in the world. The crowd had reached its boiling point by the time the last flight of skaters took to the ice.

Perhaps because of their virtuosity, fueled by the palpable excitement of the spectators, the competitors struck me as tropical piranhas in a tank that was far too small to contain them. From all reports, when a tsunami wave is about to wreak its devastation upon the land, animal life exhibits irregular and erratic behavior. Fish, for example, have been reported in such circumstances to leap out of their bowls. There were many incidents of skaters jumping too high and far, practically leaping off the ice surface into the audience.

Orser, wearing cerulean blue, was the first of the top group to skate. He performed to an upbeat, commercial version of Glenn Miller's "Sing Sing Sing" without perceptible flaws. The judging became a matter of taste, because Boitano's stately, nostalgic rendition of "Les Patineurs," choreographed by Sandra Bezic, was also flawless. Given my choice, I probably would have flashed the green light for Orser, because of his verve, lightness, and energy. Orser placed first, Boitano second. However, with the figures standings factored in, Boitano still led the competition.

I arrived alone at the Saddledome for the men's long-program competition and found my solitary seat in a prime location: center ice, row eight. As in Sarajevo, CBC was a secondary broadcaster, so I didn't provide live-to-air commentary. I could enjoy the event like any other spectator.

The competition began with a spate of stunning performances. With each flight of skaters, the audience heated up by degrees, anticipating the long-awaited showdown, the Battle of the Brians.

When the final group of skaters took the ice, the audience melted into a profound state of awe. The warm-up itself was so terrifying in its significance that my body began to tremble uncontrollably, either from excitement or fear. Although the body heat of thousands of people warmed the building, I put on my winter coat, my woolen scarf, and a pair of fur-lined mittens, preparing myself for the spectacle. Still, I could not stop shaking.

Brian Boitano was the first to skate. He performed to Carmine Coppola's score for the television miniseries *Napoleon and Josephine*, wearing a navy-blue military-style costume with gold braid. He presented an unprecedented display of virtuosity, though the program's simple choreographic grid had little nuance, finesse, or detailed footwork. It was a big slab of grade-A filet mignon without vegetables and garnish. Its essence, quite simply, was jumping strength.

Sandra Bezic had brilliantly packaged Boitano in a tailor-made program supported by appropriate music. During the year leading up to the competition, she had edited out the superficial and redundant elements of Brian's skating style. That editing was ingenious. The program itself was not.

The judging of figure skating has a lot to do with the style of the moment. In 1988, multiple triple jumps were in fashion. Choreographically, there was a dead spot at about the three-quarter point in Boitano's program. As an interested skating analyst, it bothered me greatly, yet I understood the choreographic methodology that supported it. Boitano came virtually to a complete stop and did nothing of importance for a good twenty seconds. Having regained his strength, he then accelerated into a triple Axel with such height and velocity that it seemed to be a weapon of mass destruction.

In truth, that particular jump was marred by a tiny touchdown of the free foot, but its impact on the judges constituted Brian Orser's death knoll. Even before the marks were revealed, I knew instinctively that Boitano had won the gold medal. The Canadian audience would not have agreed with me.

Orser was backstage, walking through his routine. He wore a scarlet military-style costume, designed by Frances Dafoe and similar in style to his rival's costume, and when his turn came, Brian Orser performed with no less brilliance than Brian Boitano. His choreography certainly possessed more detail, with a great emphasis on complicated connecting steps that linked element to element and jump to jump.

Brian skated to *The Bolt* by Shostakovich, a piece of music from an old program of mine (and Dennis Coi's as well). My coach, Ellen Burka, had located it among her tapes at Brian's request.

Shostakovich, like his fellow Russian composer Prokofiev, composed dramatic music, usually in a minor key. Such music falls on the listener's ears with more discordance than music written in a major key. Perhaps the minor chords exerted a subtle negative influence. Such a close contest can rest on subconscious minutiae.

Brian Orser's performance suffered from a single flaw: a triple flip jump popped into a double with a two-footed landing. Many aficionados cited that flip as the reason why Brian missed out on an Olympic gold medal for the second time in his life. To me, though, the virtuosity of the two Brians had been equal. Like Boitano, Orser received a standing ovation. He also received one perfect mark of 6.0.

One of the CTV cameras devoured the reactions of Brian's parents. It seemed to many Canadians that Joanne Orser, who did indeed suffer from medical problems, was on the verge of a heart attack when the perfect mark was announced. Joanne, the rest of the audience, and Brian himself were all apparently convinced that he had finally struck gold. 'Twas not to be.

Brian Boitano won the 1988 gold medal on a split decision of five judges to four – a tenth of a point. In the "kiss and cry" area just a second after Orser learned the outcome (the camera caught him mouthing the word *shit*), the inexperienced ABC commentator, David Santee, did a terrible thing, cruel to the extreme. Though he acted without malice, he would ultimately lose his job because the public reacted with great outrage. Live-to-air over the American network, Santee began his rinkside interview with Orser by saying, "Brian, I have good news and bad news for you. Those are tremendous composition and style marks – but you're second." Then he shoved his microphone in front of Orser's mouth and asked for a reaction.

I shall never forget the expression on Brian's face. Somehow, in that fleeting moment, his eyes or his almost imperceptibly quivering bottom lip betrayed the still-dawning realization that all the pain, suffering, and energy that he had expended over the past four years had been for naught.

A great celebration had been planned to mark Brian's gold-medal finish, but Team Orser did not drink champagne that night. Many invited guests failed to appear, including David Dore. The event exhibited all the merriment of a funeral wake. That fact in itself was as insulting to Brian as it was sad.

By any standard, Orser's performance had been as brilliant and heroic as Boitano's. In fact, Orser's achievement may have been the more spectacular and courageous because, as the favorite, under monumental pressure, he had risen to the occasion and had performed meticulously for the hometown crowd.

That men's long-program event was, without a doubt, the most phenomenal skating competition in the history of ice. There has never been anything like it. For me, on that Calgary evening, figure skating reached its highest point. To this day, when I reminisce about that extraordinary sporting event, my body is wont to shake. I just can't help it.

The day after the men's long-program event, the last skating competition of the Olympics, the traditional medalists' exhibition took place. It was one more free show that the skaters were obligated to offer the television networks (before skating off to the professional world, where their services would command handsome fees). Although I had done it myself as an Olympic medalist, when Brian Orser skated that afternoon, I couldn't help but wonder how he could muster the emotion, energy, and self-control to hit that ice surface once again.

Even while I commentated on the exhibition, the events of the previous night replayed in my head. Any serious skater who has come close to winning an Olympic medal is just the tiniest bit envious of the skating gods who do so. Nonetheless, having assessed that heroic battle, I shelved my personal feelings and genuinely wished with all my heart that both Brians would find in their forthcoming professional careers all the fame, glory, and financial rewards that they deserved. I could not have risen to the occasion as they did. I could not have faced those competitive warm-ups or delivered those near-perfect performances.

Whatever Brian Orser thought or did directly after Calgary, I never knew. I next saw him at the Worlds in Budapest three weeks later. Today I think of Brian as a good friend and confidant, but in those days I did not know him well. Battle-worn Team Orser had estranged me from him. However, Brian left much of Team Orser at home when he flew to Budapest. It was a different Brian Orser, in temperament and maturity, who entered that competition in Hungary, determined to make the most of the experience.

In the school-figure event, which I did not witness, Orser placed fifth, Boitano third. The judges probably should have been more encouraging to Orser. But what happens so often in life is that, when a god stumbles and is rendered vulnerable (this happened to me in Gothenburg after the 1976 Olympics), the hounds move in for the kill.

In the short-program event, Orser made a mistake. Boitano did not. They entered the long-program event in their Olympic order of finish.

It is fair to say that everybody involved with figure skating at that point had become supersaturated. Nobody seemed particularly interested in the results, including the Hungarian audience. Boitano skated before Orser, and his performance paled in the light of his Olympic achievement. He missed a quadruple-jump attempt and singled his triple Axel. As Orser took the ice, I felt as apprehensive as a Roman citizen watching a great gladiator face the lion.

I needn't have worried. Brian fought the last great amateur battle of his career with a brilliance that surpassed his Olympic effort. True grit and determination kicked in. Wherever the energy came from, he fought with every last drop of strength in his body. If I had been a judge, I would have tossed out the marking system and given the world title to Brian Orser. Instead, the ordinals did him in once again. Brian finished his amateur career in an uncomfortable but familiar position.

An amusing incident later occurred in the men's locker room. Heiko Fischer, the West German champion, possessed an extremely unusual physique and appearance. Though a very competent skater, he was as tall and ungainly as Herman Munster. He may also have provided the impetus for the rule that outlaws the exposure of hairy armpits. According to skating legend, Heiko moaned and whined in the dressing room. He felt that, once again, his marks had been unfairly low, and he just couldn't understand why.

Timid, meek, polite Brian Orser screamed at the top of his lungs, "The reason you didn't get the marks, Heiko, is because you are ugly. Yes, Heiko. You are ugly!"

Those competitors who were sympathetic to Heiko immediately inveighed against Brian. But Brian had finally snapped, and I couldn't blame him. Instead of suppressing his emotions, for once he said exactly what he thought. More than any other skater in history, Brian had paid his dues. He deserved the chance to express an honest (if not terribly kind) opinion.

After the Worlds, I returned to Canada, sick of skating, sick of talking about skating, sick of predicting skating results, and particularly sick of witnessing the evils of skating politics. Just one day after alighting on Canadian soil, I flew to the Divi Southwinds Beach Resort in Barbados, only to be greeted by stampedes of Canadian tourists, who recognized me, even in my Speedo, and insisted upon talking about skating.

During the summer of 1988, in the dismal desert that is Billings, Montana, Brian and I were booked to skate an exhibition together, along with other IMG clients. Having entrusted his destiny to the International Management Group, Brian was about to make his professional debut.

I made a point of watching his first pro performance, while remembering his nearly interminable amateur journey. I, and apparently only I, was aware of the momentousness of the occasion. Absolutely nobody else, including Brian, paid any attention to its significance or spoke a word about it. Maybe Brian had already become just another thoroughbred, running around the track on demand. However, turning professional is no less decisive than a vestal maiden's sacrifice of her virginity. There is no going back.

Brian's first year as a pro was action-packed, and he probably skated more than he had as an amateur. He became a principal skater with Stars on Ice, while at the same time headlining Skate the Nation, the cross-Canada tour mounted by the CFSA. The time had come to make hay while the sun shone, and the sun shone as if Brian were on a beach in Rio.

Over the years, Brian took advantage of almost every opportunity that arrived on his doorstep, and those were many and diverse. Not too long after the 1988 Olympics, he starred as the second male lead, the bullfighter Escamillo, in Katarina Witt's production of *Carmen on Ice*, filmed in Spain. Katarina's acting ability was fairly mediocre, though her visual presence on the screen was stunning. As Don Jose, Boitano fared no better. Ironically, it was Orser, Calgary's silver medalist, who gave the gold-medal performance, in my opinion. All humans with patience and fortitude eventually achieve their fifteen minutes of fame. Each of the three principals won an individual Emmy.

Professional competitions had become popular. What better drawing card for Dick Button's World Professional Championships than a replay (here we go again) of the Battle of the Brians? At the first of these annual competitions, Orser probably entertained serious thoughts of beating his archrival. After a string of defeats, however, I'm convinced that he stopped taking the competitions as seriously as he might have if he had thought that he could win. Boitano remained preoccupied with personal skating excellence. Orser acted upon a conspicuous desire, one to which I could relate: to feather his financial nest with as many feathers as he could gather.

Not immediately, but over a span of three to four years, Boitano's skating grew to be better than ever. Orser's performance level, amid a hectic lifestyle, was bound to slip. Triple Axels and Lutzes became rare, while the famously accursed triple flip evaporated into the mists of time and was never seen again.

The slow and painful death of Brian's good friend Robert McCall, highlighted in *Zero Tollerance*, was an enormous emotional drain on him. Brian proved to every member of the skating family that his kindness, generosity, and concern for Rob were Olympic-class. It was at that time, in the early 1990s, that I began to view Brian in a new way. He was not just a great skater, but a great humanitarian.

After Rob's death, Brian, along with Rob's long-time skating partner, Tracy Wilson, mounted an AIDS benefit, Skate the Dream, that took place near the end of 1992 at Toronto's Varsity Arena and featured the greatest living skaters on the planet. The phenomenon of AIDS, and particularly of AIDS within the figure-skating world, had a high media profile at the moment. *People* magazine and *Time* covered the event, which became a milestone in skating history.

Over the years, Brian was directly responsible for creating many special charitable events. There were too many to mention, but I was fortunate to be included. Among his skating friends and colleagues, Brian is known for kindness and generosity. In the figure-skating world, that is too rare.

Unfortunately, personal loss and emotional strain took their toll on Brian's skating. In a memorable professional championship, the Durasoft Colors Challenge of Champions, produced in December 1993 at the now-defunct Maple Leaf Gardens, Brian was forced by circumstances to swallow a nasty pill. I judged that particular competition, so my memories of it are pristine.

Paul Wylie finished first, with two excellent routines, *Carmina Burana* and "The Untouchables." Robin Cousins placed second, with "Busy Being

Blue" and "On the Frozen Pond." With that, Brian's traditional silver medal melted into bronze, although he clearly believed that he had out-skated Cousins. There was obvious irony in the fact that Robin had choreographed Brian's routines, "Calling You" and "Deeply Dippy."

Meanwhile, Brian had been voted the 1994 Professional Skater of the Year by *American Skating World* magazine, and I had the dubious pleasure, under the circumstances, of announcing that fact to the assembled Toronto audience. Brian, in a barely controlled rage, accepted the award from me at center ice with just enough grace to avoid public embarrassment. The crowd could not see his eyes, but I could. I thought, "If looks could kill, we'd all be dead."

In time, IMG retired the great Brian Orser from Stars on Ice. There was an inevitable changing of the guard, and Brian was bumped off the American tour. However, he had not yet sung his swan song. With the encouragement of Scott Hamilton and Tracy Wilson, he worked with a trainer, lost weight, and got back into fighting shape.

Just as Brian's career was going extremely well again, an unfortunate event in his private life made lurid national news coast-to-coast. In November 1998, he was sued for palimony. He tried in vain to convince the court to seal the file. The public revelation of the lawsuit, the airing of the dirty laundry of one of Canada's most beloved and respected sportsmen, occurred at one of the worst possible times: immediately preceding a professional skating competition in London, Ontario. Brian would be forced to meet the press just days after the scandal had erupted.

That potentially nasty episode ended in triumph when the London audience greeted Brian with a standing ovation. The legal case danced in and out of lawyers' offices and was ultimately settled out of court for an undisclosed sum of money. In a private conversation prior to the settlement, Brian had mentioned to me that one of the demands was $10,000 a month for life. Later, I diplomatically asked where, on a scale of one to ten, with ten as the highest amount, the actual settlement had fallen. Brian announced with a foxy grin and a twinkle in his eye that 1.5 was about the right point on the scale.

Among Brian's lifetime accomplishments, two remarkable recent successes come to mind. At the 2000 Goodwill Games at Lake Placid, Brian gave a performance that skaters, judges, and commentators alike widely discussed in awed tones. Armed anew with a triple Axel, his first since 1998 in Budapest, he lambasted his old adversary, Brian Boitano. At least that was my assessment. In point of fact, the judges disagreed, and the Olympic order of finish officially held once again.

More recently, at a competition in Ottawa, the Sears Open, featuring both amateur and professional skaters, Brian came from fourth place after the technical event to beat Elvis Stojko, the Terminator, and Canada's favorite cowboy, Kurt Browning, as well as U.S. and world champion Todd Eldredge and Canadian young gun Emmanuel Sandhu. That feat must be viewed as the ultimate pinnacle of Brian's career to date. He was the eldest competitor and the only representative of the Olympic classes of 1984 and 1988. I can hear him repeating, as he stood atop the podium, an inane and therefore much-quoted remark, first uttered by Canadian champion Kay Thompson: "I believe in God so much today, it's unbelievable."

To this day, Brian Orser continues to surprise and delight audiences everywhere. He will go down in history as one of the major supporting pillars of skating history. It has been my pleasure throughout the years to watch him skate, to perform with him, to commentate about him, and to judge his work. But more than that, I am proud to have been privileged to call him my friend.

Skate Canada, London, Ontario, 1985

CHAPTER 15

JOZEF SABOVCIK

✲

Born in the Wrong Country

J ozef Sabovcik was born on December 4, 1963, in Bratislava, Czechoslovakia, a nation that no longer exists. His parents were Alexandra, a prima ballerina, and Jozef, a retired dancer and principal choreographer with the National Volks Opera in Vienna, Austria. Jozef's grandmother cared for him while his parents rehearsed and performed less than forty miles from Bratislava. He lived with her on weekdays and with his parents on the weekends. From the time he was six, his grandmother took him to figure skate, day after day, on an outdoor rink.

The Communist system usually weeded out the less promising skaters, and it took Jozef longer than most children to learn each new element. Besides, even at six, he was considered too old to begin treading the path to international success. His persuasive grandmother interceded for him with the establishment, however, and he was allowed to continue. His passion was jumping.

At the age of fifteen, Jozef attended his first Worlds. Starstruck at seeing all the mature skating talent in Vienna, he placed a humble nineteenth. That placement would rise in subsequent years to sixteenth, twelfth, sixth, and finally fourth. By 1984, Jozef had an Olympic bronze medal hanging from his neck, but he never took the giant step onto the Worlds podium.

In 1985 in Gothenburg, Jozef won his first European title. The following year, he won again and executed what most observers thought should have been certified as the first quadruple jump in the record book. He landed it on one foot, then slightly scraped the heel of his free foot coming out.

The day after the event, after viewing a videotape that had been shot from such a poor angle that it failed to show Jozef's free foot at all, the judging panel claimed that he had two-footed the landing and wouldn't be credited with the quad. Commentator Scott Hamilton offered to give the judges a copy of the American videotape, showing the jump cleanly landed on one foot, but the officials had made their final decision.

Two months later at the Worlds in Geneva, Jozef stood in second after the figures and the short program. Then his coach forced him to try a quad during the long-program practice, before he was properly warmed up, and he tore the ligaments of his already-damaged landing knee. Forced to compete in spite of the injury, Jozef gave the worst long-program performance of his life and hobbled off the ice.

After several rounds of surgery, Jozef had to give up his quest to compete at the 1988 Olympics. During the summer of 1987, when he made the decision to quit amateur skating, he effected another change in his life. He married two-time Canadian champion Tracey Wainman, with whom he had been involved since Skate America 1985. They lived in Germany for a year, while Jozef recuperated and eased back into skating, then moved to Canada. During their on-again, off-again relationship, Jozef and Tracey had a son, Blade, born in the spring of 1992.

Once Jozef's knees were sound, he enjoyed a brilliant second career as a professional skater, touring and competing under the *nom de guerre* "Jumpin' Joe."

ℒℰℒℰℒℰ

I n 1973, it appeared to the figure-skating world that it was about time for me to finally win a world title. Everyone around me – coaches, fellow skaters, and even judges – reassured me that the gold medal would fall into my pocket at the forthcoming Worlds in Bratislava. After adequately completing my school figures, and after winning the short program (I never lost a short-program event in a major competition), I was inches away from that goal.

Because of an unsavory incident the night before the men's long-program event, described in depressing detail in *When Hell Freezes Over, Should I Bring My Skates?*, I experienced one of the great disappointments of my life. Instead of winning the gold medal, I ended up in fourth place.

The skaters whom I've always admired the most are those competitors who have been singled out by their home countries as heavy favorites to win. When those extraordinary athletes actually accomplish what they are expected to do, they achieve the purest form of sporting glory. Unpredictable creature that I was, I forever disappointed those who expected me to achieve great things. Conversely, I often surprised those same people by achieving a goal that nobody suspected I could reach. I danced that dramatic jig throughout my skating career.

Only competitors who have experienced the same torture at the end of a long-program performance can appreciate the pain that comes with the realization that an entire year of hard work, discipline, and sacrifice has just exploded, leaving a great void. From one second to the next, a fantasy dies.

At the end of my disastrous Bratislava long program, a small, thin, ten-year-old boy skated out to meet me, carrying a few sad, limp tulips. I looked down into his enormous china-blue eyes and accepted his gift of flowers, but I was too emotionally depleted to offer my thanks. The child was certainly aware that his Canadian skating hero had failed. We didn't exchange a word, but I always remembered him.

Thirteen years later, at the 1986 Europeans in Copenhagen, one of my jobs as CBC commentator was to conduct post-competition interviews in a living-room-like set located at the official hotel. Jozef Sabovcik, after a long and turbulent quest for gold, had just won his second European title. During our interview, he reminded me of that little blue-eyed blond who had given me flowers in Bratislava. That boy had been Jozef.

Jozef was the rare skater who possessed almost too much talent. The son of dancers, he was tall for a skater and painfully thin, with extremely long, lean legs. However, his wide shoulders gave him an imposing presence on the ice. His face was extremely Slavic, finely molded, but overwhelmed by those enormous blue eyes. His hair was flaxen, and he couldn't have been more Aryan in appearance. Only one thing surprised me: from that refined, dancer's body emanated a deep, resonant, masculine voice.

It is difficult to write objectively about a skater for whom one feels great admiration and affection. It would be easy for me to use up all the superlatives I know. I first became aware of Jozef, the competitive skater, at the 1982 Europeans in Lyon, where the West German champion, Norbert Schramm, surprised the audience by winning his first European title. It was also at Lyon that Torvill and Dean made an indelible impression, Alexander Fedeev cracked the top five for the first time, and Katarina Witt leapt onto the medal stand.

Jozef's rather naive performance might have gone unnoticed in such an atmosphere, except that his natural jumping ability was unlike anything that I had ever seen. He had mastered all the triple jumps at an early age, and he executed them in an almost casual, lazy way. His jumps were not marked by blinding rotational speed, but by their propensity to hover above the ice, while Jozef rotated in what looked to me like slow motion.

I'm convinced that no judge ever fully appreciated Jozef's unique talent. He waged a battle throughout his career, amateur and professional. Because every aspect of his skating simply appeared too natural and easy, few could discern the difficulty of what he did.

Training in Communist Czechoslovakia was exceedingly challenging. Proper coaching, sufficient ice time, adequate costumes, sophisticated choreography, and the money with which to acquire them were all but nonexistent. What would Jozef have been able to achieve if he had been born within the nurturing environment of North America? Surely he would have become a World and Olympic champion.

Jozef won the bronze medal at the 1984 Sarajevo Olympics. His performance there, although of high quality, was overshadowed by North American exploits. Spectators and commentators alike were entirely blinded by the excellence of Brian Orser and diverted by Scott Hamilton's uncharacteristically poor performance.

One event in Jozef's amateur career stands out starkly in my memory. At the 1986 Europeans in Copenhagen, he won his second European title with a brilliant technical display. In the first minute of his long program, he successfully executed a triple Axel, a triple flip, a quadruple toe loop (he landed the quad convincingly, but his free foot briefly touched the ice), and a somewhat over-rotated triple Lutz. The remainder of his program included many more jumps, among them an additional triple Axel and better-than-adequate artistry. At the end of the program, every judge but one declared Jozef the champion. The Russian judge even posted a perfect 6.0. The sole dissenter was the British judge, Sally-Ann Stapleford.

Later I asked Stapleford why she had given Jozef such low marks. She told me that she had awarded him the mediocre technical mark of 5.6, because most of his fireworks had come at the beginning of the program. She also made light of the quad by informing me that Jozef had almost imperceptibly touched down his free foot on the landing.

I have found that British judges often display unwarranted pretension in light of the historically poor showing of that nation's free skaters (with the exceptions of Curry and Cousins) that persists even today.

Stapleford's own amateur career was based entirely on a certain talent for school figures. My memory is frighteningly archival. I do recall that, during her not-so-golden age as a skater, she lightly trailed her free leg to ensure more accurate school-figure tracings. She also delivered primitive long-program performances. Anyone who had been such an inferior skater should have had the eyes to see and understand genuine virtuosity. Sally-Ann Stapleford was a generally intelligent judge, but I found her evaluation of Jozef at Copenhagen petty, silly, and cruel. For years I have wanted to admonish her. Now that burden is off my chest.

A little more than a month later, at the 1986 Worlds in Geneva, Jozef was one of the favorites for a medal. With the exception of Brian Boitano, the male competitors performed particularly poorly at that event. Jozef, with his acutely ailing knees, was barely able to execute a jump. I remember watching him on television and believing that his great talent had burned out prematurely. I was wrong.

Jozef retired then from the amateur world and found himself in an unenviable position. Once he had recuperated from several rounds of knee surgery, he had the potential to make big money as a professional skater. However, there were no fortunes to be made in Europe. Even Holiday on Ice, once a money-making machine, had begun an economic downslide.

Jozef would have been a jewel in the crown of Stars on Ice, but the cruel reality was that Stars on Ice, like other North American ventures, based its success upon featuring American and Canadian stars.

Meanwhile Jozef had fallen in love with Canadian champion Tracey Wainman. He married her in 1987, and they lived in Germany for a year. Then Jozef immigrated to Canada and began a new life with Tracey in Toronto. For some reason, I didn't see them often. Whenever I did, though, it was with the greatest of pleasure. Jozef was always immensely humble, polite, and respectful. For years I thought of Jozef as the son that I never had.

Jozef, the young husband, soon found himself in a volatile marriage. To make matters worse, he could not be too discriminating in accepting professional engagements. On at least two occasions, he performed as a chorus skater in Brian Orser's television specials. Imagine the indignity of a European champion and an Olympic bronze medalist skating for a paltry sum in the chorus of a competitor's show.

In 1992, Tracey and Jozef had a son whom they named Blade. I counseled them against that name choice. It reminded me of an executioner's blade. I did, however, suggest in vain that they call the boy Grenade, a reference to explosive lethal power. The Sabovcik marriage dissolved, and eventually Jozef, who had always been the more devoted caretaker, moved with little Grenade to Salt Lake City.

After some dead-end skating jobs during his marriage to Tracey, Jozef arrived at long last, albeit through the back door, in the top echelon of the North American professional skating circuit. Because of his talent, professionalism, and excellent results at pro competitions (not to mention his enthusiastic fans), he was finally received as a card-carrying member of the A group. It had been an arduous journey, as difficult as his climb to amateur renown.

I last saw Jozef in 1997 at my skating tribute in Toronto. All my favorite skaters and best friends attended the event. My only real disappointment that evening was that Jozef was ill and could not skate. I had very much wanted him to be part of my last hurrah.

I received a pleasant surprise while watching the opening ceremonies of the 2002 Salt Lake City Olympics on television. Lo and behold, there was Jozef, weaving in and out as a principal character among the other performers on the ice. His sensational back flip brought the ceremonies to a close.

Perhaps it was poetic that Jozef's talents were used once again in a major production, closing the circle that had opened for us, the competitor and the flower-bearer, in Bratislava. My memories of the phenomenal Jozef Sabovcik will dance in my mind until I take them to my grave. What a talent!

Jimmy Fund Benefit, Cambridge, Massachusetts, 1987

MARTHA LOWDER KIMBALL.

CHAPTER 16

ELIZABETH MANLEY

✒

Inherit the Whirlwind

A self-confessed "army brat," Elizabeth Manley was born in Belleville, Ontario, on August 7, 1965, Joan and Bernard "Red" Manley's fourth child and first girl. Not surprisingly, she was drawn to boys' games as much as to girls' activities. By grade one, the athletic child was taking daily skating lessons.

When Elizabeth was nine, the family moved to Ottawa, one of the traditional power centers of Canadian skating. There she joined forces with Bob McAvoy, who coached her to senior national medals.

Elizabeth's two eldest brothers moved away from home to pursue hockey careers, a blow to a young girl who liked to stay close to her family. Then her parents separated, and her third brother chose to remain with his father in the Ottawa family home. Elizabeth and her mother moved together to an apartment near the Gloucester Figure Skating Club and became inseparable, as Elizabeth climbed from Juvenile Ladies all the way to the Senior ranks and a national silver medal.

When normal teenage distractions contributed to inconsistency on the ice, the CFSA arranged for Elizabeth to leave her beloved coach and move to Lake Placid to train. Desperately homesick and feeling uprooted from everything that she knew, Elizabeth developed clinical depression, intractable weight gain, and near-total hair loss.

By the spring of 1983, Elizabeth had left Lake Placid, determined to give up competitive skating. Her saving grace was the arrival from New York of Sonya and Peter Dunfield, who persuaded Elizabeth to allow them to train her. They moved their entire family to Ottawa in order to do so. The Dunfields' faith in Elizabeth's potential restored her shattered confidence and allowed her ailments to heal.

The culmination of their work together, the 1988 Olympic silver medal and the freestyle title, topped off the three Canadian titles that Elizabeth had already won. She went on to an energetic career with Ice Capades and participated in the full range of professional opportunities that opened up after the highly popular Calgary Games.

ᘯᓂᘯᓂᘯᓂ

I heard about Elizabeth Manley many years before I ever laid eyes on her. One of her first and most influential teachers was Canadian pairs skater Bob McAvoy, a childhood friend of mine, who died of AIDS in December 1994.

While Bob taught skating in Ottawa, I occasionally saw him at various events, and the premier subject of his interest was his young pupil Elizabeth Manley. At the time, I paid little attention to Bob's rhapsodic praise of Elizabeth, because it was so excessive that I nearly suffocated from boredom. If Elizabeth Manley was truly the greatest living skater in the world, why had *I* never heard of her?

In 1984, at the height of my commentating career, I saw at long last the reputed greatest female skater in the world at the Sarajevo Olympic Games. She gave an exceedingly forgettable performance, wearing a boring purple dress, displaying no discernable personality. I remember announcing to the Canadian public that this particular skater (the world's greatest) had a great deal of homework to do once she returned to Canada.

Her defects, in my mind, and her thirteenth placement, had nothing to do with skating and everything to do with focus, discipline, and priorities.

After Sarajevo, at least in my view, a tsunami wave of oblivion swallowed Elizabeth. Had I given the matter any thought, I would have predicted that she would never be heard from again in international competition. I was very much mistaken.

My next recollection of Elizabeth seared itself upon my memory like a branding iron. My career, unbeknownst to me, was nearing its apex. I was training at Lake Placid for the opening of Ice at Radio City Music Hall.

Lake Placid Village boasted at least three ice surfaces, all within the same complex, the Olympic Center. As though it were yesterday, I remember standing in the corridor that links the Lussi rink with the old 1932 rink and hearing my name called. Because I was convinced that Radio City and New York would be mere stepping-stones to Hollywood screen tests and discovery by movie moguls, I dressed with an eye to standing out in the crowd. Encased in my floor-length white wolf coat, I felt a tug at my furry sleeve.

"Hi," said a tiny waif with a gray pallor, dull eyes, too much chubby padding, and very little hair on her head. It was Elizabeth.

It crossed my mind that a single square inch of my wolf coat boasted infinitely more hair than Elizabeth's entire head. That tragic revelation stunned me. I instantly presumed that the poor girl suffered from leukemia and had undergone chemotherapy. A great compassion welled up within me. Evidently she planned to skate bravely on until the very end of her life.

My diagnosis was completely erroneous. Elizabeth's problem, as I found out years later, was not physical but emotional. In a fragile, nervous state, she had lost her hair to alopecia areata. Once again, she was as far away from international skating glory as anyone could possibly be.

My next encounter with Elizabeth was electronic. I witnessed her 1986 Worlds long-program performance, broadcast from Geneva on Canadian television. That women's competition marked the true beginning of the international rivalry between reigning world champion Katarina Witt of East Germany and American champion Debi Thomas.

Debi, who had placed only fifth the previous year, won the 1986 round.

The two skaters representing Canada were Tracey Wainman and, lo and behold, Elizabeth Manley. Elizabeth's performance was so important on all levels – technical, emotional, and historical – that an entire chapter could be devoted to its description. Manley, for the first time in her life, revealed a level of virtuosity and competitiveness that the world had never seen.

To this day, Elizabeth's Geneva long program has to be included as one of the most important female performances of the twentieth century. Beyond flawless presentation, its overwhelming attributes were confidence and speed of a sort that I have never seen in another woman and rarely in a man. Elizabeth could have medaled in the men's competition that year. Since she performed in the third of four groups, her marks were conservative. Still, she finished third, to move up from tenth after the short to fifth overall.

At her very moment of glory, I flashed back to the distracted Elizabeth of Sarajevo and to the hairless Elizabeth of Lake Placid. Those unfortunate twins passed through my mind like frozen ghosts as I watched the present-day Elizabeth skate across my television screen. The Delphic prediction of Bob McAvoy echoed in my ears: "The greatest female skater in the world!"

Nancy Greene Raine, a Canadian Olympic gold medalist in skiing whose career was as erratic as Elizabeth's, once noted in a magazine article, "Confidence breeds success." All that an unsuccessful-but-talented athlete must do is taste success – just once. Then success will come again. Elizabeth's Geneva performance was to be her first big hint of great things to come.

For the most part, Elizabeth failed to recapture the essence of that performance. Nobody, including Elizabeth, knew how to trigger the phenomenon. Even so, that triumph contributed to a major change in perception. The CFSA regarded Elizabeth in a new light. Judges, officials, and other skaters were forced to acknowledge her as a legitimate podium wild card.

A little less than a year before the 1988 Calgary Olympics, Cincinnati hosted the Worlds. Those were to be, at least for me, among the great

Worlds in the history of figure skating. Elizabeth, though still lacking a world medal, was very much a player. She was taken seriously. In fact, David Dore announced to her that the CFSA expected her to win.

School figures were still part of the equation, and Elizabeth performed them well enough (fourth best) to be within range of a medal, perhaps even gold. The next day she performed her short program to music from *The Fantasticks*, wearing an extremely peculiar sleeveless canary-yellow dress with black trim and black feathers. (My photographic memory is sometimes an albatross.) Rated second best to Katarina Witt, Elizabeth moved up two notches, from sixth place into fourth.

Something occurred the next afternoon that happens to skaters from time to time without their knowledge and beyond their control. I remember the incident like a scene from a familiar movie.

Cincinnati's Riverfront Coliseum was enormous. It had a seating capacity of something like twenty thousand. I arrived at the building fully made-up, coifed, and dressed in a tuxedo, prepared to do some on-camera interviews. Although I had no official reason to watch the women's practice, anyone who has ever competed at the Worlds is irresistibly drawn to the action on the ice.

At the precise moment of my arrival on one of the upper levels, the top female skaters were taking their final long-program practice before the evening's competition. Canadians and Americans are the greatest of all skating fans, and the practice was packed. Thousands of eyes watched as Elizabeth prepared to begin a run-through of her long program.

At that moment, she was a thoroughbred racehorse. The starting gate opened, and all the year's energy, passion, virtuosity, and magic surged forward. Knowing that Elizabeth was giving the performance of her life, and knowing that she would have nothing left for the competition itself, I tried to get down to the ice level to stop her, but the crowds and the security guards prevented me from arriving in time. I could only watch with horror, powerless to help.

I didn't mention to my television colleagues what had happened that afternoon in practice. Whenever a CBC technician or a Canadian fan predicted a big win for Elizabeth that night, I refrained from comment. I knew that such an outcome was unlikely.

Indeed, the glory of the afternoon run-through faded away. Skating aficionados cited her tragically flawed performance as just another example of silly Elizabeth blowing it again. That was not the case at all. Her teacher should have assessed the problem as soon as it reared its head and pulled his student off the ice.[*]

The evening ended with Elizabeth running into my arms, crying and apologizing for her sixth-rate performance. She could not understand what had happened. I was deeply disappointed for her, and I tried to make her understand that, some day, she would have it all. She truly could be the greatest female free skater in the world.

From a Canadian standpoint, the home stretch for the 1987–88 Olympic season began at the Canadians in Victoria. Canadian sportswriters lambasted Elizabeth for her inferior performance. They had long forgotten her brilliance in Geneva. I had not.

Elizabeth's disappointment in Victoria was an important element of her Olympic experience. I believe that it was psychologically necessary for her to fail before she could triumph.

Many skaters in history (I'm at the top of the list) have found it impossible to seize the medals that were virtually conceded to them in advance. They have triumphed only when the press and officialdom have ignored them. Sarah Hughes is the latest example of that principle.

Although I was still the premier figure-skating analyst and commentator for the CBC, we were not the host Olympic broadcaster in Calgary; CTV had that honor. A CBC skeleton crew, of which I was a part, broadcast one-hour nightly roundups of the day's events after the CTV coverage had already aired.

The energy in Calgary was electrically charged. For Elizabeth's fans, Victoria was forgotten. As the highest-ranking Canadian in the women's competition, Elizabeth was the clear home-crowd favorite. However, she was able to avoid the pressure of gold-medal expectations, because of the irresistible melodrama playing out between American champion Debi Thomas and reigning world champion and sex bomb Katarina

---

[*] Coach Peter Dunfield called Elizabeth Manley off the ice after twenty minutes of practice, but any damage had already been done.

Witt. Debi and Katarina had chosen nearly identical music, excerpts from Bizet's *Carmen*, so their showdown was predictably labeled the Battle of the Carmens.

As in Geneva two years earlier, nobody paid much attention to Elizabeth. Nobody harbored great expectations of her. Yet a skating analyst and expert could certainly have argued that she was at least as talented as the co-favorites.

After her school figures (fourth-ranked) and short program (third-ranked), Elizabeth held her own in third place overall. Still, even though she entered the long-program event within reach of a gold medal, the press and crowds continued to fixate on the Carmen divas.

An unexpected event proved very advantageous for Elizabeth: the exit of fabulous American skater Caryn Kadavy. Caryn's unfortunate withdrawal from the long-program event, due to severe influenza and a dangerously high fever, knocked a major player out of the game. Prior to her illness, Caryn had been among the favorites to win a medal at Calgary, because of her bronze-medal finish a year earlier at Cincinnati.

I might modestly note that I designed and costumed Caryn's brilliant but grossly undermarked fifth-place short program.

As a television commentator, I had easy access to the areas frequented by competitors and their trainers. Probably because nobody had ever done so for me, I always made a point of going backstage to wish my favorite skaters good luck. Charlene Wong, Elizabeth's fifth cousin, was the second Canadian ladies' competitor in Calgary. After a few encouraging words with her, I concentrated on strategizing with Elizabeth and her coach, Peter Dunfield. Then Elizabeth and I spent a private moment together.

Elizabeth's persona and charisma could permeate any arena. Real stars manifest that ability. Backstage at the Saddledome, however, Elizabeth appeared small and timid as I stared into her alert but frightened eyes. She began to sing a tired song that so many Canadians are guilty of singing at competitions: *I just want to go out and have fun.*

Hearing her absurd rhetoric and wanting to deck her on the spot, I grabbed Elizabeth by the shoulders, pinned her to the wall, and admonished her that this was absolutely *not* the time in her life to have fun. This was the time to rise to the occasion and go in for the kill. I instructed

Elizabeth that, just before her music started, as she stood before eighteen thousand people in the Saddledome and millions of television viewers, she was to say as loudly as she could, "Fuck off, everybody!" Then she was to go straight for Carmen's jugular.

I don't know whether Elizabeth said those magic words before executing her memorable and dazzling performance to music from *Irma la Douce* and *A Canadian Concerto*. To say that Elizabeth seemed divinely inspired – or perhaps more accurately, divinely protected – would be an understatement. The alacrity and confidence with which she skated announced to everyone with any sensitivity that those four minutes on the ice constituted the performance of her life.

Skaters who have experienced similar performances will agree with me that it is like skating within a secret womb that nothing external can penetrate or influence: four minutes of virtuosity, condensed into a few seconds of perceived time. There is never a feeling of fatigue or a lack of stamina. Pure magic takes over.

Elizabeth's performance was a textbook illustration of the out-of-body performance. On that thrilling night in Calgary, the color of her skating dress was especially effective: electric cherry pink, an aggressive color, a color with which to be reckoned.

After Elizabeth's long-program performance, the Calgarians erupted in sheer euphoria. A fan tossed a cowboy hat from the stands. Elizabeth, deafened by the thunderous ovation, donned the hat at center ice. That gesture so endeared her to the audience that her image in the cowboy hat became her trademark.

I knew that, in order to present my nightly commentary at the CBC headquarters, I would need to leave the building immediately, before the final two competitors, Kira Ivanova and Debi Thomas, performed. I had watched the competition from an exceedingly luxurious private box, suspended from the building's rafters. The quickest way to reach the ground was by elevator. Traveling alone in that elevator, I could hear Elizabeth's marks read over the audio system. There was such a plethora of 5.9s that, before I arrived at the bottom of the shaft, I was convinced that little Elizabeth Manley had just won an Olympic gold medal.

Whatever the mathematics were, at the end of the night Elizabeth had won the free-skating gold medal but had finished second overall. As far as I was concerned, however, she had just fulfilled Bob McAvoy's prediction. She had demonstrably become the greatest female skater in the world.

In the light of Olympic hoopla and media frenzy, the world championships soon afterward are anticlimactic. Olympic placements often guarantee Worlds placements, regardless of actual performances.

Although the 1988 Worlds in Budapest seemed monotonous through and through, one incident struck me as particularly pathetic. In the school-figure event, the judges had the effrontery to give Katarina Witt first place. Like many fine free skaters, Katarina was capable of executing some of the worst figures in the history of the sport. Elizabeth, bolstered by her new silver-medal confidence, executed the best figures of her life. Her loop was especially good. Its quality was such that it towered over Katarina's.

Although the judges boosted Elizabeth's modest Calgary marks up just a notch to reflect her Olympic medal, by a fluke of the ordinals Katarina still received first place. In a just world, Elizabeth would have won the figures and earned the best shot at the world title, but political maneuvering and protocol judging once again clouded the judges' evaluations.*

So the cards fell in the preordained pattern. As an unpopular and iconoclastic voice within the figure-skating world, I stood alone in my campaign to crown Elizabeth world champion. Nobody else stepped forward to enlist. The Olympic silver medalist would have to be content to place second again, in the good old Canadian tradition.

Winning a world title is such a unique privilege. The event in Budapest was truly Elizabeth's best chance. But the big war machine did not work in her favor. Katarina, with an entirely forgettable performance, won the world title on a night when not one of the top ladies gave her best effort. Perhaps the judges reasoned that Katarina deserved to win based on her stellar track record.

---

* Elizabeth Manley won the first and second figures, placing second in the third, but a quirk of the ordinals left her in second overall.

After the competition, the big guns left the battlefield and new warriors unsheathed their weapons to fight for the next four years. So ended the turbulent amateur career of Elizabeth Manley.

Beyond the glory of Olympic success and the world silver medal, Elizabeth's future was rife with possibilities. Although she did become one of the most sought-after female stars, second only to Katarina, Elizabeth's professional career was as erratic as her amateur journey had been, marked by extreme highs and equally extreme lows. Only the reasons were different.

Monetary success and fame can result in a nasty whiplash. Elizabeth's highs resulted from her skating triumphs, while her lows resulted from multifarious broken relationships, depression, and a flirtatious dance with an illegal substance.

Elizabeth famously invited Brian Mulroney, prime minister of Canada, and his wife, Mila, to her wedding reception in Ottawa. She intended to wed Paul Hendrickson, technical coordinator of the Tom Collins tour. She raised more than a few eyebrows when she found herself in the unenviable position of having to uninvite Canada's first couple less than a month before the ceremony, having realized that she was not yet ready to marry and settle down in Minneapolis.

Over the next decade, my encounters with Elizabeth were few. Details of her professional career came to me second-hand. I did encounter Elizabeth once at an AIDS benefit at the New York Armory. Anybody who mattered had been invited to perform. I was coming back from my twenty-seventh retirement.

Elizabeth was chosen to close the show, a sign of great respect and honor. Silently watching this woman who had blossomed into a major skating star – enhanced by fabulous costumes, makeup, and choreography – I couldn't help but ponder the long journey that had brought her to such professional heights.

However, I do remember hearing certain female stars mutter about Elizabeth's breathless anticipation that David Letterman would soon phone to book her on his late-night talk show. Her tedious hubris ultimately drove some of the women into the men's dressing room.

I last bumped into Elizabeth at my skating tribute in Toronto. The cast, all special friends, came from among figure skating's elite. Elizabeth's performance that evening was typical in so many ways. It mirrored her personality, her passion, and her soul.

Elizabeth opted to perform a Western number, and the famous cowboy hat from Calgary appeared. Somehow, on that special night, Elizabeth gave to me, through her skating performance, everything that she was, everything that she had been, and everything that she wanted to be.

The acid test for any skating star is longevity. In that department, Elizabeth has more than earned her spurs. In her private rodeo, she has been bucked off the bronco more than a few times. Undaunted, she has always remounted.

Today, Elizabeth teaches skating in Florida, keeping one foot in the active performing circle and one foot just outside it. Without question, she ranks with the best athletes Canada has ever produced. The turbulent odyssey that she experienced remains equally unique in Canadian history.

Cincinnati, Ohio, 1992

CHAPTER 17

KATARINA WITT

Between East and West

K atarina Witt was born to Kathe and Manfred Witt on December 3, 1965, in Staaken, East Germany, and raised in Karl-Marx-Stadt (called Chemnitz before and after Communist rule). Her elder brother, Axel, would eventually marry the 1980 Olympic figure-skating champion Anett Pötzsch.

Katarina, enamored of the ice from her first skating experience at age five, gained acceptance into her city's elite state-sponsored sports school, Sport Club Chemnitz. By age nine, she was being taught by Jutta Müller, whose daughter, Gabriele Seyfert, was a world silver medalist.

In East Germany, winning sports medals was equivalent to achieving Cold War victories. The Müller regime was stringent, on and off the ice. Katarina's diet was so restrictive that other skaters smuggled food to her – in particular, rich desserts – during competitions and tours.

Otherwise Katarina was the perfect disciple, adhering without question to athletic discipline. Success in sports was one of the keys to a good life for her and her family, although her parents were not allowed to

189

watch her compete outside East Germany until the 1988 Worlds in Budapest, safely behind the Iron Curtain.

Katarina's greatest achievement was competing at three Olympics. She won the gold medal in Sarajevo in 1984 at age eighteen, defeating the American champion, Rosalynn Sumners. In 1988, at age twenty-two, she became the first woman since Sonja Henie to defend an Olympic title, taking home a second gold medal from Calgary after edging out Elizabeth Manley and Debi Thomas. Then, at age twenty-eight, in a free and united Germany, Katarina reinstated as an eligible skater for the 1994 Games in Lillehammer. She moved audiences with her tribute to Sarajevo and finished seventh. Along the way, she amassed four world titles.

After the 1988 Games, Katarina became the first East German champion to be allowed to travel somewhat freely outside the country in order to continue to skate professionally. Pressing the point with the government, which originally objected, she invoked her exceptional status as a two-time Olympic gold medalist. After a run with Stars on Ice, she hired an East German defector to produce *Carmen on Ice* for a West German film company. She was in Seville, Spain, in the autumn of 1989, filming a scene for *Carmen on Ice* with Brian Orser and Brian Boitano, when the Berlin Wall fell.

At first the effects of that signal event were more negative for Katarina than positive. Because of her sports successes, she had enjoyed a relatively high degree of freedom, along with more conveniences and consumer goods than the average East German citizen. Her newly free compatriots became strident critics of athletic privilege.

Worse, Katarina was falsely accused of informing for the Communist East German government. With the opening of the Stasi files, the data collected by the East German secret police, 1,600 pages of reports on Katarina's activities came to light. During her amateur skating years, Katarina had been followed, spied upon, and taped. Her telephone line had been tapped. She was the victim, not the informer.

Katarina's next project was an arena tour with Brian Boitano. The skating shows featured higher concepts, better choreography, and more proficient casts than the run-of-the-mill touring spectaculars.

The ever-buxom, flirtatious Katarina went on to ap]
sional competitions, commercials, television shows, movi
the glossy pages of *Playboy* magazine. At this writing, her (
full gear.*

⅃ℸ⅃ℸ⅃ℸ

T he reader will forgive me, I hope, if I digress more than usual in
discussing Katarina Witt, a good friend and a woman whom I
admire enormously. In many ways she is a useful symbol, not only of East
Germany at a certain point in history, but also of the Communist bloc
as a whole. Her career, both eligible and professional, spanned the
dissolution of those monoliths. The way things used to be is fading from
twenty-first-century memory. It is instructive to recall those circumstances.

I was unable to see any of the live 1980 Worlds competition in
Dortmund, East Germany, even though I was performing with Holiday
on Ice in Cologne, a little more than an hour away. The television coverage at the time was certainly not of the quality that it is today, and,
because my time schedule conflicted with what little coverage there was,
I didn't even see the broadcasts. I did, however, receive almost hourly
telephone updates from my former coach, Ellen Burka, who trained
Canadian skater Tracey Wainman.

Tracey was causing a great stir in Dortmund because of her phenomenal talent and extreme youth. Another child prodigy, from East
Germany, shared the stage with Tracey. Although Tracey ended up in
fourteenth place and the other young skater finished tenth, many knowledgeable members of the skating community speculated that both had
promising futures. The East German skater was Katarina Witt, and both
she and Tracey were indeed destined to move dramatically up the ladder
of world competition.

---

* Katarina Witt declined the opportunity to corroborate the accuracy of the factual
material in this chapter, remarking, "Why answer questions? Toller will write what he
wants anyway."

I made my debut as a commentator at the Europeans in 1982 in Lyon, and my initial impression of Katarina remains crystal clear in my mind. First impressions can haunt the memory. Her aristocratic countenance was straight from a fifteenth-century Florentine portrait. As young as she was, barely seventeen, she stood out dramatically from all the other female competitors. Her trim, leggy, thoroughbred body and her athletic ability, coupled with aggressive and fearless competitiveness, set her apart.

One rarely saw triple Lutzes and flips in those days, but Katarina performed a perfect triple flip at Lyon, the one and only triple flip that I ever saw her execute over what is now a period of some twenty years.

The East German competitors seemed to lust more than others did for the high drama of international competition. It was rare that a skater from East Germany performed poorly. Perhaps Sonja Morgenstern and Evelyn Grossman gave some inferior performances, but those were exceptions. Katarina in particular – remarkable for any competitor, anywhere, at any time, in any sport – virtually never gave a bad performance.

Not surprisingly, we competitors from the capitalist free world of North America viewed East Germany as a factory that produced top athletes on an assembly line. We were led to believe that the discipline and training of those athletes were more stringent than our own, and that their coaches and facilities were superior. It was all a myth, but we believed it wholeheartedly.

One factor that we did not consider was that East Germany, an extremely poor and underpopulated country, was renowned on the global stage for producing top sports heroes – but for virtually nothing else. Any honors won by East German athletes in Olympic and world competition accrued to the glory of the East German propaganda machine. Otherwise, life was rather bleak. Over the years, I often performed in East Germany, both as an amateur and as a professional. Of all the Communist countries, I found it the most authoritarian and frightening. It possessed virtually no resources or industry, as the West Germans found out when the two halves eventually merged.

It compensated in strategy for what it lacked in resources. The East German figure-skating federation almost invariably designated one particular judge (in Katarina's case, it was Walburga Grimm) to follow a skater through every competition throughout his or her career. That was a clever ploy. Knowledge is power.

Something else that we North Americans failed to fully consider, because we didn't know it for a certainty, was that the East Germans had perfected performance-enhancing drugs. One summer, at a skating exhibition in East Berlin, I accidentally entered the wrong dressing room and found myself surrounded by gigantic East German hockey players. They were so enormous that I did wonder if those homegrown skating monsters had been fed growth stimulants.

Rumor suggested that the brilliance of some East German athletes at international competitions lay in their ability to mask performance-enhancing drugs. Because that ability far outstripped the capacity of Western officials to trace the substances, for a number of years the East Germans were able to beat the system.

Beyond drugs, there was the phenomenon of blood doping, allegedly much used under the East German sports system. Apparently an illegal pre-competition injection of highly oxidized blood, taken from the athlete months earlier, results in a boost in stamina and a rush of competitive aggression that minimizes feelings of nervousness and vulnerability.

Blood doping was a hot topic at the 1988 Calgary Olympics. A Canadian hockey coach was virtually hung out to dry when he accused the East German hockey team of the practice. Behind closed doors, most people within serious hockey circles agreed with the Canadian coach's theory. But when push came to shove, he stood alone in launching the accusation. He was left with egg on his face and made to apologize, because he had no proof.

At a European competition in Sarajevo, I had raised the question with a top-ranking U.S. skating official from Boston. If blood doping were to be prevented at the 1988 Olympics, why couldn't Canadian customs officials explore the personal baggage of East German team doctors? Surely, if the offense were planned, officials would discover vials of athletes' blood. Nobody picked up on my suggestion.

I remember listening to the CBC color commentator rhapsodize about the East German swimmer Kornelia Ender, who won four gold medals

at the 1976 summer Games in Montreal. In all her events, Ender finished
miles ahead of the pack. There have been no comparable strings of East
German victories since the dissolution of the German Democratic
Republic, and I have always wondered why those superhuman feats were
not scrutinized after the fact. I suppose that it is much easier, more convenient, and less expensive to forget.

Specific to figure skating, the East German concept of a pairs couple
was completely different from the West's understanding of the perfect
pair. In East Germany, the ideal male partner usually possessed the
silhouette of an orangutan, while his female counterpart inhabited a
ten-year-old's body. North Americans certainly speculated that growth-
retarding drugs were given to the young women, but an athlete was guilty
only if she tested positive.

The pair Sabine Baess and Tassilo Thierbach aroused my suspicions.
I remember asking Sabine's age, because I found it macabre that a child
of eleven would skate with a twenty-five-year-old man. I learned to my
surprise that the child of eleven was actually a teenager. Over the years,
I incorrectly assumed that other skaters and spectators saw what I saw
and were equally troubled.

Today we could open a can of worms by launching an international
review of East German medical records, if anyone had the money or the
interest to exhume the unsavory details. It is my opinion that many big
wins in various sports had more to do with illegal drugs and/or blood
doping than with superior talent.

This is not to suggest that Katarina Witt herself took performance-
enhancing drugs or submitted to blood doping. Only Katarina knows the
truth. However, other East German athletes have admitted to doing so,
including at least one female figure skater.

Many phenomenal skaters sprang from the East German system.
Almost without exception, it was Katarina's coach, Jutta Müller, who
taught them. Their successes stoked the fires of the Müller myth. Years
later, we North Americans discovered that, because of Müller's government connections, no skater had a real chance of leaving East Germany
to compete internationally unless Müller was the trainer.

Perhaps a more somber irony is that the many champions who arose under the East German umbrella – Gabriele Seyfert, Christine Errath, Anett Pötzsch, Jan Hoffmann, all world gold medalists – virtually disappeared when their amateur careers ended. There was nothing for them to do as professionals within East Germany. They were simply retired by the state to make room for up-and-coming talent. Even more tragically, Anett, as an Olympic gold medalist, is largely unknown today. She has become the answer to a skating-trivia question.

Athletes from totalitarian states like East Germany lived in fear. They couldn't trust anyone. Certain subjects of conversation were dangerous or forbidden. Skaters attending competitions abroad were like caged birds, only briefly released from their prisons, and one of the major police officers was Jutta Müller. She was on the inside track at a high level of East German politics, and she also happened to be the lover of a certain Herr Grunwald, the head of the East German figure-skating association. Those twin credentials made a lethal combination.

To the best of my knowledge, only one figure skater ever defected from East Germany: eighteen-year-old Gunter Zöller. Gunter was an excellent school-figure skater, far superior to his main competitor, Jan Hoffmann. Although Gunter couldn't jump well, because he suffered from major knee injuries, he managed to finish second behind Jan at the 1971 East German Nationals. That gave him his last opportunity to attend the Europeans outside East German borders and escape before the state retired him to a dusty shelf full of skating has-beens. No one, least of all his coach, Frau Müller, suspected his intention to defect. I know about this particular incident only because my childhood friend and competitor Haig Oundjian assisted in the caper.

Just before the draw for skating order in Zurich, Gunter escaped custody of the East German authorities and plunged to safety through a hotel laundry chute, assisted by Haig and future European dance champion Erich Buck. From all reports, the incident caused a major sensation at the championships. After that, the East German skaters were monitored even more carefully and were rarely allowed to wander unchaperoned through a Western city.

Anett Pötzsch missed her chance to escape after winning the Olympic gold medal in Lake Placid. She was escorted home to East Berlin. Nobody from skating circles saw her again for many years. I suspect that her forced retirement had everything to do with young Katarina's rising star.

Persistent rumors had Anett attempting to escape to the West on a skiing holiday. Allegedly she was shot at and captured by East German police and incarcerated for a number of months. The problem with any rumor involving events in East Germany was that there was virtually no way of learning the truth. Everyone within the system feared for his personal safety and livelihood.

Katarina, because she was East German and because she was taught by Frau Müller, behaved obediently. She willingly accepted the influence of monstrous East German taste. It was as a beautiful and seductive athlete, a sex bomb on ice, that she captured the imagination, first in Europe and then throughout the world. I felt that, had a mentor with refinement and culture coached her in the West, she would have gone down in history as the most sensual and remarkable skater ever. Thanks to her teacher's vulgarity and chronic bad taste, she fulfilled only half of her potential.

Above and beyond great skating talent, a killer's competitive instinct, and a beautiful face and body, chronological circumstances carried Katarina to glory. She owed her six consecutive European titles, at least in part, to the fact that there were few bona fide competitors.

Athletes might be surprised to learn how closely television commentators observe them during their warm-ups. At the 1988 Europeans in Prague, I scrutinized Katarina's long-program warm-up, sensing that, although she was not currently in first place, she didn't take any of her competitors seriously. Perhaps incorrectly, I viewed her body language through the prism of personal experience.

I remember being stymied by her aggressiveness. Moments before my long program at international competitions, I was invariably intense and serious. Katarina, on the other hand, seemed like a filly ready to burst eagerly through the starting gate. In all my years of competing, commentating, and observing skaters, I have never seen anyone so hungry and eager to compete as Katarina was.

Several things always amused television spectators who were familiar with the character and quirks of Frau Müller. While waiting for the marks in the "kiss and cry" area, she seemed to make love to her pupils on-camera: patting hair, touching faces, holding, kissing, stroking, and caressing. At such moments she also displayed her latest rings and bracelets, clothes, and maquillage. A former Olympic champion, Ondrej Nepela, first pointed out to me those particular idiosyncrasies. After Ondrej clued me in, I took great pleasure in anticipating the richly dramatic Academy Award–winning cameos. Even if the skater was the lovely Katarina, Frau Müller stole the show.

East Germany passionately embraced figure skating as an athletic sport (and therefore rejected ice dancing as legitimate, which led to a dearth of competent teams). The antithetical philosophy that I shared with such skaters as Oleg and Ludmila Protopopov and Jayne Torvill and Christopher Dean held that figure skating on the highest level was the perfect mixture of sport and art.

Katarina's impressive, almost superhuman, European, world, and Olympic victories have melted in my memory into a great golden puddle. She was neither an artist nor an innovator. Her programs, choreography, and musical choices were not usually particularly memorable. Like me, she was an inferior practitioner of school figures, those compulsory exercises that died a quiet death two years after Katarina turned professional. She was able repeatedly to win simply by being stronger, more aggressive, and more athletic than anyone else.

At the 1984 Olympics in Sarajevo, Katarina won convincingly over American Rosalynn Sumners. Her long-program performance made the choice easy for the judges. In addition to her superior athletic performance, Witt's appearance, attitude, charisma, and costume all spelled *Olympic champion.*

In 1987 at the Cincinnati Worlds, Katarina won fair and square in enemy waters, those of American Debi Thomas, by presenting the most complete package of skating talent. Her appearance was particularly stunning on that occasion. She wore a conspicuously understated short black dress with billowing silver-trimmed dolman sleeves, and her hair had been tightly double-braided and studded with small silver bows. Her music was a medley from the score of *West Side Story*, a decidedly hokey choice for a skater of Katarina's caliber. Yet, with her gorgeous appearance and refined charm, somehow Katarina made that middle-of-the-road musical choice work to her advantage. She performed her long program after Debi had finished competing, and the crowd acknowledged her superiority with a standing ovation.

The 1987 Worlds were an extremely important event. The results had a great bearing on the competitive pecking order as the 1988 Calgary Olympics drew near. Katarina's victory in Cincinnati positioned her as a heavy favorite to win her second Olympic gold medal.

When Katarina arrived in Calgary for the Olympics, she caused a sensation. More than 180 journalists attended her standing-room-only press conference. It was as though a genuine movie star were competing. When a journalist asked Katarina about her sexuality and sensuality on the ice, she responded, in essence, that if an attractive young woman had a beautiful body, why shouldn't everyone enjoy it?

Italy's heartthrob, the great giant slalom skier Alberto Tomba, announced to the press, "If Katarina doesn't make the gold medal, I'll give her one of mine." Katarina, in a rather typically well-bred German schoolgirl way, rebuffed Alberto, because she had every intention of winning her own. When the two met formally backstage at the arena through the Italian Carlo Fassi, Katarina turned down Alberto's romantic gift of a single rose.

As a commentator for the CBC (again, not the host broadcaster), I had a lot of free time to observe, interrogate, converse, and spy. I chatted with many skating luminaries about potential outcomes. At the school-figure competition, I even ran out onto the ice to inspect the final tracings before the Zamboni could lick them off with its mechanical tongue.

Few of the figures that I saw were particularly noteworthy, including Debi's. Katarina's were decidedly weak compared to some of the others, but her popularity and track record put her within reach of a gold medal. Had she been any other skater, she would never have placed within the top ten. When the compulsories ended, the top-five finishers were Kira Ivanova, Debi Thomas, Katarina Witt, Elizabeth Manley, and Jill Trenary.

Katarina won the short program. Debi finished in second, though she still led overall going into the long-program event. Elizabeth Manley lay in wait in third place.

Remember, the women's long-program competition centered to a large degree on the coincidental fact that Debi and Katarina had chosen near-identical musical scores from Bizet's *Carmen*, so the women's competition was the Battle of the Carmens.

The final flight of women ostensibly contained the medal winners. However, the phenomenally athletic Japanese virtuoso, Midori Ito, skating at the end of the second-to-last flight, had already made a forceful statement. When the big guns took the ice at Calgary's Stampede Corral, they appeared to have been unnerved by Ito's challenge. Midori would not medal, but her performance rattled the podium like an earthquake.

Jill Trenary was first to skate in the last group. She performed a conservative routine that left her in fifth place for the long program, fourth overall. Then came the opening salvo in the Battle of the Carmens. Katarina's performance was not particularly superior, either artistically or athletically, but she did look gorgeous in red and black, and she gave everything that she had. Her triple jumps – toe loops, Salchows, and a popped loop – paled in the light of Midori's athletic accomplishments. Katarina's marks were respectable but beatable.

Then came Elizabeth Manley's surprise performance, a dazzling spectacle proffered to her adoring Canadian fans.

Midori and Elizabeth had truly stolen the show, electrifying the audience to such an extent that, when Debi finally skated last in the competition, on the always-dull heels of Kira Ivanova, the audience had short-circuited. There was no energy left in the arena for Debi to draw upon. Her sad performance will go down in history as the gold-medal firecracker that never ignited. It sparked, then fizzled, ending in a pile of ashes.

I felt particularly sympathetic to Debi. The failure of her long program was not entirely her fault. The audience mood and prior superior performances had contributed substantially to what must be viewed as a competitor's worst nightmare. Whenever Debi made an effort, she found no strength, no stamina. She did win the bronze medal, but even that was probably a gift.

Computer experts could explain better than I can just how Katarina won her second Olympic gold medal. I never did understand the mathematics of that victory over Elizabeth Manley, but Katarina triumphed by the skin of her teeth, certainly not by a majority of first placements. The point remains that she did win. While the free-skating performance itself is generally forgotten, that second gold medal shines as brightly as the first.

As a result of her triumph in Calgary, Katarina was crowned the imperial empress of figure skating. At the 1988 Worlds in Budapest, she was ready to launch her professional career in a major, international way. Her amateur career had been unrivaled by any skater in recent memory. It seemed that, as a professional, she was destined to tread in the footsteps of triple gold medalist, movie star, and international femme fatale Sonja Henie.

With the power and leverage that she possessed as a double Olympic gold medalist, Katarina obtained permission to travel to the West. Unlike her predecessors, she was too internationally famous, too powerful, and too well connected to allow herself to be held under house arrest in East Germany, shelved and retired prematurely.

Katarina soon parlayed her *Carmen* long-program role into a theatrical film, *Carmen on Ice*, that co-starred Brian Boitano and Brian Orser. Many skaters whom I knew personally participated in the project. The movie (which later became an HBO special) was filmed on location in Seville, Spain, on tanks of ice that were installed in a bull-ring and in the ruins of an old castle.

Meanwhile, Communist regimes throughout Eastern Europe were beginning to crumble. During the summer of 1989, the Hungarian reform government began to allow East Germans to escape through Hungary's Austrian border. At that point, the wall that separated East and West Berlin became practically useless. On November 9, the East German government announced regulations intended to allow those who wanted to travel to the West to do so directly from East Germany – but only with official permission. When citizens optimistically misinterpreted that bulletin, they gathered in crowds at the Brandenburg Gate, demanding to be let through. Guards were forced to comply. Thousands of East Germans poured through the Wall's various crossing points, jubilantly tearing it to pieces.

Katarina was filming a night scene, a dream sequence, with Brian Orser when word came that the Berlin Wall had begun to crumble. Many of the caterers, drivers, and runners on the film set had recently escaped from East Germany, so the buzz was deafening. Most East Germans could hardly believe what they saw on television. It was as baffling to them as it was overwhelming.

Carmen on Ice had been financed with German money. However, a curious fate awaited its Dresden premiere and subsequent West Berlin showing. Katarina naively expressed sympathy for the plight of East German chancellor Erich Honeker, who had been taken into custody by his own people. Her sentiments riled the German public to such a degree that there was genuine risk to the security of the theaters that showed her film.

Katarina was not at all popular at home for a time: a striking parallel to Sonja Henie in postwar Norway. (Brian Boitano was concerned enough to invite Katarina to take refuge in San Francisco.) However, both Sonja and Katarina rode out the wave of unpopularity and ultimately found themselves embraced as heroines.

When the two Germanys merged, the stars of the East German system found themselves in a precarious position. From one day to the next, the bosses and power-brokers had no influence whatsoever. Peter Crick, long-time head of the West German figure-skating association, told me an anecdote that I took great pleasure in hearing. It related to the political demise of Jutta Müller.

When a German television network mounted a skating show in the small town of Weiden, FRG, Frau Müller, as was her habit, demanded to personally receive any fees owed to East German skaters. Peter told her, in essence, to take a hike. That practice was no longer current. Skaters' money would be given directly to individual skaters. That was the beginning of the end of an internationally important career, and it had arrived none too soon, in my opinion.

Katarina was the only 1988 Olympic champion who found a genuine market among both European and North American audiences. However, her professional skating career was based more on celebrity and entertainment than on the further honing of her skating skills. Brian Boitano and Kurt Browning are two prime examples of skaters who became greater as professionals than they ever had been as amateurs. Katarina, although she continued to skate credibly, preferred to make use of other gifts.

In one of my last Stars on Ice engagements, I shared the bill with Katarina. During that tour through Canada, I finally got to know her on a personal basis, and I observed that her good German upbringing and her proper European schooling influenced her character and behavior. She was conspicuously different from her American contemporaries: always polite, refined, and amazingly down-to-earth. She possessed a charming, honest naturalness and a sense of humor that was neither prudish nor vulgar.

One thing that amazed a number of us was the voracious appetite that she brought to the catered buffet in each arena before the show. I always ate lightly for fear of appearing too heavy on the ice. Katarina was a healthy German girl with an even healthier appetite.

In Vancouver, during the Stars on Ice rehearsal period, the ice was too wet and too thin. Jumping was impossible. I observed Katarina in her blackest humor, cursing about the conditions. She threw a fit worthy of a diva. During her performance that evening, however, she executed with ease every element that she had failed to complete in practice. I realized that her earlier outburst had served to rev her up to triumph over the challenges, goading her into accomplishing the kind of performance she wanted to give.

One afternoon in Calgary, Katarina and I happened to stroll through the local shops together. When we ate at a small café, many people recognized her (and a certain sprinkling of the public noticed me as well). I was impressed by the way Katarina treated her fans: with naturalness, courtesy, and an enormous display of humility. I have never known

Katarina – unlike certain others stars – to act any differently among her fans from the way she behaves among her friends. Her character and personality are entirely consistent.

In 1993, for reasons that only Katarina truly knows, she decided to put her professional career on hold in order to reinstate as an eligible skater and compete at the Lillehammer Olympics. Many athletes are unable in their subsequent lives to recapture the elation of winning an Olympic gold medal. Perhaps that was part of her motivation. The discipline and hard work of everyday training for such a lofty goal can also be thrilling.

Because of Katarina's decision to represent Germany once again, it seems to me that the tide of popular opinion changed once and for all. Overnight, the German people adored her.

Unfortunately, Katarina became one of the many casualties of the Tonya and Nancy melodrama. Without that *cause célèbre*, her more-than-respectable comeback performance would have made front-page headlines. As it was, nobody could compete with Tonya and Nancy for newspaper ink, so Katarina received honorable mention on the back pages of the sports section.

At the end of the Lillehammer Olympic year, when I broke my leg in Vail, Colorado, the professional figure-skating conglomerate essentially put me out to pasture. In the spring of 1995, therefore, I was particularly pleased when Jay Ogden of IMG telephoned to ask if I would be interested in performing in a television movie, *The Ice Princess*, starring Katarina Witt. Whether or not I would be able to skate in the film, the opportunity was too good to miss.

I arrived during midsummer on a rather extraordinary set at Studio Babelsburg outside Berlin. Neither the director nor the producer, and least of all Katarina, had any real sense of what my role would be. It turned out that my role was rather minor, and I spent many days at the studio among a large cast of characters, doing nothing. To while away the boredom (filming movies involves the most excruciating boredom on earth), I practiced on the ice surface every day during the lunch hour. I hadn't skated for seven months, and at first I was not at all sure that I still could.

Over a period of two-and-one-half weeks, my acting ability remained statically melodramatic, but my skating ability improved dramatically. One day the director, Danny Huston (son of John, half-brother of Anjelica), came to see me practice. He was impressed to the point of creating a skating role that, up until that moment, had not existed. Once the scene had been filmed, I decided that I had never performed better in my life. I am deeply indebted to Katarina for requesting my participation and allowing me the privilege of making a comeback when virtually everyone else had written me off.

Katarina's long professional career had begun to wind down as well when something occurred that completely revitalized it. In 1998, she agreed to pose nude in *Playboy* magazine. The photo spread, which delighted and scandalized the skating world, was one of the cleverest marketing ploys in history. If the press is to be believed, that particular issue sold out immediately and became an instant collector's item for anybody lucky enough to have found a copy.

The photos themselves said a lot about Katarina. True, she was as naked as the day is long, but the photographs were beautiful and completely natural. They caused a sensation. Katarina was on top of her game once again.

I'll close with a sticky point in my relationship with Katarina, one that we have not yet discussed. I was asked to judge a professional competition, the Gold Championship in Edmonton. Kristi Yamaguchi, Oksana Baiul, and Katarina Witt, all Olympic gold medalists, were hired to fight it out on the ice for enormous sums of money. There were also three male gold-medal competitors.

In the technical event, Kristi skated without flaw, executing every triple jump in the book except a triple Axel. Katarina's routine contained only one difficult element, a shaky double Axel. As a serious judge, I could not possibly give Katarina a score that approached the sum I awarded Kristi. My marks for Katarina were the lowest on the panel.

I later heard that, on the telecast, Katarina had remarked that she couldn't believe that I would give her low marks. We were such good friends. I certainly understood her emotional reaction, but what she did not understand was that friendship couldn't influence the marks I deemed appropriate. Friends are friends and judges are judges. The two relationships cannot overlap.

Katarina has dedicated her life to figure skating. Although, like Sonja Henie, she has had her fair share of lovers over the years, I imagine that even love affairs have played second fiddle to her enduring romance with skating. One day, like all of us, she will be obliged to leave the sport forever, to embrace an existence away from the ice. That will be the most difficult decision of her life.

Worlds, Paris, 1989

CHAPTER 18

KURT BROWNING

℘

The Incredible Cowboy from Caroline

C onceived on a fall hunting trip, Kurt was born to Neva and Dewey Browning on June 18, 1966, in Rocky Mountain House, Alberta, the youngest of three children. Growing up on a 325-acre ranch in tiny Caroline, he got his first horse when he was four and enjoyed all the outdoor pursuits that an active boy could imagine.

When Kurt was six, the town constructed the Caroline Arena, where he played hockey avidly and figure skated. When Kurt's skating coach recognized his competitive talents, he took his student on the road to find extra ice time.

At thirteen, Kurt began lessons with Czech émigré Michael Jiranek, a farmer with a degree in mechanical engineering who taught figure skating part-time. Several years later, Jiranek convinced his pupil that, if he wanted to skate seriously, he should move to Edmonton and give up hockey. Though gifted, Kurt was expected to be too small for a pro hockey career.

At the 1982 Canadians, Kurt placed twelfth in the novice division. His results soon improved, and he first competed at the Canadians as a senior in 1986, placing fifth. In subsequent years he moved to second, repeated as silver medalist, then won three consecutive titles. Kurt debuted at the Worlds in 1986 in fifteenth place. He finished sixth the following year, then won three consecutive titles before falling to second in 1992 after facing severe back problems. By 1993, he was on top again.

Kurt turned pro after a disappointing 1994 season, and found his true métier in Stars on Ice and as a professional competitor. In April 1995, he proposed to his future wife, Sonia Rodriguez of the National Ballet, from the ice surface of Maple Leaf Gardens in front of a packed house. Sonia came down from the audience to accept. Their collaboration resulted in the full realization of Kurt's potential as a premier ice artist.

ᘓᘖᘓᘖᘓᘖ

On many levels, both positive and negative, the 2002 Olympics caused the figure-skating world to open its eyes to certain realities. One such revelation was that the talent reservoir within the Chinese population, reputed to be more than one billion, is rich and seemingly limitless. It is simply a matter of time until Chinese skaters win every world and Olympic title. At least, that is the presumption of many informed skating enthusiasts.

The theory makes sense, yet it is flawed. Supreme talent and genius in any field, whether art, literature, politics, or sport, can spring up like a magic mushroom at any time, in any climate. Kurt Browning is a magic mushroom.

Kurt rose within the figure-skating world from an improbable environment and cultural background. In the remote town of Caroline in northern Alberta, he first learned about skating on a small frozen pond that his father flooded in front of the family home. Like Bill Clinton from the one-horse town of Hope, Arkansas, who grew up to become president of the United States, Kurt left the one-horse town of Caroline to become a four-time world champion and one of the most important male skaters of the twentieth century.

At the 1987 Worlds in Cincinnati, Brian Orser was the great Canadian hope in the men's competition. After many years of placing second to various champions, he finally won his one and only world title.

Somewhat removed from the Canadian skating scene, I had never heard of the other two men who represented Canada in that event. The second Canadian men's competitor was a Calgarian, Michael Slipchuk. His performance was memorable not for its brilliance, but because his skate blade caught the boards, causing Michael to take a major fall. (He was allowed to restart his program.) The third Canadian man was another Albertan, Kurt Browning.

As a CBC commentator, I was obliged to be extremely diplomatic and encouraging in my analysis of Canadian skaters. I learned years later, when the CBC fired me, that veracity can be unpopular. Canadians have always worshiped their skating icons, meeting any criticism, however valid, with antagonism and disapproval.

I remember pepping up my on-air schtick by saying something to the effect that both Slipchuk and Browning lacked maturity, but seemed to possess genuine talent and bright futures. I was not at all convinced, but that's what I said. Time would prove my instincts wrong and my words correct.

I do not recall meeting either Michael or Kurt in Cincinnati. Both were young, naive, and thin. They trained at the Royal Glenora Skating Club, where Kurt's teacher, Czech Michael Jiranek, worked. That struck me as odd. Kurt was a world competitor, yet I had never heard of his coach – not to discredit Jiranek's coaching talents. When I learned that his other job was that of a farmer, I was more surprised. Diversity is valuable, but I found the idea of raising livestock incongruous with teaching artful figure skating.

At the 1988 Calgary Olympics, Kurt made a splash in the B-class pool. Calgary hosted a phenomenal competition. Skater for skater, there were more superlative performances there than at any other Olympic competition I can recall.

After such events conclude, agents, promoters, and television moguls pounce upon the major talents. My former IMG manager, an American named Mike Halstead, who had left IMG to form his own agency, was quick to pick my brain. Who among the lower-ranked skaters did I think were the children of destiny, fame, and fortune? The big guns had already aligned themselves with various agents.

I told Mike, and I should have charged him a fee for my advice, that the skinny little cowboy from Caroline, Alberta, was his best bet. Kurt would certainly have been my number-one choice. For whatever reason, Mike didn't sign him. That was probably the biggest financial faux pas in the history of the sport.

At the 1988 Worlds in Budapest, Kurt dramatically improved his reputation by executing the first quadruple jump ever landed in competition. In my book, the quad that he performed, however daring, was not without flaw. He had landed on one foot, yet had made several gratuitous revolutions on the ice. Technically, he had over-rotated the jump (not unlike another Canadian, Vern Taylor, in landing the first certified triple Axel).

Brian Orser retired after the Budapest Worlds, removing a major roadblock from Kurt's path. The next year, Kurt became the Canadian champion. Michael Slipchuk, his colleague and friend, also moved up the ladder.

In 1989, the Worlds took place in Paris. Few of the previous generation of skaters had remained amateur (Viktor Petrenko was one of the few who did), so the chessboard was clear, ready for a new game and a new skating king. Kurt threw down the gauntlet and amazed the figure-skating world by winning the event.

I found that outcome oddly interesting. My professional career probably owed at least some of its success to the fact that Brian Orser had remained amateur for so many years, through two Olympics and eight senior men's Canadian championships. Brian, for his part, immediately lost some of his luster when Kurt won the world title right out of the blocks and came to rival Brian as premier Canadian male skater. Once again, Brian slipped into second position.

Whereas Brian had rarely performed poorly in competition, Kurt rarely performed extremely well. No matter how poorly he skated, though, he was able to pull the rabbit out of the hat at the Worlds. It seems to me that his phenomenal ability to channel energy at the important competitions was the number-one bullet in his gun. Several victories, specifically in Munich and in Halifax, Nova Scotia, were questionable in my opinion, but gold is gold.

Kurt was polite and friendly to me, but he certainly knew that I was not his biggest fan. His greatest adversary was Viktor Petrenko, a refined, passionate, and athletic skater, who positively reeked of Soviet discipline. Kurt's style was erratic and casual by comparison to Viktor's, although Kurt was undeniably a virtuoso. I arrived at the conclusion that Kurt's successful performances were based on guts and luck, not on hard-core training like Viktor's.

In November 1991, I attended the Lalique pre-Olympic event in Albertville, since I was training the Canadian ice-dance team of Mark Janoschak and Jacqueline Petr. The three of us were lodged at the same hotel as Kurt, and I observed him carefully. On the night before his long-program appearance, I recall that his hotel room was the venue for pillow fights and other teenage antics involving a female Canadian pairs skater. I found that behavior entirely inappropriate prior to an important competition.

Kurt's performance the next evening was decidedly flawed. Alexei Urmanov put on a dazzling show. The dark, good-looking Russian with perfect American teeth executed in vain a quadruple toe loop and a triple Axel/triple toe-loop combination. He skated without flaw, yet placed second to Kurt.

At breakfast the next morning, I sat with the Canadian contingent that included Kurt's Canadian judge, a woman from Vancouver. I listened to her explain to Barbara Graham, the Canadian team leader, the marks that she had given the previous evening. With the wide-eyed innocence of Bambi, she reported that, by giving her first placements in the short-program event and the long-program event to two different skaters, she had been able to squeeze Kurt into first place by a majority of second ordinals.

Listening to that odious confession, I wanted to say (but didn't), "You are the living example of what skaters fear judges to be. Shame on you!"

Some years later, at the Worlds in Edmonton, this particular judge was forced to flee the competition and return home to Vancouver after awarding the lowest mark on the panel to Canadian champion and folk hero Elvis Stojko. I was asked to comment on national television the morning after the men's competition, and I took pleasure in excoriating her. I am convinced that the only credible judges are former skaters with international reputations.

During the late 1980s and early 1990s, Edmonton became a major training center, first because of Kurt's international successes and later because the Royal Glenora Club hired American coach Christy Ness – teacher of Kristi Yamaguchi, who became the 1992 women's Olympic champion in Albertville. As a student, Kristi demonstrated the Asian understanding of discipline that had been imparted by her parents. She obeyed instructions with extreme reverence. Incidentally, Kristi was the first of a series of world champions from Asia or of Asian descent who dominated the world stage for a decade. Others included Midori Ito, Lu Chen, Yuka Sato, and Michelle Kwan.

On the men's side, Kurt was the Canadian great white hope at the Albertville Olympics, even though he had spent two months in physiotherapy for an ailing back. For his short-program routine, he wore one of the most peculiar costumes ever seen on ice: cartoon-like yellow bloomers that melted into scarlet around the ankles, conjuring an image of Scheherazade gone terribly wrong. He fell apart, making an egregious error that prevented him from entertaining any serious thoughts of a gold medal.

The Canadian judge, Jean Matthews, embarrassed her country by ignoring the mistakes and placing Kurt second, though no other judge placed him higher than fourth. She also placed Viktor Petrenko third, while seven other judges put him first. She was obliged to offer the ISU a written explanation.

· What Canada's international judges seem not to understand is that marks may be inflated only for good performances. In the wake of disaster, judges are obligated to give appropriately low scores. The skater has guaranteed his own failure.

Kurt's long program was no better than his fourth-rated short, but once again the Canadian judge made a serious mistake. She continued to promote Kurt as Canada's number-one male competitor at the expense of brilliant performances by Elvis Stojko and Michael Slipchuk. Both Elvis and Michael dropped a place.* Kurt finished the competition in sixth.

Although Kurt was a world champion, his inability to win an Olympic medal certainly came as a major disappointment. He returned home to Edmonton with his tail between his legs, but with a head that was actively analyzing his future. Before the Worlds, he broke in a new long free-skating program to Stravinsky's *Firebird Suite*.

At the 1992 Worlds in Oakland, California, a humiliating error in the men's short-program judging gave Kurt a leg up on the competition. Canadian judge Jane Garden (and three of her cohorts) marked Kurt's accidental double Lutz, executed in a corner, as if it had been a triple. Her rationalization after the fact was that, even if Kurt hadn't done the required triple, it didn't matter, because his program was better than anybody else's.†

With skating mistakes in short programs, the draconian rule is to punish any incomplete element with a mandatory deduction. In the case of that particular error, the recommended deduction was .5, to be subtracted from the technical-merit mark. Jane Garden awarded 5.9 out of a possible 6.0. Three other judges scored Kurt either 5.6 or 5.7. Judges who can't tell doubles from triples should find something else to do with their volunteer time.

So Kurt went into the long-program event third behind Petrenko and Peter Barna, then managed to move up to second place, despite a popped triple Axel. A difficult season had finally come to an end.

Once, while I was performing in Edmonton with Stars on Ice, I had the opportunity to see how Kurt lived when he wasn't engaged in

---

* Elvis Stojko slipped from sixth to seventh, Michael Slipchuk from eighth to ninth.

† At the press conference after the event, Kurt Browning expressed his belief that the judges had made honest mistakes.

competition. He invited me, along with the rest of our cast, to the house
that he rented in downtown Edmonton with two male friends.

Their environment, reminiscent of a fraternity house, bespoke a
lifestyle that was moderately out of control. I was amused. The casual,
carefree existence that his milieu implied was at odds with the champion's maintenance of a disciplined routine on the ice. However, one of
Kurt's many talents was his finely honed ability to take in the big picture.
He also possessed a large dollop of common sense.

Some time after the 1992 Olympics and Worlds, Kurt left that
halcyon existence and defected to the east (of Canada) to train with
Granite Club coach Louis Stong in Toronto. Sandra Bezic, as choreographer, was part of the equation. Her ability to reinvent and edit Kurt's
skating was probably much more valuable in the long run than any
coaching that Stong, however gifted as a coach, could have offered.*

With Kurt's defection from the Royal Glenora Club and Kristi
Yamaguchi's retirement from the amateur world, Edmonton's glory as a
training center all but came to an end. Christy Ness eventually left
Edmonton as well, so the waves of the Red Sea flowed back together,
leaving the Royal Glenora a backwater once again.

Kurt arrived in Toronto with little fanfare, in spite of his illustrious
credentials. The press certainly did not react dramatically to his decision
to embrace a new environment and a new coach. I skated at the Cricket
Club, a mere fifteen minutes from the Granite Club, yet I never saw Kurt
or heard anything more about him until the Canadians in Hamilton,
Ontario. Kurt won the men's title there, despite intense heat from Elvis
Stojko. He performed new programs with an entirely new look, master-
minded by Sandra Bezic.

At the 1993 Worlds in Prague, Kurt experienced, in my opinion, the
greatest victory of his career. The commentators who analyzed his long
program failed to detect its real significance. What was clear to me was

* The 1992–93 season was not Kurt Browning's first opportunity to collaborate with
Sandra Bezic. She first choreographed for him in 1987, producing Kurt's humorous,
romantic cowboy persona for his long-program performance to selections that included
the "Grand Canyon Suite."

that Kurt had undergone a complete metamorphosis of image and skating style. Simply put, he now competed as a mature, savvy professional within a field of amateurs. A number of his rivals were able to execute more triple jumps than Kurt, but his ace in the hole was that, whatever he did, he did it with more style and élan than anybody else possessed. It wasn't what he did but how he did it that won the day in Prague.

It was in Prague that Kurt performed his most memorable choreography, sporting a white dinner jacket and skating to "As Time Goes By" from the Humphrey Bogart and Ingrid Bergman film classic *Casablanca*. His professionalism and emotional maturity made the other male competitors look like novices.

The year leading up to the 1994 Olympics in Lillehammer was exciting worldwide. Former Olympic champion Brian Boitano had chosen to reinstate as an amateur and to compete once again for the gold. I'm convinced that his return was an attempt to relive the euphoric exultation that his 1988 Olympic gold medal had provided. That intense euphoria, like a potent illegal drug, is so extreme that virtually everything in one's subsequent life becomes anticlimactic and disappointing.

Viktor Petrenko, the 1992 Olympic champion, had also elected to continue, perhaps because his victory over Paul Wylie in Albertville had been tenuous rather than convincing.

Kurt, as four-time world champion, hungered for the gold medal as well. It was the major piece that was missing from his medal collection.

Kurt's quest had begun with a loss to Elvis Stojko at the Canadians. Just before boarding the plane for Lillehammer, he surprised me with a phone call. I was deeply moved that he wanted to talk to me about his Olympic strategy, but I sensed that he harbored a seed of self-doubt. Deep down, he wasn't convinced that he could win the gold medal.

I assured Kurt that he possessed all the tools to fulfil his dream, both in mind and in body, but his confession of doubt worried me. I have frequently wondered if one's destiny is predetermined. Our conversation that day certainly raised the possibility that Kurt's subsequent failure to win a medal had been preordained; that his fate had been sealed before his arrival on Norwegian soil.

Brian, Viktor, and Kurt, because of the enormous pressure exerted upon them, both from without and within, all bombed abysmally in Lillehammer. Kurt's appearance in the short-program event was by far the most memorable, but not because of his skating. After Kurt fell on the triple flip and singled an Axel, after the announcer read his twelfth-place marks, as his dream lay in shards around his feet, a CTV commentator conducted an interview. It is difficult for anybody, during the aftermath of a personal disappointment of such magnitude, to explain to the Canadian populace what went wrong and why.

Kurt's mother had found her way backstage and was visible on-camera, waiting for her son to finish his interview. When it ended, Kurt fell into his mother's arms. He revealed through his body language that, although he had given everything that he could, he had failed. He had disappointed himself, his family, and his country. Mrs. Browning, in turn, demonstrated that the love between mother and son was unconditional. Her feelings for Kurt had nothing to do with medals. The incident caused the entire Canadian nation to galvanize on Kurt's behalf.

I happened to watch Kurt's short program and its aftermath in the first-class departure lounge of the Halifax airport. The episode affected all the passengers waiting for their respective flights in the lounge. Compassion flooded the room. I found myself speaking in a most famil-iar manner with perfect strangers. By the time I left the lounge, I was seconds away from missing my plane.

Meanwhile, Elvis had made a major move. After the short-program event, he stood in second position, a stone's throw away from Olympic gold. Kurt must have found Elvis's brilliant short program a particularly bitter pill to swallow.

Kurt's long program was excellent, but the damage had been done. He had no hope of a gold medal, however much he might have deserved it. He placed third for the long program, fifth overall. Elvis won the silver medal, behind Alexei Urmanov.

I believe that most Canadians hoped that Kurt would rise from the ashes and set the record straight by bringing home a fifth world title from the 1994 Worlds in Tokyo, Japan. A CBC interviewer asked me on-air what counsel I would offer him, and my advice was that, rather than end his amateur career on such a sour note, Kurt should dig deep and make one last attempt to embrace amateur glory. Had Kurt heard my suggestion, it would have fallen upon deaf ears. He had already decided to forfeit his right to redeem himself, and would never again skate as an amateur.

Kurt had already achieved a level of success that few skaters in history can claim. What nobody knew at the time was that, as a professional, he would achieve far more glory and respect. His amateur life was a warm-up act for one of the most stunning professional careers of the century.

Shortly after the 1994 Worlds, Stars on Ice mounted a cross-Canada tour with Kurt as its principal star. I had also been asked to perform in that production, so I viewed Kurt at close hand, both on and off the ice.

The tour began in Halifax, after approximately three days of practice. The skating fans of Halifax have historically been among the most devout in Canada, and they received all the members of our cast warmly. But it wasn't until Kurt appeared in Quebec City and Montreal that I became fully aware of the fanatic adoration that he provoked.

In the opening number at the Montreal Forum, Kurt and fellow Canadian Olympian Josée Chouinard spoke to the spectators with hand-held microphones, introducing the rest of the cast. That opening was extraordinary; I had rarely seen a more excited crowd. It reminded me of the audiences that came to Toller Cranston's The Ice Show at the Montreal Olympic Vélodrome. The crowd approached hysteria in revealing both love and respect for the failed but forgiven Olympic hero.

Devoted female Kurt Browning fans from across Canada somehow found each other and sent their wedding rings and other gold jewelry to be melted down and formed into a piece of art that included the Canadian maple leaf and a map of Canada, with a diamond marking Kurt's hometown. They presented the piece to Kurt as compensation for his lost Olympic medal.

Kevin Albrecht, Kurt's manager, indicated that the sculpture was worth in the neighborhood of $250,000. Had I received that gift myself, it would certainly have hit the melting pot, but I'm sure that Kurt has kept his extraordinary talisman in a place of honor.*

---

* The golden gift resides in the Alberta Sports Hall of Fame in Red Deer, Alberta.

Kurt possesses the ability to render himself emotionally transparent to his audience. Like peering voyeurs, spectators are able to experience intimacy with Kurt while he performs. Many fans make the mistake of thinking that they know him, because his personality fuses with his art.

The greatest performers in figure skating are those who possess fundamental self-knowledge. Scott Hamilton and Robin Cousins are prime examples, but Kurt's self-knowledge and skating vocabulary are no less profound than theirs. He is so comfortable with his masculinity that he has never been afraid to reveal his feminine side. With the androgynous appeal of a Mick Jagger, David Bowie, or Billy Idol, he plays to both female and male audience members.

I have always prided myself upon being profoundly honest and accurate in evaluating skaters and their performances. In my last tour of duty as judge at the World Professional Championships in Landover, there were only four skaters in the men's competition, yet I found myself in the unenviable position of having run out of marks.

Viktor Petrenko, the 1992 Olympic champion, skated first in the artistic competition. A tired game that judges play all too often involves reserving high marks for subsequent skaters, no matter how well the first performs. I didn't feel like playing that game, so I gave Viktor a perfect mark of 10.0 for a performance that was technically and emotionally extraordinary. All other judges on the panel held down their marks, and wisely so.

When Kurt skated last, he was even more extraordinary than Viktor, but there were no more marks left to give. I considered awarding 11.0, but I would have been instantly disqualified from the panel.

The profound knowledge of skating, which of course I possess, is somewhat different from the profound knowledge of judging, as I found out. I was forced to tie Viktor and Kurt, though that wasn't what I wanted to do. I concluded that judgments made in error are forgivable if they result from honest mistakes. Deliberate judging mistakes, incidentally, are far more prevalent.

I was the first Canadian male to conceive of and star in my own televised skating specials. Kurt subsequently followed suit. Perhaps feeling somewhat bitter about Kurt's failure to invite me to participate, I peevishly made a point of not watching them. However, I did manage to witness a clip of his extraordinary remake of Gene Kelly's famous dance routine from *Singing in the Rain.*[*] When the number ended, it crossed my mind that nobody had ever been more fabulous than Kurt was in that number. It was pointless to try. All the male skaters in the world might as well retire.

I asked IMG to invite Kurt to perform with me at my 1997 farewell tribute. However, Kurt and some of the other performers felt hurt because of my failure to telephone them personally with an invitation. At the time, I was experiencing a great deal of emotional and professional turbulence, and I was simply unable to phone anyone about anything, especially if the call involved asking a personal favor.

Perversely, I waited to see who, if anyone, would show up without an individual request. Kurt's decision to participate may have been nip-and-tuck, but the fact remains that he did skate, more fabulously than ever before. I watched his performance from backstage, recognizing that his style had reached a level that couldn't be eclipsed by anyone, anywhere.

That style has been subject to many influences over the years, but perhaps none has been so important as the influence exerted by his girlfriend and now wife, Sonia Rodriguez. Kurt met Sonia in Edmonton when the National Ballet of Canada toured the west. From all reports, it was love at first sight. Sonia, a classical dancer, exposed Kurt to the refinement of balletic movement. Over the years since their meeting, his creative and conceptual approaches to his material have become increasingly diverse, increasingly refined.

A strange thing happened to me after my retirement from professional skating. I felt that I no longer belonged to the skating world's royal family, so I deliberately distanced myself from all my friends and colleagues, including Kurt. During that time in my life, I made a point of

---

[*] That number was originally part of Kurt Browning's television special "You Must Remember This."

collecting information about everyone in skating who was important to me, but I made no contact with any of them.

Then in late December 2001, I received a call from a woman at Insight Productions in Toronto. She was about to produce and direct a Kurt Browning special, and she planned to interview four former Canadian men's champions in their respective domiciles. Could Kurt and his wife, Sonia, plus a skeleton crew, come to San Miguel de Allende for three days? Of course I agreed, but I confessed that I was apprehensive about meeting Kurt after our long separation. By Kurt's own admission, he, in turn, was somewhat apprehensive about flying to San Miguel.

Kurt was the first A-class skater to visit me in Mexico, but since we had shared so many common experiences on and off the ice, after thirty seconds we were right back where we had left off. The filming included conversations between Kurt and me, and we publicly exposed our feelings for one another. Kurt told me, "Toller, I've always been intimidated by you." I countered, "How peculiar. It was I who was always intimidated by you."

The filming ended with a dramatic visual image. Kurt, Sonia, and I mounted horses and rode into the Mexican sunset. I experienced an overwhelming sense that we were all in perfect harmony, different yet the same. In the silence of that ride, surrounded by the beauty of the desert landscape, I felt a sense of peace, an emotional tranquility that I had rarely known. I was honored to be with Kurt and Sonia, sacred members of a special family. I shall never forget that late-afternoon ride, when the sound of silence said everything that there was to be said among us. I suspect that Kurt and Sonia felt the same.

Skate America, Buffalo, New York, 1990

CHAPTER 19

MIDORI ITO

℘

Japanese Jumping Phenomenon

M idori Ito was born on August 13, 1969. Early in her life, she became one of Japan's most highly acclaimed sports heroes and national treasures, carrying the burden of a nation's hopes into competition. She trained in Nagoya, where she lived with her coach and surrogate mother, Machiko Yamada.

At sixteen, Midori developed the triple Axel that became her calling card, and in the fall of 1988, she entered the record book as the first woman to land that jump in competition. A decade and a half later, only Tonya Harding has followed suit.[*]

At four feet, nine inches and ninety-seven pounds, Midori won her only world title in Paris in 1989, using her powerful triple Axel to silence those who criticized her lesser artistic gifts. The following year, her poor compulsory figures cost her the chance to repeat as gold medalist.

---

[*] In 2002, it has been a full decade since a female skater has landed a triple Axel in competition. A number have tried, most recently Yoshie Onda.

The 1991 Worlds in Munich were perhaps Midori's most memorable, but for all the wrong reasons. After a painful and damaging collision with Laetitia Hubert of France during the warm-up period, she jumped too close to the barrier while launching her short-program combination jump and flew right off the ice through a gap in the boards carved out for a television camera.

At the 1992 Olympics in Albertville, Midori missed her combination jump in the short program, but came back strongly enough to place second to Kristi Yamaguchi and win the silver medal. She then turned professional, touring Japan in exhibitions and returning to amateur events only to provide commentary for Japanese television.

In 1993, Midori became the first and only woman to land a triple Axel in professional competition.

〜〜〜〜〜〜

J apan's Midori Ito was one of the most peculiar squares in the patchwork quilt of figure skating. She was a phenomenon. There was never anyone like her, and I doubt that anyone like her will appear in the future. She possessed such extraordinary athleticism that it seemed she could reign uncontested as world champion for as long as she wished. This wasn't the case.

I first heard about Midori from British journalist Alexandra (Sandra) Stevenson, who had seen Ito's winning performance at an international competition in Japan. Sandra indicated that Midori would have been equally successful in the men's competition. She was able to jump like no other human.

I had my first up-close look at Midori at the 1987 Worlds in Cincinnati. She was tiny in stature, with a somewhat stocky build. Her short, muscular legs were conspicuously bowed. However, like Paul Wylie, she skated with such speed and strength that her diminutive size ceased to matter. She became a giant. She executed triple jumps with the ease that others brought to singles.

School figures were still part and parcel of a competitor's life, and Midori was not proficient at compulsories (and who really cared?), so she didn't often enjoy the advantage of competing in the last free-skating flight. She left a stunning impression at the end of her long program in Cincinnati, but no judge dared to give her the scores that she deserved for fear of running out of marks before the last flight competed. Like Beatrix Schuba in school figures, Midori could rarely be scored fairly.

Once, at Carnegie Hall, I heard Vladimir Horowitz play Rachmaninoff's Concerto Number 3 for piano. At the end of his performance, the audience exploded into applause of a volume and frequency that I had never experienced before. Similarly, in Cincinnati and again in Calgary, Midori received an ovation that was unlike the applause accorded to any other competitor. The audience moaned in awe, creating a sound that seemed to emanate from the base of a human volcano.

In 1989, I watched Midori win her first and only world title in Paris. She placed sixth in the compulsories and first in the short-program event. Once again, the virtuosity of her long program could not be accurately marked on the mathematical scale reserved for other competitors. She executed a flawless triple Axel, so enormous that it left me speechless. I was commentating for the CBC, and I'm sure that my audible gasps, followed by silence, must have confused many Canadian viewers.

The 1990 Worlds were held in Halifax. It was considered a foregone conclusion that Midori would win her second world title there. However, she put her foot down while executing one of the three school figures. (Those were the last Worlds at which figures were contested.) The catastrophe landed her in tenth place going into the short-program event, which she won, followed by Kristi Yamaguchi, Holly Cook, Natalia Lebedeva, and Jill Trenary. Entering the final, Natalia and Holly stood first and second, but were unlikely to remain there. Jill and Midori were third and fourth.

Midori once again skated a fabulous long program and stood a chance to win the overall competition, but only if Jill placed lower than third in her final free skate. A peculiar incident then occurred. Midori ran out to the boards and devoured Jill's performance in a most obvious and unladylike fashion. Her intimidation tactics, if that is what they were, did not succeed. Jill placed second to Midori in the long-program event and won her first and only world title. Midori took home the silver medal.

That particular Paris competition featured another unusual character in skating history: Holly Cook, an American from Bountiful, Utah. She earned the bronze medal in Halifax, her first Worlds, then was never seen again in competition.

At the 1991 Munich Worlds, Midori performed a historical short program. Because of her speed and athleticism, when she jumped into her triple Lutz/double toe-loop combination, she flew off the ice surface through a gap in the boards, momentarily disappearing from view. She then came running back onto the ice to finish her program.

Midori certainly knew how to take advantage of the crowd's response to her dramatic unplanned exit. I watched her carefully, marveling at her aptitude for milking the audience dry. With a charming smile, she tried to compensate for the incomplete element, and she may have succeeded. She finished a surprising third for the short program and fourth overall, while all three medals went to Americans: Kristi Yamaguchi, Tonya Harding, and Nancy Kerrigan.

In 1992, Midori was a serious contender for the Olympic gold medal. She was the kind of skater who could virtually terminate competitors if she performed without error. However, she entered the final event in fourth place, so it was mathematically nearly impossible (but don't tell that to Sarah Hughes) for her to win the overall event.

In a sensational interview, live to Japan, Midori felt compelled to apologize to her countrymen for her poor short-program showing. That apology ran utterly counter to North American sensibilities, but as a Japanese gesture it was almost routine. Midori had lost face and felt humiliated. Culturally and athletically, she was Japanese through and through, unlike a later Japanese champion, Yuka Sato, who became thoroughly westernized by training in Canada and later marrying an American.

In a long-program performance that will go down in history for its sheer virtuosity and guts, Midori missed her opening triple Axel yet threw in another one, landing it perfectly, during the last twenty seconds of her program.

Kristi, who had won the short program, offered a more complete long free skate than Midori. However, Midori's overall virtuosity, coupled with the late triple Axel, made the long-program event difficult to decide. Had I been a judge, I would have posted a tie. The panel gave Kristi the long-program victory and the gold medal. Midori finished second in the long-program event and took home a silver medal from Albertville.

At the 1996 Worlds in Edmonton, Midori, at age twenty-six, returned to amateur competition. Her appearance and personality had changed dramatically. She had lost a tremendous amount of weight and had ceased to present herself as an athletic dynamo. She was small, wan, and un-smiling as she clutched her rib cage in pain.

It was my understanding that Midori's personal life in Japan was rocky, and her physical appearance in Edmonton certainly confirmed such rumors. Her return to the eligible ranks had been a grave mistake. Her performances were more mediocre than memorable. She finished seventh and was never seen again in amateur competition. She returned to professional skating and commentating.

The one and only time that I judged Midori at the World Professional Championships in Landover, I placed her first in the technical program and last in the artistic event. Unfortunately, Midori had never developed much artistic ability. Perhaps she possessed sensitivity and artfulness, but her coach had not polished the rough edges. As I saw Midori's situation, the glory was entirely her own, based on hard work and innate talent, while the blame for her failures lay at the feet of those who had trained and counseled her.

In 1997, I was invited to Nagano to work with the Japanese figure-skating team prior to the 1998 Olympics. Midori and I both performed at an exhibition for the team's benefit. I had not seen her since Edmonton, and I was glad that the audience received her with a show of profound love.

In a perfect world, Midori would have developed into a more rounded and complete skater. As it was, she achieved a level of greatness that is within the reach of very few. She is a unique part of the texture of figure-skating history.

With training mate, Paul Wylie, Tom Collins Tour, 1992

CHAPTER 20

NANCY KERRIGAN

⁂

The Whack Heard 'Round the World

N ancy Kerrigan came from Massachusetts, on the Atlantic Coast. Tonya Harding came from Oregon, on the Pacific Coast. When they met in the middle in Detroit at the 1994 U.S. Nationals, they became inextricably linked in skating lore, whether they liked it or not. Thus will they intrude on each other's chapters.

Nancy was born on October 13, 1969, in Woburn, Massachusetts, and raised in Stoneham, ten miles from Boston. Her close-knit working-class family consisted of Daniel, a welder; Brenda, a legally blind homemaker; and two elder brothers, Mark and Michael, who liked to play ice hockey. Although Nancy enjoyed joining her brothers in hockey scrimmages, she focused primarily on figure skating, because that was what girls were expected to do.

Nancy was shy and quiet, keeping to herself at school, as she moved deliberately up the skating ladder, and her family sacrificed greatly to finance the effort. In 1986, while Nancy was still a junior skater, her coach moved away and passed the promising student to Evy and Mary Scotvold. The husband-and-wife coaching team analyzed and improved Nancy's technique and taught her about artistry.

Nancy graduated from Stoneham High School in 1987 and, after a one-year hiatus, went on to earn an associate's degree in business from Emmanuel College. It took her four years to do so, because she continued to skate full-time and to progress through the ranks, if somewhat erratically.

It was Tonya Harding who grabbed the 1991 U.S. title by landing the second-ever triple Axel performed by a woman in competition, but Nancy answered a month later with a world bronze medal. By the end of the 1992 season, Nancy was an Olympic bronze and world silver medalist. Her own national title followed a year later, after Kristi Yamaguchi's retirement from the amateur ranks.

Early in their careers, Tonya had outpaced Nancy. Then Nancy began to pull ahead. Thus twenty-four-year-old Nancy became the primary obstacle standing in the way of Tonya's Olympic ambition. That led to the infamous clubbing incident that occurred at the U.S. Nationals in Detroit on January 6, 1994. As Nancy left a practice session prior to the short program event, a large man wielding a bludgeon attacked her from behind, administering two forceful blows to her right knee. He fled the building by crashing through a chained Plexiglas door and sprinting away into the snowy afternoon.

Nancy withdrew from the Nationals but stayed to watch the events, sequestered in a private box. Then she headed home to Stoneham with serious bruises to her right thigh and knee.

Ten days after the incident, Nancy returned to the ice, avoiding jumps in the early days of recovery. She ultimately made a spectacular public return at the Lillehammer Olympics, placing a close and controversial second to Oksana Baiul of the Ukraine.

Nancy began dating her manager, Jerry Solomon, who was being sued for divorce. A year after the Olympics, the couple became engaged in spite of their fifteen-year age difference. They were married on September 9, 1995.

On December 17, 1996, Nancy found her truest vocation as the mother of her son, Matthew. Today the Solomons live in Lynnfield, Massachusetts. They produce skating shows and ice videos.

꒰꒰꒰꒰꒰꒰

N ancy Kerrigan possessed everything a great champion might desire: a slim, athletic body; refined, almost aristocratic, brunette good looks, not unlike those of Katherine Hepburn, to whom she was compared; a flair for skating; and a single-minded determination to succeed. Those admirable traits were cultivated within a lower-middle-class background.

Fabulous skaters often surface as if by magic in the American skating pool, and sometimes they appear first on the international scene as fully mature and seasoned competitors. I had never heard of Nancy when I encountered Ellen Burka, my former coach, in a remote, freezing-cold suburban practice rink at the 1990 Goodwill Games in Seattle, Washington. Ellen was teaching Canadian champion Karen Preston. Karen could be a difficult, emotionally taxing pupil.

Ellen possessed a meticulous and discerning eye for skating talent, and she rhapsodized about a phenomenal but unknown American competitor, Nancy Kerrigan. I remember Ellen asking rhetorically, "Can you imagine teaching anyone so gorgeous and talented? And she doesn't even complain. Wonderful!"

Fifteen minutes later, my eyes alighted upon Nancy, and I noticed that everything Ellen had reported was accurate. It seemed to many of us that it was just a matter of time before Nancy became a great skater and a champion.

The next season, Nancy qualified for the U.S. World Team and won the bronze medal in Munich. However, during the months that followed that promising achievement, as I watched Nancy skate, either live or on television, I found her performances, whether in competition or in exhibition, consistently flawed and disappointing. The 1993 Worlds were Nancy's nadir. The glory that Ellen and I had predicted now appeared unattainable.

At the Jimmy Fund benefit at Harvard in the fall of 1993, Nancy and I both performed with Peter and Kitty Carruthers, 1984 Olympic silver medalists in pairs. Peter, Nancy, and I chatted in the dressing room before one of the three shows. Peter and I wanted to know how Nancy's Olympic training was going. We wondered about her state of mind.

Peter assured Nancy that she had an excellent chance to become the 1994 Olympic champion at Lillehammer. Her skating was great, and her positive attitude was even greater. We both wished her good luck.

In San Miguel de Allende, Mexico, just before the women's competition began at the 1994 U.S. Nationals, I received an early-morning phone call from a Canadian journalist. He asked me what I thought about the savage attack that a fanatic had perpetrated upon Olympic hopeful Nancy Kerrigan. After Nancy's free-skating practice at Cobo Hall, an unknown assailant had savagely smashed her right kneecap. The incident horrified me. Like anyone who learned its grisly details, I was appalled, shocked, and depressed.

The obvious question, and the very next question that the Canadian journalist posed to me, was "Who could possibly have committed such a crime?"

I assured the journalist that I had no idea, but I did utter one prophetic remark. I said I did not believe the incident was a random crime committed by a stranger. I was convinced that the monster was somehow a member of the figure-skating world. In the deepest recesses of my mind, I suspected that the act might have been conceived and financed by a rabid European skating mother. Several leapt to mind, but I will not name them.

It occurred to me that the willful destruction of a beautiful young athlete's career, and potentially her health, was particularly vile, and I viewed the attack as attempted murder. The event sent shock waves through the worldwide Olympic community. Many athletes must have considered hiring bodyguards.

Nancy, with remarkable composure, answered the endless questions posed by the American media. With similar composure, she watched the women's competition in the days following her attack. Her number-one competitor, Tonya Harding, won handily, with a nerveless performance.

The USFSA was quick to issue a statement naming Nancy as Tonya's Olympic teammate, based on her competitive credentials, even though she had been unable to skate to qualify. Under the terms of the unanimous decision, newly crowned U.S. silver medalist Michelle Kwan, age thirteen, would serve as first alternate. Of course, as the Games drew closer, Nancy would need to prove her physical ability to compete.

So Nancy returned home and began what must have been a depressing and emotional period of rehabilitation. Although members of the press were forbidden to enter her training rink, hordes of ravenous journalists camped outside the facility and near Nancy's home.

At first, the attack was generally perceived as an act of fan violence, similar to an earlier assault on tennis star Monica Seles. However, in relatively short time, evidence pointed to a bodyguard in the employ of Tonya Harding and her then-husband, Jeff Gillooly. What remained to be decided was whether Tonya herself was complicit.

Meanwhile, while Tonya trained for the Olympics, she exhibited the behavior and attitude of Richard Nixon during his impeachment. To get through any given day, she apparently blocked out negative thoughts and focused on the certainty that she had been an innocent bystander.

It was clear to me that Tonya was involved in the attack, whether directly or indirectly, because both her husband and her bodyguard were influenced by her. I gave some thought to the situation of Henry II of England, who famously remarked to his knights, "Is there no one who will rid me of this troublesome monk?" He referred to the Archbishop of Canterbury, Saint Thomas à Becket. Wishing to curry favor with the king, the knights then rode to Canterbury Cathedral and brutally murdered the Archbishop. Henry II was later appalled that they had interpreted his wishes as a command.

Similarly, I mused, perhaps Tonya had indicated to her husband and her bodyguard that, if Nancy were removed from competition, the way would be clear for her to win the Olympics. Perhaps Tonya's wish had been interpreted as a command. I'm not sure that I believed my own argument, but it offered Tonya the benefit of the doubt. Although both Henry II and Tonya Harding pleaded innocence, history held them accountable.

Under the circumstances, I felt that the influence Tonya would exert on her fellow Olympic competitors, and on the very Games themselves, could only be negative and counterproductive. Based on my long-time friendship with IOC member Carol Ann Letheren, an expert in Olympic protocol, I believed that every national governing body had the right to send whomever it chose to the Olympics. No reasons had to be specified.

However, American officials caved in to the threat of lawsuits. I'm convinced that they also caved in to a far greater pressure, a pressure exerted behind closed doors. Host broadcaster CBS had a vested ratings interest in Tonya's participation, so it was important to the network executives that Tonya be approved to go to Lillehammer.

If the incident had occurred in any country other than the United States – Canada, Russia, Great Britain – Tonya would not have been allowed to compete. Her inclusion in the Games flew in the face of everything that the Olympic creed represented and that "Olympism" purported to be.

American team leader Gale Tanger, whose responsibility was to see to the needs of the members of her contingent at Lillehammer, truly must have found herself between a rock and a hard place: reconciling the U.S. contingent's palpable resentment of Tonya with Tonya's needs and her own personal feelings. The IOC irrationally assigned Tonya and Nancy to the same practice sessions and refused to budge on the issue.

Tonya dropped herself out of contention early in the proceedings with a tenth-place short-program performance. Nancy won that round, followed by Oksana Baiul, the wispy Ukraine orphan who had been badly hurt in a practice collision.

When it came to the final showdown between Nancy and Oksana, who deserved to win? The simple fact that Nancy was able to perform both her short and long programs without a single mistake was nothing short of a bona fide skating miracle. She gave the two best performances of her life. In my opinion, she demonstrated character and the will to triumph against all odds over a horrendous situation.

However, if the gods on Olympus were to evaluate Oksana Baiul's suffering as well, they might fairly conclude that she had paid as dearly, both in life and on the ice. Call it a draw on the emotional scale.

Leaving aside the affective content to focus on the technical, Oksana's long-program performance did not equal Nancy's in strength and jumping skill, in spite of the fact that Nancy's physical stature and body type made performing her jump content more difficult. Cede that round to Nancy.

Finally, Nancy stood in first place before the long-program event. If the judges found Oksana's and Nancy's long programs approximately equal, then perhaps Nancy should have been given the edge for her better short program.

As it was, the five-four decision in favor of Oksana split hairs. It probably rested on her lightness and her ingenuous grace.

Almost immediately, events began to go awry for Nancy once again. When the medal ceremony was delayed for close to half an hour, she erroneously assumed that the weepy gold medalist was composing herself and restoring her makeup. As Nancy waited backstage, CBS cameras and microphones caught her remarking petulantly to Lu Chen, "Oh, come on. So she's going to get out here and cry again. What's the difference?" Those words set off round one of a public-relations nightmare.

Obviously feeling peevish, but citing "death threats," Nancy left Lillehammer early and returned to America to begin her professional career. As the closing ceremonies took place in Norway, Nancy was in Florida, riding in a parade at the Walt Disney World Magic Kingdom Park. There she endangered her important endorsement contract with Disney Productions by making a casual, thoughtless remark about the "corny" situation in which she found herself. Again microphones picked up her words. Apparently she hadn't learned her lesson in Lillehammer.

What happened to Nancy next, as a result both of the Harding incident and of her own Olympic disappointment, is a long, complicated tale. She had never been particularly motivated by money. Mary Scotvold once astounded me by quoting Nancy as saying something like, "I don't want all this money, and I don't need it. What am I going to do with it?" Nonetheless, Nancy made millions. It was her failure to parlay Olympic renown into a solid professional career that I found sad.

At her first professional competition, Ice Wars in Uniondale, New York, in November 1994, Nancy gave what were characterized as "uninspired" performances. Her Christmas on Ice tour in December drew sparse crowds. A children's book project was postponed. A movie about her life was canceled. There was widespread speculation that the recent figure-skating glut had saturated the market. Enough was enough.

When I skated in an exhibition with Nancy in Virginia, I found that talking to her was like trying to communicate with a wounded bird. She seemed sensitive and vulnerable.

Some time later, I judged Nancy at Dick Button's World Professional Championships in Landover. Her performance was frighteningly amateur and unglamorous compared to the slick sophistication and virtuosity of Kristi Yamaguchi and Yuka Sato.

Backstage, Nancy's manager and new husband, Jerry Solomon, asked me what seemed to be the problem. As diplomatically as possible, I informed him that the winning equation at that particular competition involved glamor as well as serious technical and choreographic preparation. For the record, Nancy received last place out of five competitors, performing a rather silly Irish jig. The audience, though certainly aware of Nancy's tribulations, offered just a trickle of applause.

If Nancy had won an Olympic medal without having to circumvent the Tonya Harding roadblock, perhaps she might have become a major professional star. Instead she became a wealthy young woman but an undisciplined and inferior professional skater. That is a class-A American tragedy.

On the other hand, Nancy may now possess what she always wanted most of all: a husband and a child to care for, a figurative trip back in time to Stoneham, Massachusetts. If so, then dreams do come true.

Harding (left), with Kristi Yamaguchi and Nancy Kerrigan, Tom Collins Tour, 1992

CHAPTER 21

TONYA HARDING

ᘒᘒ

A New Low for Figure Skating

T onya Maxine Harding was born on the wrong side of the tracks in Portland, Oregon, on November 12, 1970. Al Harding would eventually become just one of LaVona's seven husbands, and although Tonya was her mother's fifth child, one had died in infancy and the others had left home by the time Tonya arrived. It was a peripatetic childhood. LaVona changed addresses more often than she changed spouses.

Tonya started skating at age three, showing remarkable early promise and tenacity. Two years later, she owned her first hunting rifle, and her happiest times were those she spent in Al's company, hunting, fishing, and tinkering with cars.

Tonya dropped out of high school during her sophomore year and later earned a General Equivalency Diploma. There were many other bumps in her road. LaVona left the family on one occasion and threw Tonya out of the house on another. Tonya's half-brother attempted to sexually molest her. She defended herself by burning him with a curling iron and whacking him with a hockey stick. He went to jail.

The only real constants in Tonya's life were her coach, the generous and unstinting Diane Rawlinson, and her time on the ice – inhibited by exercise-induced asthma.

Not surprisingly, Tonya lacked the finesse and gentility of the typical female skater, offending the establishment with her inclinations toward beer, cigarettes, pool, drag racing, and pickup trucks. Athletically, however, Tonya was a tigress. She made her first mark on the international scene when she placed second at the 1991 Skate America event in Portland, Maine.

In 1990, at age nineteen, Tonya married Jeff Gillooly, a conveyer-belt operator for the Oregon Liquor Control Commission. The couple's relationship was rocky from the start. They separated twice. In 1992, Tonya received a restraining order against Gillooly. She filed for divorce, then reconciled with him.

Meanwhile, the 1991 U.S. women's champion by virtue of her astounding triple Axel finished third at the 1992 Nationals, fourth at the 1992 Olympics, sixth at the 1992 Worlds, and fourth at the 1993 Nationals. Tonya was skidding down a slippery slope.

There were two final straws: Tonya's poor marks at the NHK Trophy event, an international competition in the fall of 1994, and her perception that the USFSA had favored Nancy Kerrigan by featuring her on the cover of *Skating* magazine. Those humiliations led directly or indirectly to the ill-conceived clubbing plot involving Gillooly; his friend and dim bulb Shane Stant; Shane's uncle, Derrick Smith; and Shawn Eckardt.

In the years since Tonya's conviction (she pleaded guilty to hindering the investigation), she has served probation, told tall tales, clashed with the law, remarried (to Michael Smith in November 1995), and divorced again. She has also taken tentative strides toward rehabilitation as a skater.

✠✠✠✠✠✠

I first saw Tonya Harding at a practice session in Sun Valley, Idaho. Her conspicuously masculine virtuosity rendered me speechless. That kind of talent inevitably winds up on the international stage. It was just a matter of time.

In 1991, I was again privy to a Tonya Harding performance, this time at the U.S. Nationals at the Target Center in Minneapolis. Tonya astounded the figure-skating world by executing the first triple Axel ever performed in competition by an American woman, and the second woman after Japan's Midori Ito. The judges unanimously chose Tonya over Kristi Yamaguchi, defender of the national title.

Tonya was an unusual specimen within the ladies' ranks. Because she possessed the physical strength and athleticism of a male, her international skating performances would be taken seriously.

Tonya made her Worlds debut in Munich later the same season. I remember being impressed that, as a complete unknown, she skated second in the short-program event, yet received second-place marks. Normally judges award conservative marks early in an event in order to "save room" on the mathematical scale for the rest of the field. With the help of another triple Axel, Tonya went home from Germany with a silver medal in a one-two-three American sweep, sandwiched between Kristi and Nancy Kerrigan. Midori Ito placed fourth.

Tonya made the mistake of taking a cavalier position toward her coaches. She was the boss. The coach, her employee, was subservient to her wishes – ironic since Tonya received many, many free lessons. But Tonya was the captain of her own ship. Historically, when a skater overrides a coach's authority, the ship sooner or later ends up on the rocks.

When Nancy won the American title in 1992, Tonya began to view her rival as a major obstacle on her path to the Olympic gold medal. Just before Christmas 1993, Tonya and her cohorts conceived a plot and set it in motion. Shane Stant made his infamously fruitless trip to the Tony Kent Arena on Cape Cod, Nancy's training rink, then ultimately tracked down his prey in Detroit. As a result of the clubbing incident, Tonya won the short-program event on all nine judges' cards, skating to – if you can believe it – *Much Ado about Nothing*. She left Detroit with her second U.S. title.

I'm certain that Tonya, although outwardly tough and brazen, must have experienced some unpleasantness as a result of the media sideshow that surrounded her pre-Olympic training in Portland, as the press speculated about her involvement. On the other hand, more than a

thousand spectators typically turned up to watch her practice and
to root her on. When I saw her television interviews, she sounded to
me like a brainwashed cult victim. Revealing no genuine emotion,
she delivered upbeat Olympic predictions that I found indigestible. She
repeatedly assured the American public that she would bring the gold
medal home from Lillehammer.

Meanwhile, a check stub and handwritten notes referring to the Tony
Kent Arena turned up in a Portland Dumpster. Phone records reflected
calls to that rink from Tonya's home. Further phone records tied Tonya's
credit card to Stant, the hired henchman. A Detroit television station
revealed that Tonya had requested Nancy's room number at the competitor's hotel in Detroit. Finally, Gillooly's lawyer issued a statement that
left little ambiguity about Tonya's complicity.

Ultimately, Gillooly accepted a plea bargain, pled guilty to one rack-
eteering charge, served six months in the Shutter Creek Correctional
Institution, a prison boot camp, and paid $100,000 in fines. Then he
changed his name to Jeff Stone (over the official protests of several other
Jeff Stones), remarried, and got on with his life.

Prosecutors chose to delay action on Tonya's case until after the
Olympics, so the USFSA and the United States Olympic Committee
(USOC) were faced with a difficult legal, ethical, and public-relations
dilemma: whether to send Tonya to Lillehammer. She made their decision easier by suing the USOC, demanding $25 million in punitive
damages if the national governing body kept her off the team.

Tonya did not travel to the Olympics with the rest of the U.S. contingent. Purportedly for a large fee or equivalent enticements, she traveled
to Norway in a first-class seat with television anchorwoman Connie
Chung, granting an exclusive interview. Chung was assigned to Tonya for
the duration of the women's competition. The American media provided
their ravenous viewing audiences with unlimited junk food.

I remember seeing an interview in which Tonya meekly expressed the
desire to hug Nancy and apologize. Since Nancy and Tonya never spoke
a word, apart from a brief hello at the team photo shoot, I very much
doubt that the kiss-and-make-up strategy panned out.

Even before competition got under way, the bizarre saga took on a new dimension: Gillooly had sold *A Current Affair* the pornographic video that he and Tonya had taped on their wedding night. It was not a pretty sight. Photographic out-takes appeared in all the newspapers. Tonya was incensed, but she had cried wolf once too often. Some cynical detractors speculated that she had released the video herself as a publicity ploy.

The short-program event drew a record Nielsen television ratings share, the highest audience share in Olympic history. It became the third-most-watched sports show of all time, following two Super Bowls, and the sixth-highest-rated show of any type.

Nancy placed first. Tonya missed her combination jump and fizzled to tenth. It was all over but for a little more shouting.

Tonya was nearly late for her long-program performance. She didn't immediately appear when her name was called. Then she showed up, skated for just over one minute, missed a jump, and stopped. She went to the referee and announced, in tears, that her lace had broken. To millions of people watching worldwide, that seemed to be just another cheap ruse to garner attention.

I suspect that the situation was innocent enough, but ultimately it tarnished Tonya's image – if that was still possible. Any serious Olympic competitor carefully checks her skate laces before the most important performance of her life.

Canadian Josée Chouinard was a second casualty of the skate-lace incident. Although top competitors can often handle wrinkles in the script, Josée simply couldn't on that occasion. Forced to skate early, while Tonya found a new lace, she gave an inferior performance and placed ninth.

Tonya restarted her program, finishing seventh in the free skate, eighth place overall. With Baiul in first, Kerrigan in second, and Lu Chen of China in third, the medalists were finally ready to stand on the podium.

As a direct result of the Harding-Kerrigan coverage, which one wag dubbed Frozen Watergate, skating temporarily became the second-most-watched sport in the world, second only to basketball (thank you,

Michael Jordan). Because of the extraordinary coverage, skaters' salaries and fees worldwide increased dramatically. It seems curious to me that Tonya, in her forced professional exile, was able to proffer an enormous gift to all skaters.

Eventually, after the Olympics concluded, Tonya agreed to a plea bargain. Prosecutors accepted a guilty plea for hindering prosecution, which carried no jail time. In return, Tonya would have to pay hefty fines and legal fees, perform five hundred hours of volunteer work in her community, serve a three-year probation, undergo psychiatric treatment, attend school or find a job, and resign from the USFSA.

Tonya continued to pop in and out of the press. A Chicago firm offered $5 million for a head-to-head Tonya-Nancy skate-off. A paperback biography was rushed into print. A made-for-television movie aired.

Tonya often created her own news. She threw a punch in a bar brawl. She alleged that a dark-haired stranger had abducted her at knifepoint and had forced her to drive him across town. After a dustup with a boyfriend, she was jailed for disorderly conduct and malicious mischief. She filmed a B movie, the action-thriller *Breakaway*. She was even subject to eviction from her Vancouver, Washington, apartment for nonpayment of rent.

Dick Button is a businessman who does his own marketing survey before making professional decisions. In 1995, at a private dinner for the judging panel at his Landover competition, he asked each judge whether he or she felt that Tonya Harding should be invited to compete in the future at his prestigious event.

Some judges were ambivalent and made no comment at all. I, for one, was extremely vocal in asserting my reasons why Tonya had no right to compete.

Two-time Olympic gold medalist Irina Rodnina was the only judge who supported Tonya's invitation. Irina is a particularly intelligent and experienced skater, and, although I disagreed wholeheartedly with her position on Tonya, I thought that it spoke volumes about Irina's humanitarian sensibilities.

Tonya's long-awaited professional figure-skating comeback came in the form of a two-minute routine, performed in Reno, Nevada, prior to a minor-league hockey game. Among the gifts tossed onto the ice were two rubber clubs.

In October 1999, Tonya made a more legitimate skating appearance at the ESPN Pro Championship, which took place the same week Mike Tyson returned to boxing. Their planets must have been aligned.

Tonya descended to the very depths of poor taste in March 2002, when she met – and easily defeated – Clinton accuser Paula Jones in a televised boxing match on the Fox network's "Celebrity Boxing" special. A *Newsweek* wag quipped before the event, "There'll be no knee-whacking allowed." Such is Tonya's legacy to figure skating.

In his trademark crossfoot spin, Champions on Ice, Syracuse, New York, 1995

CHAPTER 22

PHILIPPE CANDELORO

✍

Chippendales Dancer in Skate Boots

M arie-Thérèse, a young woman from Normandy on a visit to Italy, met Luigi Candeloro. They married and eventually settled in a Parisian suburb named Colombes, the French word for *doves* (or *pigeons*, if you prefer). Luigi, a bricklayer, built the home where he and Marie-Thérèse raised their family. Philippe, the youngest of their four children and the couple's third son, was born on February 17, 1972.

Philippe was good at jumping on the trampoline and swimming. When his elementary-school class went to the ice rink, it turned out that he was good on skates as well.

Figure skating was expensive for a family of six to support. According to legend, Philippe stole the first pair of skates that he owned. His mother later reimbursed the sporting-goods store.

Eventually, Philippe showed enough promise to receive some support from the Fédération Française des Sports de Glace, but his relationship with the establishment was rocky from the start.

Philippe loved the technical aspects of figure skating, but his masculine ego shunned the artistic side. He learned that, by creating characters, he could project "artistry" with less embarrassment. That was the beginning of his long succession of characters: Conan the Barbarian, Rocky Balboa, Don Corleone of *The Godfather*, Tony Manero from *Saturday Night Fever*, D'Artagnan, Tom Jones, George of the Jungle, and Braveheart.

Philippe, with other young French skaters, participated in the closing ceremonies of the 1988 Calgary Olympics as the torch passed to Albertville. Inspired by the Battle of the Brians, he went on to senior competition two years later. In 1991, he stunned audiences with his freewheeling "Conan the Barbarian" routine, which launched one of his signature moves, a cross-foot spin, in which he descended onto his shins and the sides of his skate boots, continuing to rotate.

Philippe locked horns a number of times with the French federation over his training and lifestyle choices. In 1992, he was placed fifth at the national championships (as punishment, he felt) and failed to make the Olympic team. The one good thing that came from that painful year was his meeting with ballet dancer Olivia Darmon, whom he married six years later.

The spoils of Philippe's amateur career included four national titles, world silver and bronze medals, and two Olympic bronze medals.

Philippe, always a man of the people, once confided to a fellow skater that he aspired to launch a hot, lightly clad lounge act on skates in the style of the Chippendales dancers. He attacked his professional career voraciously, taking the term *crowd-pleasing* to new heights – as well as depths.

❧❧❧

P hilippe Candeloro is the only skater in the world of any current significance whom I do not recall meeting. If I was introduced to him during his earliest years as a competitor at the Europeans, I have forgotten. We had no occasion to bump into one another. Moreover, Philippe was one of the very few skaters whom I had no desire to meet (and if he reads this chapter, I suspect that he will reciprocate the feeling). It was clear to me that we had absolutely nothing of mutual interest to discuss, even though, as a Montreal native, I spoke fluent French.

My earliest remembrance of Philippe does not center on his skating or choreography. What I particularly recall is the image of an elderly male coach hovering at the entrance to the ice with his pupil, an extremely young and naive Philippe, wide-eyed and bushy-tailed, hungering to compete.

There is a famous painting in the Musée du Louvre, Florentine Domenico Ghirlandaio's *An Old Man and His Grandson*, *circa* 1480. The double portrait depicts an elderly man gazing lovingly into the eyes of a young boy with golden curls. It's an eternal theme: old age smiling down upon youth. Philippe's early coach looked benevolently down at his young student in just the same way, but that was where the resemblance to the portrait ended.

The point is that Philippe's early influences and training couldn't have come from a coach who was more out of touch and out of the loop. As far as I know, this teacher's one and only claim to fame was Philippe. I discussed that situation with a well-known French international judge who is no longer involved with skating, having been caught with her hand in the till at one of the Lalique competitions. She agreed with my assessment, then remarked, "But Philippe has so much talent." On that point we agreed.

Philippe was an amazingly talented, athletic, and charismatic skater. Despite his excellent credentials, however, I believe that he never matured.

I once heard an analysis of why China, in modern days, was left behind in the wake of Western progress. However advanced China might have been in ancient times, its writing system was virtually impossible to master. The entire Chinese civilization therefore spun its wheels and went nowhere for centuries.

To me, that is a metaphor for Philippe. Though a skater of great talent and potential, he began to spin his wheels at the peak of his career for lack of effective tools of communication. He ceased to progress, either in style, self-expression, or technique.

Philippe's strengths were two: his talent for high-level competition and his phenomenal jumping ability. It is also fair to say that, for a certain sort of spectator (usually young and female), Philippe possessed enormous charisma. But there the positive attributes ended.

Because of his complete lack of mature pedagogical influence, sense of body line, and refinement, sophistication, and musicality, Philippe achieved impressive victories but never won a World or Olympic title.

At the Goodwill Games in Leningrad, the publisher of a French skating magazine asked Philippe if he was aware of the inventiveness of Soviet skater Igor Bobrin. Philippe responded that, no, he had never heard of Igor Bobrin, but what did it matter? Everyone would remember Philippe Candeloro.

That answer was telling. In some ways it was accurate, but the trouble was that the figure-skating world would remember Philippe Candeloro for some of the most monstrous and tasteless performances in history.

Philippe won a bronze medal at the 1994 Olympics in Lillehammer, skating both his short and long programs in his *Godfather* persona to different segments of Nino Rota's film score. At the Worlds three weeks later in Chiba, Japan, he caused a major sensation among the teenyboppers in the audience, and he took full advantage of that support base.

It was at about that point in his career that Philippe began to remove his clothes during exhibitions – to the squealing delight of those teenyboppers and to the absolute horror of the ISU and the skating world at large. For several years, just the shirt came off. Eventually the pants followed suit. I'm told that Scott Hamilton once remarked, "Philippe really wouldn't be too bad if he could just skate with his clothes on."

Philippe was an interesting thorn in the side of the figure-skating world and particularly its governing establishment. In spite of the base level to which Philippe sank in the name of self-promotion, he had to be treated with a certain deference because he was a celebrity with the ability to draw crowds to the box office.

Philippe, of course, was not the only skater to offer cheap entertainment. There were numbers of others, including Elvis Stojko, Christopher Bowman, and even sometimes Olympic champion Viktor Petrenko. The difference between Philippe and the others was that their corny exhibitions never crossed the line of decency, while Philippe took great pleasure not only in crossing the line but in leaping right over it and playing jump rope.

When Philippe competed at the 1996 Worlds in Edmonton, he wove his magic as Lucky Luke, performing to a medley of songs from TV westerns. Even as a world and Olympic medalist, he placed a lowly ninth. The French celebrity was completely out of his depth, and he paid the price.

I was surprised that Philippe did not retire after Edmonton and go on to skate professionally in France. However, he rose from the ashes and won his second Olympic bronze medal in 1998 at Nagano. That was his amateur swan song.

It was only then that his frighteningly grotesque skating routines began to appear at professional competitions and on television screens. The tragedy is that an athlete with so much talent and potential did not have a creative mentor to mold him into the skater he could and should have been.

In December 2001, Kurt Browning and his wife, Sonia, visited me in Mexico directly after the World Professional Championships. Kurt, one of the most solid and intellectual professional skaters of our age, admitted that watching Philippe compete, holding a phony gorilla and wearing little more than a pair of men's briefs, made him physically ill. That repellent performance, immediately preceding Kurt's routine, prevented Kurt from skating as well as he might have. Watching the videotape that my former pupil Lucinda Ruh sent to me, I was certainly able to understand Kurt's reaction to the Candeloro schtick. When Philippe plunged, nearly naked, over the boards and onto one of the judges, I felt that he had violated a taboo.

I'm convinced that Philippe's compete lack of good taste is not altogether his fault. Perhaps because of his huge number of young female fans, or perhaps because of hungry managers anxious to make a buck, or perhaps because of differing cultural interpretations of humor, Philippe may not believe that his behavior is unseemly.

His artistic crimes, I conclude, result from bad influences around him and a lack of intelligence and sensitivity on his part. We can only imagine what such an exceptional talent could have achieved under the influence of great trainers, gifted choreographers, and creative costume designers. We will never know what Philippe could have become. What a pity.

Tobel (centre), with his sister and ice dancer Gwendal Peizerat

CHAPTER 23

LAURENT TOBEL

%

Turning Lemons into Lemonade

L aurent Tobel was born on June 24, 1975, in Savigny, France. He began skating at age three, but, as he grew up, he also enjoyed ice hockey, soccer, and even judo.

In 1993, Laurent debuted in the senior division of the French Nationals, placing tenth. By 1997, he had placed third, then moved up a medal at each of the next two championships. He competed at the 1997 Worlds in Lausanne, finishing thirteenth.

Over the next year, Laurent grew an incredible eighteen inches. The dramatic height change affected his balance, caused knee trouble, and produced shin splints. At the 1998 Worlds in Minneapolis, he dropped to sixteenth, his signal to turn professional.

Laurent is known for his comedy routines, notably "The Pink Panther" and "Swan Lake." To perform the latter, the six-foot, two-inch skater dresses as a rather unlovely ballerina.

$\mathcal{L}\mathcal{T}\mathcal{L}\mathcal{T}\mathcal{L}\mathcal{T}$

I always have been sensitive to names that begin with the letter T. I believe that, if one knows nothing about a thoroughbred's background, for example, it is a good bet to risk one's money on a horse whose name starts with T. Tara, Tommy, Tamara, Tonya, Tim, Torvill, Tatiana Tarasova, and Toller are some examples from the figure-skating world. Tobel is another.

In 1996, while living in San Miguel de Allende, I received a telephone call from the president of the French figure-skating federation, a friend and fellow skater, Didier Gailhaguet. He and I had competed together at the 1972 Olympics. (I placed ninth; he was thirteenth.) Didier asked me if I would be interested in traveling to the French training center that summer to teach and choreograph for the French team for a period of one week.

Upon my arrival in Montpellier, I learned that the airline had lost my luggage. Embracing what the French call joie de vivre, I simply went out with Didier for a divine three-and-one-half-hour lunch. By the time we had finished dessert, my luggage had somehow materialized at my hotel.

Later that evening, I was presented to the French team and invited to describe my strategy for the week's training. It was at this meeting that I first encountered Laurent Tobel. Judging by his physical appearance, he was entirely miscast in the sport of figure skating. Laurent was an enormous young man whose body type would have been more suited to football or the shot put. His head sprouted less than one millimeter of hair, and his face, at a glance, was not at all the countenance of an intellectual.

Laurent's personality and body language suggested buffoonery. I recall being completely dazzled by the length of his feet, and it crossed my mind that even custom-made skate boots would be difficult to find in that size. In short, Laurent Tobel was not, in my opinion, a candidate to play the role of Prince Charming.

The next day I watched Laurent skate, and I wondered why his blades did not snap in two from supporting his weight. Stylistically, Laurent's skating lacked refinement. His landing position was particularly rigid and ugly, something that I count as a serious flaw. Good landing positions mark great skaters.

Over the course of the week in Montpellier, I asked Didier about Laurent's history, and I innocently suggested that another sport, like soccer or football, might be more suitable for this Incredible Hulk.

Didier explained to me that Laurent's career path had taken a somewhat tragic turn. As a young skater, he had been a prodigy, supremely talented and capable of performing every triple jump with ease. But as a teenager, he suddenly had started to grow – and grow and grow. When I met Laurent, he was still growing. He actually outgrew his ability to skate and had to relearn the elements from scratch.

Laurent and the other French skaters revealed the influence of government-employed coach and choreographer Allen Schramm, an American who will go down in skating history as one of the sport's most unique and original performers. Allen exerted a direct influence on Gary Beacom, among others, through his freewheeling, unconventional vocabulary of movement.

On the last day of my seminar, I staged an interpretive competition, an exercise in performing without inhibition in front of an audience. Viewing Laurent's creative performance, I suddenly recognized his phenomenal talent and range of emotional expression. At the end of his routine, my mouth hung open. I was awestruck.

Laurent was able to lose himself in the music, expressing his innermost feelings in the most profound way. Many of the other skaters, male and female, performed excellent routines, but Laurent's possessed unique and rare genius.

I next saw Laurent at the 1997 Worlds in Lausanne. I enjoyed unique credentials and access because I had been invited by the ISU as their honored guest. In conjunction with the Worlds, I was presenting a painting exhibition at the Olympic Museum.

The initial round of the men's qualifying event was Laurent Tobel's world debut. Above and beyond phenomenal jumping content (including a triple Axel/triple toe-loop combination), he performed with a comedic sense that enthralled the audience in a way that no competitive skater in the sport's history has ever done.

A master comedian, Laurent poked fun at himself (and at the judges as well, I thought). The real genius of the routine, choreographed by Allen Schramm, lay in the fact that every member of the audience seemed to comprehend Laurent's thoughts and underlying motivations. When the performance ended, the crowd erupted into a prolonged standing ovation. As they applauded, all the members of the audience wore huge smiles.

Laurent did not receive high marks, a fact that dismayed me. Later that evening, he entered the skaters' dining room with other members of the French team. All the athletes in the room stood up and offered a second standing ovation. To the best of my knowledge, that had never happened before.

Laurent skated even better in the next round of the competition than he had in the qualifier. The audience clearly anticipated his long-program performance. I watched it with Stephanie Grosscup, a unique and original skater in her own right. Laurent did not disappoint us. Once again, he made skating history in his own original way.

During Laurent's standing ovation, Stephanie said, in an offhanded way, "He is so beautiful." That remark struck a chord with me. It was true that, because of his authentic passion and soul, Laurent was indeed a beautiful performer. Stepping onto the ice and immersing himself in his music and choreography, he somehow underwent a physical metamorphosis and became a god. Laurent's long program in Lausanne ranks among my three favorite skating performances of all time.

The next summer, the French federation again invited me to work with the national team, this time in the Hautes-Alpes. Again it was my privilege to choreograph for Laurent. This time, I did not make the mistake of judging the book by its cover. I discovered a magnificent skater and an extremely intelligent man with a devastatingly clever sense of humor.

That was the last time that I saw Laurent skate. He turned professional shortly thereafter. It seems a pity to me that Laurent did not continue as an amateur. His inventiveness could have served the skating world as an example of pure art. Sometimes greatness is achieved over a long period of time through many memorable performances. Sometimes it is achieved in one fell swoop.

Laurent surely has many admirers throughout the world, but I will challenge anyone who claims to be his number-one fan. I reserve that honor for myself, and I will fight for it.

Out on the town, a magnet for paparazzi, circa 2001

CHAPTER 24

OKSANA BAIUL

❧

The Tormented Swan

O n November 16, 1977, in Dnepropetrovsk, Ukraine, Marina and Sergei Baiul welcomed their only child, Oksana. Two years later, Sergei disappeared from his daughter's life, leaving her to be raised by her mother and grandparents.

Marina, who had been a dancer, wanted her daughter to become a ballerina, but instead, at age four, Oksana began to skate. By the time she reached the age for classical ballet training, she was too much in love with figure skating to devote herself full-time to anything else. As a precocious nine-year-old, she was landing triple Lutzes.

When Oksana was ten, she lost her beloved grandfather. Less than a year later, her grandmother died as well. The most crushing blow came in 1991, when Marina, who had remarried, lost her battle against ovarian cancer. Feeling alone in the world and uncomfortable with her new stepfather, Oksana left her mother's funeral and ran to the ice rink for solace.

Stanislav Korytek, Oksana's coach, provided some sense of continuity until the day, about a year after Marina's funeral, when he secretly left the Ukraine for a chance at a new job in Canada.

Oksana was shuffled three hundred miles to Galina Zmievskaya, celebrated trainer and new mother-in-law of 1992 Olympic champion Viktor Petrenko. Galina took Oksana into her home in Odessa. In new skates that her surrogate brother, Viktor, had bought for her, Oksana won the national championship of the Ukraine and took home a silver medal from the Europeans in Helsinki, Finland. The next stop was Prague, where Oksana stunned the figure-skating world by capturing the world title the first time she entered the event. She became the second-youngest world champion (after Sonja Henie).

For the 1994 Olympic season, sixteen-year-old Oksana fulfilled a wish of her mother's by performing her short program as the black swan in *Swan Lake*, placing second to Nancy Kerrigan. The next afternoon, at a training session, Oksana and German skater Tonya Szewczenko, both skating backwards at high speed, collided painfully. Oksana injured her back and spiked a gash in her own leg that required three stitches. Until the long-program warm-up, she was not certain that she would be able to compete.

To a Broadway medley, Oksana delivered a light, lyrical, free-spirited program, tossing in a last-minute triple toe loop to make up for the one that she had doubled. Then she threw in an extra jump combination. That was enough to barely ensure the gold medal, five judges to four. Oksana returned to a heroine's welcome in the Ukraine.

The new Olympic champion turned professional in October 1994 after recovering from arthroscopic knee surgery, finding enough work to become a millionaire. She moved into an upscale condominium in Simsbury, Connecticut, the small city that recently had erected the International Skating Center of Connecticut. In November, her life story aired on CBS: *A Promise Kept: The Oksana Baiul Story*.

Sudden wealth, celebrity, and freedom didn't sit lightly on Oksana's shoulders. Moreover, her sudden late-teen growth spurt caused intransigent injuries. Oksana spent more than a year away from public performing. During that time, she lived life in the fast lane. She developed a drinking problem that the press publicized in January 1997 after she drove her speeding lime-green Mercedes into a tree on the way home from a bar. She was arrested on charges of driving while intoxicated.

Sometime after resuming her interrupted career, Oksana left the Tom Collins tour to check herself into a rehabilitation facility for several months of treatment. Today she is a recovering alcoholic, trying to reassemble the pieces of a difficult, and still young, life.

ぇ৵ぇ৵ぇ৵

L ong before I ever saw Oksana Baiul on the ice, I heard about her sensational debut at the 1993 Worlds in Prague. Seemingly from out of nowhere – as it turned out, she was from the Ukraine – she descended onto the world stage and snatched a gold medal on her first time out of the blocks. As far as I know, no competitor, male or female, had ever done such a thing in the history of figure skating. Oksana had placed second to Nancy Kerrigan in the short-program event. She then edged out Surya Bonaly in the free-skating event in which Nancy choked like George Bush eating pretzels.

I eventually saw a video of Oksana's triumph, and, although I was deeply impressed by her performance, I was not at all convinced that France's exotic Surya should not have won on the basis of superior athleticism and speed. It seemed, however, that the young Ukrainian virtuoso had arrived to dominate women's skating for many years to come.

That was not to be. Oksana retired from amateur skating the very next year, after the 1994 Olympics in Lillehammer.

Members of the IOC told me that the Lillehammer Olympics were the best Winter Games in recent memory. I couldn't understand that viewpoint. For me, the most memorable element of those Games was the fanatic attention the press accorded to Nancy Kerrigan's battle against she-devil Tonya Harding. That showdown eclipsed every other aspect of the women's competition, and perhaps of all the skating events in Norway.

During the Games, I hosted a painting exhibition in Vancouver, where a local television station proposed to film my live reactions to the performances of the female competitors. It is rare for me to find myself ambivalent, but I was not completely convinced that Oksana deserved the gold medal instead of Nancy. Today, considering what I know in hindsight, I believe that Nancy would have been the worthy winner on the day. However, neither woman subsequently made the most of her Olympic experience.

Oksana chose not to compete at the Worlds in Chiba, Japan, three weeks later, just as Tara Lipinski passed on the Worlds in Minneapolis following her Nagano victory. On bad advice, both chose to grab the medal and push those golden chips under the cashier's window. In my opinion, they committed a regrettable error in opting for the get-rich-quick scenario. It was their privilege and obligation to continue as eligible skaters, advancing the art of figure skating for all young athletes.

Oksana's history was as fascinating as her multifaceted ability to charm judges and spectators. Virtually orphaned as a young girl, she was adopted by her famous coach, Galina Zmievskaya, the teacher of renowned Olympic champion Viktor Petrenko. After winning her Olympic gold medal, Oksana went to train in Simsbury, Connecticut, an American city that had become, overnight, Ukraine West. Dozens of former Soviet amateur and professional skaters gravitated to Simsbury, post-perestroika, to study with the famous Russian skating coaches who settled there.

For an erstwhile penniless Russian orphan, America offered many Dionysian temptations that resulted in Oksana's temporary self-destruction.

In mid-1994, IMG asked me to fly from Toronto to New Orleans to meet with Chinese ladies' champion and Olympic medalist Lu Chen, with an eye to concocting the strategy that would ultimately result in her world bronze medal. It was there in New Orleans, in an enormous sports complex during a Tom Collins tour stop, that I first met Oksana and watched her perform.

I have always been uncomfortable prowling around backstage, fearing that I will know either too many people or none at all. Tom Collins treated me with great deference, and it turned out that I had a personal connection, or at least some familiarity, with all but two of the skaters: Philippe Candeloro, France's heartthrob, and the reigning Olympic gold medalist, direct from Lillehammer, Oksana Baiul.

Oksana skated second from last, while Viktor Petrenko closed the show. Although the ice wasn't good by the end of the evening, Oksana performed with a rare brand of charismatic star quality. She projected a larger-than-life image, skating one of her signature numbers, "The Dying Swan" from Camille Saint-Saëns's *Carnival of the Animals*. Like a Bolshoi prima ballerina, Oksana held the audience spellbound with every movement she made – and even when she made no movement at all. In all my life, I have not seen anything quite so mesmerizing and fantastic.

At the end of Viktor's number, Oksana joined him to perform in tandem. Oksana, new to professionalism, was no less professional than Viktor, the seasoned entertainer.

I was presented to Oksana as a middle-aged god from Mount Olympus, with hat in hand, and in today's vernacular, I was "dissed" by the goddess Oksana. It was obvious that she had never heard of me – and, furthermore, she didn't care if she hadn't.

Oksana and I next met at an AIDS benefit in Toronto that had been created by its host, Brian Orser. There, Oksana and I had a tête-à-tête. Her personality, charm, and outrageous naivete held me enthralled. I felt an instant attraction to her personality and to her offbeat, original sense of humor.

Oksana's fabulous Russian skating technique had begun to reveal signs of wear and tear, if not utter disintegration. During the two performances that I witnessed, she camouflaged the lack of a relatively easy double Axel by employing theatrics and displaying eccentricities.

During her free time, Oksana fluttered off to the Versace boutique in Toronto's Yorkville area to spend $40,000 Canadian on clothes – clear evidence to me that she was flying out of control.

Some time later, I judged Oksana at the 1995 Gold Championship in Vancouver, in which the field consisted entirely of past and current Olympic champions. Oksana placed second to Kristi Yamaguchi, the 1992 gold medalist. In our discussions after the competition, I learned that most of the judges had preferred Oksana's overall skating (to "Meditation" from *Thaïs* and "The Feeling Begins"), yet she had made too many errors and displayed too many flaws to topple the exquisite, technically perfect, and somewhat mechanical Kristi (who performed to "The Seasons" and "Gonna Be Strong"). Oksana's nearly new career had already begun its descent.

That was the last time I spoke to or saw Oksana. Her reputation in the figure-skating world began to take on negative overtones, flabbergasting and depressing her peers. Her perfect body changed dramatically. Her approach to the sport became less than serious. Her behavior on and off the ice grew bizarre and troubling. Oksana was a textbook embodiment of what can happen in the wake of instant fame, a huge bank account, and lack of parental supervision.

People with more knowledge and first-hand experience could write a book about the rise and fall of Oksana. Certainly her coach and adopted stepmother, Galina, from whom Oksana declared her independence, could relate a hair-raising tale of tragic proportions. Oksana received international press coverage when she arrived at a Simsbury courthouse to answer a charge of drunken driving. Can anyone imagine Peggy Fleming, Dorothy Hamill, or Kristi Yamaguchi in such a mortifying situation?

The Oksana Baiul scenario was a bona fide American tragedy. The champagne will never taste the same. Its bubbles can't regain their lost effervescence.

Oksana, by all reports, has sincerely tried to improve herself in all aspects of life. But for a young woman who took the world by storm and galvanized the media as recently as early 1994, her current obscurity is tragic. As someone famously said (I believe that it was Oscar Wilde), we should be careful what we wish for, because our wishes may come true. In Oksana's case, the wishes that were granted exacted a terrible cost.

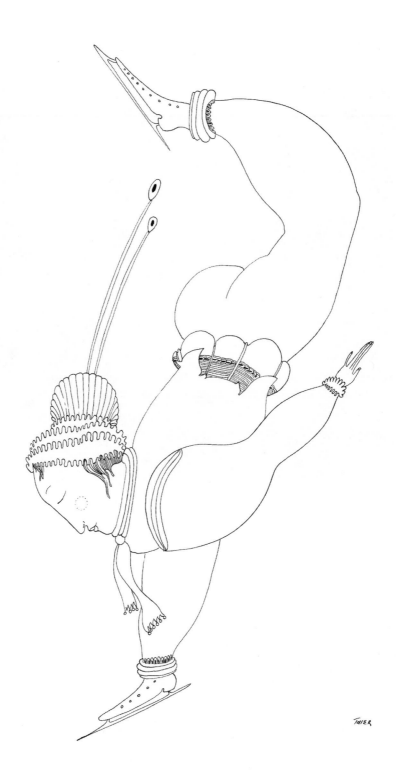

Recent publicity photo

CHAPTER 25

LUCINDA RUH

❧

The Princess of Spin

L ucinda Ruh, world citizen, was conceived at the start of a revolution in Tehran, Iran, and born in Zurich on July 13, 1979. Her father, René, the president of Sika, Ltd., moved his wife, Silvia, and his two daughters around the world as business dictated. Meanwhile, they maintained a home base in their native Zurich.

The family moved to Japan when Lucinda was four. Two years later, she joined her sister on the ice and was soon coached by Nobuo Sato, father of Yuka, the 1994 world champion.

Sato taught his Swiss pupil that good spinning would help her to center her jumps. She spun, and spun, and spun some more, until she could accomplish 270 revolutions per minute. In 1996, she became the Swiss champion, the most recent and greatest practitioner in a line of remarkable Swiss spinners that included Denise Biellmann and Nathalie Krieg.

As a child of seven, Lucinda was offered a scholarship to train with the Royal Ballet in London, England. She turned down the offer in order

267

to continue to skate, but her classical training became manifest in every move that she made on the ice.

Lucinda's quest for the perfect training situation took her to Toller Cranston in Toronto, Christy Ness in San Francisco, Hongyun Liu in Harbin, China, and Oliver Höner in Switzerland. After the 1999 Worlds in Helsinki, where she placed thirteenth, Lucinda was invited to join the German tour of Stars on Ice.

As a professional, she went on to dazzle audiences and judges at the 2000 World Professional Figure Skating Championships with routines choreographed by Lea Ann Miller. *International Figure Skating* magazine named Lucinda one of the sport's "Top 25 Most Influential People."

Lucinda repeated her World Pro success one year later with costumes and choreography by Toller Cranston. During the 2001–2002 season, she received enthusiastic ovations while touring with the U.S. Stars on Ice company.

Highly intelligent and linguistically gifted, Lucinda speaks fluent English, French, German, and Japanese, as well as some Chinese and Russian. Her mastery of Japanese is so advanced that she is certified to teach the language.

While touring with Stars on Ice, Lucinda is based in New York City. Her elder sister, Michèle, lives in London, England, while René and Silvia currently reside in Dubai.

ﾂﾂﾂﾂﾂﾂ

Lucinda Ruh's parents, although Swiss, have lived throughout the world as a result of René Ruh's position as CEO of a multinational company. When I first met Lucinda, the family was based in Japan.

When Yuka Sato came from Japan to Toronto so that I could choreograph new programs and design new costumes for her, Lucinda and her mother, Silvia, came along, and I met them for the first time. Lucinda's skating coach was Yuka's father, a well-known Japanese champion who had placed fourth at the 1965 Worlds in Colorado Springs. Yuka and Lucinda were like sisters.

Lucinda possessed an absolutely charming personality and a stunning, leggy body. Her face was lovely and interesting, but not beautiful in the classical sense. Perhaps her most engaging physical quality was the dazzling smile that revealed bright white Chiclets teeth.

During my week with Yuka, Lucinda trained at the Cricket Club as well. I suggested to her that, during her stay in Toronto, I design some skating costumes for her that Angela Arana, master costume seamstress with the National Ballet of Canada, could sew. Lucinda's tall, trim body was a dream to dress.

I also offered to choreograph a small exhibition number for Lucinda. I used music from the movie *Sleepless in Seattle*, a two-minute violin piece entitled "An Affair to Remember." As a pupil, Lucinda was attentive, disciplined, and gutsy. For me, our short time together was memorable.

After Lucinda, her mother, and Yuka flew back to Japan, I did not see them again until the 1996 Worlds in Edmonton. I was in Edmonton to perform a bat number (on artificial ice) in the middle of the Edmonton Opera's production of *Die Fledermaus*. Lucinda and her mother took time out of their busy schedule to come to see me one night as Dracula in drag – at least that was how I viewed my operatic look. I tried to incorporate into my exotic dance everything that I had taught Lucinda about performing without inhibition, and I skated just for her.

Lucinda's debut at the Worlds provoked a certain interest among skaters and officials. I was particularly pleased that she wore the two dresses that I had designed, and that those dresses drew notice and positive comment.

The most extraordinary aspect of Lucinda's repertoire was her ability to spin. She possessed phenomenal and unique talent in that regard. No skater in the world could compete with her.

When a skater displays an outstanding ability within the standard vocabulary of skating technique, why do judges consistently ignore it? Why do judges hold the insular point of view that "technique" is equal to nothing more than triple jumps? If Lucinda Ruh (with somewhat mediocre jumps) could astound audiences with her many spin variations, why wasn't she the equal of Tara Lipinski (with mediocre spins by comparison), who astounded audiences with her triple jumps? When a skater on any level thrills an audience with a unique approach, when that audience spontaneously jumps to its feet in enthusiasm, why then is that accomplishment not reflected in the marks?

Skating must be viewed as a combination of art and sport, as I have repeatedly insisted. Those skaters who have been most admired historically are the well-rounded athlete/artists who pay attention to every aspect of the medium. Lucinda represented everything that is fine and admirable in figure skating. She simply could not perform a triple Lutz.

After the Worlds, the Ruhs traveled with the Japanese team from Edmonton to San Francisco en route to Tokyo. Silvia and Lucinda phoned me from San Francisco to thank me and to say goodbye. I had returned to Mexico by then, and I spontaneously invited them to visit me in San Miguel de Allende.

That would involve an expensive change in airline tickets. Silvia thanked me but declined, citing the difficulties and complications. But Lucinda's last words to me were, "See you in Mexico tomorrow." True enough, she and Silvia arrived the next day.

It was during the extremely pleasant week that the three of us spent together in San Miguel that we somehow agreed that Lucinda would leave Japan and come to train with me at the Toronto Cricket Club. (I was then in the habit of splitting my time between Mexico and Canada.) I am certain that, because of my fondness for Lucinda and her mother, I must have solicited their business quite flagrantly.

When the Ruhs arrived in Toronto, I embraced Lucinda's metamorphosis with as much passion and integrity as I could muster. My former coach, Ellen Burka, became Lucinda's co-teacher. I focused on artistry, while Ellen focused on technique. Although Lucinda made great progress, acquiring interesting new numbers and costumes for the upcoming season, the two jumps that were missing from her repertoire, triple flip and triple Lutz, never became secure.

Nonetheless, our collaboration was a positive experience for Lucinda. She won the Central Ontario Summer Competition, an international event. It seemed that we were all heading straight down the road to success.

During the fall, I accompanied Lucinda and Shin Yamato, a former Japanese champion, to an international competition in Vienna. There, my career as a coach began its decline. Lucinda performed her short program well, placing seventh within a group of twenty-three (I thought that the placement should have been higher, but seventh was respectable). However, the next afternoon's long-program event offered my first dose of professional humiliation: Lucinda barely landed one triple jump.

At dinner that night, the Ruhs informed me that the reason why Lucinda had not performed well was that the previously gorgeous program that had in fact won the summer competition was now an inferior and badly choreographed routine.* A ton of bricks dropped from the sky and flattened me on the pavement. To say that I did not react well is a masterpiece of understatement.

When I become angry, I don't erupt into a red-hot fury. Rather, my temperature drops to below freezing, and I say nothing. Any number of people, within and outside of the figure-skating world, have experienced this treatment. I abandoned the Ruhs and locked myself in my hotel room with a crushing headache. There were many knocks on my door that night and many kind entreaties that I slink out of my hole, but I pretended that I was not there. I lay in state on my bed like a mummified Tutankhamen.

The next morning, I greeted everyone with frightening politesse, and we all headed back to Toronto via Zurich. We were to spend the night at the Ruhs' lovely Swiss apartment and travel together to Toronto the next day. Just before our plane landed in Zurich, I fantasized about sensational, Houdini-like escapes. I would lose the Ruhs in the crowd at the airport and hop a plane for Canada a day early.

Like an unlucky Alcatraz inmate, I found no avenue of escape. By evening, my fury had cooled. After a pleasant dinner with the Ruhs and their friends, I bounced back to what, for me, might be described as normal.

Just before Lucinda, Silvia, and I boarded our plane for Canada, I witnessed something that I will remember always: the farewell embrace

---

* According to the Ruhs, two international judges had told Lucinda to change the program by moving some difficult technical material from the second half of the number to the first. Toller didn't wait to hear that explanation.

between Lucinda and her father. Even in the movies, I have rarely seen so emotional and loving a hug. In that moment, a hypodermic needle pricked me: the realization that such a show of warmth could never have happened in my dysfunctional family.

The next day I went to the rink and began to pare down Lucinda's program. Like custom-made clothes, my choreography had been designed to fit the character and skating ability of the individual. However, I stripped off the detail and nuance, leaving a generic program grid that didn't camouflage Lucinda's jumping difficulties. I did not enjoy the process. A good teacher or coach is (almost) always right. That certainly was the doctrine underlying my relationship with Ellen Burka. But in this case the customer was right.

Within less than a month, Lucinda and I had a major falling-out. Whatever the reasons, there was enough blame to go around on both sides. I began to realize, to my chagrin, that I had committed the cardinal sin of becoming too emotionally involved. One afternoon, after a particularly bad lesson, I received my pink slip. By evening, I was en route to San Miguel, vowing to forever abandon the noble coaching profession.

Shortly thereafter, Lucinda and Silvia flew to San Francisco to engage Christy Ness, former teacher of Kristi Yamaguchi, before returning for Skate Canada in London, Ontario. I did not see Lucinda skate in London. However, based on Ellen's and my meticulous work (and charms of her own), Lucinda won a bronze medal. Unfortunately, that was the last international medal that she ever won.

I met Lucinda later that season at the 1997 Worlds in Lausanne. She and her family greeted me warmly, but I'm afraid that a few stubborn crystals of frost still hung in the air around me. One afternoon I went to see Lucinda's practice. The program that I had choreographed was barely recognizable. As a creative genius, I found that hard to take.

I did not see Lucinda again in person for several years, but I heard that her relationship with Christy Ness didn't last, and she moved on to former Swiss champion Oliver Höner. Because of injuries, Lucinda temporarily disappeared from international competition. She was not chosen to represent Switzerland at the 1998 Olympics in Japan. That was surely a harsh blow.

I did watch Lucinda's performance broadcast from the 1999 Worlds in Helsinki, where she placed thirteenth, and it was clear to me that she had blossomed into a gorgeous young woman. Wearing a beautiful strapless yellow-and-blue dress, she gave an excellent performance. My ire had evaporated by then, and I wanted to leap out of my seat and tell her how great she had been. What a pleasure it was to see her skate as Ellen and I had always known she could. I was outraged by Lucinda's low freeskating marks. She had clearly been one of the crowd's favorites.

The years slipped by. During the summer of 2001, I received a telephone call from Silvia Ruh, phoning from Dubai. I was pleased to make contact again, and particularly interested in hearing news about Lucinda. Silvia seemed concerned about her daughter's future. Lucinda had suffered some sort of breakdown, and was living by herself in Japan. She continued to skate, but apparently she had become depressed and fragile.

I immediately phoned Lucinda in Tokyo at what must have been three o'clock in the morning. We spoke like family for half an hour. (Don't ask how much that cost.) Our last words before saying goodbye were, "Let's try to work together again."

Lucinda came from Japan later that summer and established residency in New York City. Our conversations became more frequent. We made plans. During the World Trade Center crisis, I was terribly worried about the Ruhs, but unable to reach them. Their apartment was right across the street from Ground Zero.

I heard from Lucinda a week later and received a first-hand account of what had happened in New York and how it had directly affected their lives, both logistically and emotionally. Fortunately, Lucinda and Silvia had been at Sky Rink when the planes hit the World Trade Center. As they left the building at Chelsea Piers, they noticed people running toward them. Unable to return to their apartment, they were forced to move in with friends for a number of weeks, with only the few possessions that they were able to gather during a brief visit to their home under police escort.

By then Lucinda had turned professional and had signed a one-year contract with IMG's Stars on Ice. She had a window of opportunity, about one week of free time, between rehearsals and professional commitments, and she needed new costumes and choreography for two upcoming professional competitions. I flew to Toronto in mid-October of 2001, designed the costumes, and choreographed two programs.

I was happy to see that Lucinda's skating had reached maturity, like a perfect rose in full bloom. She no longer needed a teacher. What she needed was creative input. It is a joy for any creative person to work with such a finely tuned instrument, sensitive and gorgeous. During our week together, it seemed like old times, a great and memorable pleasure. However, I had learned a lesson from my earlier coaching days. A teacher, while giving everything that he can, must maintain a professional distance.

Lucinda performed splendidly at the professional competitions, placing third in both. The response from my skating colleagues was glowing. Lucinda was the embodiment of beauty, grace, and unique gifts that are rarely seen on the ice.

Lucinda is truly a child of destiny. Often people who possess unusual talents are afforded many creative opportunities. That is what I wish for Lucinda. If the gods permit, she will enjoy a brilliant career and a multifaceted life. It was my privilege to have been part of the creative molding process.

I include Lucinda among the greats in this book for the same reason that IMG has included her in the topnotch cast of Stars on Ice. She is simply the most refined and proficient spinner that the world has ever seen – and we may never see her like again.

Michelle Kwan (top) and Sarah Hughes at a press conference, 2002 Nationals, Los Angeles

EPILOGUE

✍

A Salt Lake City Retrospective

The Olympic Games symbolize for me far more than ultimate achievement in figure skating. In my mind, they have an almost religious or spiritual connotation. It has sometimes seemed to me that a divine hand has chosen the gold-medal winners to carry the torch of advancement and enlightenment.

The 1998 Olympics in Nagano, however, struck me as largely forgettable. As proficient as the gold medalists were at their moments of glory, their specific performances have since been all but forgotten. At those Games, figure skating was treading water. None of the champions changed the sport or left behind vivid visual memories. The ice-dance event was a particular blight.

Because of my involvement with this book, I was determined to watch all the television coverage from Salt Lake City in February 2002. It was important for me to see exactly what skating had become within its historical context and to find out to what extent, if any, the current competitors were innovators and artists.

The pairs competition certainly captured the imagination of the global public. The long-program performances of Russians Elena Berezhnaya and Anton Sikharulidze and of Canadians Jamie Salé and David Pelletier were both of splendid quality. While Elena and Anton were excellent on that night, Jamie and David were sublime.

When five of the nine judges cast their votes for the Russian couple, the international press had a field day decrying the injustice and conveying the outrage of spectators and commentators. Even serious programs like *Crossfire* aired segments featuring the pairs imbroglio between pieces on Afghanistan and the U.S. economy.

Before the 2002 Games began, IOC corruption had already sullied Salt Lake City's reputation. Had the new president of the IOC not forced the powers-that-be to award a second set of gold medals to Salé and Pelletier, those Olympics would have been tarnished forever.

What was most peculiar and distressing about the judging of the pairs event was that the French judge, Marie Reine Le Gougne, who had placed the Russians ahead of the Canadians, actually admitted to being involved in a certain amount of collusion or at least subjected to undue influences as yet to be publicly specified.

I have known the occasional Frenchman to be hysterical and erratic, but it boggles my mind why this judge admitted her crime. Had she quietly stuck by her decision to place the Russians first, at least she was in good company. Four other judges – from Russia, China, Poland, and the Ukraine – had reached the same conclusion, and no doubt could back it up in writing.

What most journalists and television commentators failed to acknowledge or address was the question of how long such illegal collusion had been going on. How many world and Olympic medals were won through deception?

I cannot help but question, for example, some of the many judgments that catapulted Katarina Witt to six European titles, four world titles, and two Olympic gold medals. The jury is out. Or, to be more precise, the jury will never enter the courtroom to hear testimony about what really went on behind closed doors amongst the judges, federation officials, and coaches who all suckled from the same Communist cow.

With Le Gougne's unseemly admission, old fears and suppressed knowledge surfaced in the conscious minds of skaters of the past, igniting in them a white-hot fury. It was a huge I-told-you-so moment for many of us. For me, the public exposure of collusion and duplicity among international judges savagely ripped off the emotional scab that had covered a very deep wound.

In my amateur heyday, I twice won free-skating gold medals only to finish third or fourth overall. My pathetic claim to fame consists of one paltry Olympic bronze medal and one sad little world bronze medal. The Salé-Pelletier scenario made me painfully aware once again that I might have been a victim of the same crime that affected their results.

I considered launching an official protest to have the IOC review the tapes of my world and Olympic competitions. I believe that such a review would show that the Soviet bloc prevented me from receiving a gold or silver medal on several occasions. If I were to follow through with my quest for justice, I can only imagine how many dozens of other wronged skaters would tread in my footsteps.

It is true that there have been many deserving world and Olympic champions. However, the way those results were obtained lacked credibility and integrity. I believe in great skating and great skaters, but I will never believe in judges.

The Salt Lake City men's competition, with the exception of the top three skaters, was rather pedestrian. The nobility and virtuosity of Olympic champion Alexei Yagudin commanded respect and awe from anyone who witnessed it. Evgeny Plushenko dazzled me with his magnificent and aggressive performance, and an ardent passion for skating surged through my veins. Timothy Goebel certainly did not perform on Alexei's or Evgeny's artistic level, but when he jumped flawlessly, my mouth dropped open in amazement.

The ice-dance event was the low point of the Games, both technically and emotionally. Grotesque costumes and choreography, coupled with frightening makeup and hair, horrified anyone unlucky enough to be a witness. Well, at least I can speak for myself. Unless the rules governing costuming, music, and choreography are changed immediately, ice dance is in serious jeopardy of losing its status as an Olympic sport. It has become little more than a farce.

The women's competition was a fitting end to the fortnight. It became obvious that the future of skating is brilliantly vital. The long program of sixteen-year-old American Sarah Hughes ignited a flame of ecstasy in my heart and soul. Her ingenuousness melded with scandalous virtuosity and grace as she offered four minutes of global inspiration. For skaters and non-skaters alike, Sarah was a convincing example of limitless human potential, leaping from fourth place to the top of the podium.

Michelle Kwan's failure to win a gold medal may have disappointed her, but the outcome was just. Michelle exemplifies all the finest qualities, both of character and of skating ability. Her bronze medal was certainly not a tragedy. It was one more honor that this exceptional athlete and artist can add to her countless other awards.

The future of California skater Sasha Cohen burns bright. It is clear that skating greatness waits for her around the corner, only slightly out of reach.

With the brilliant influence of skaters like Alexei, Jamie, David, Michelle, and Sarah, the next decade of competitive skating is sure to be magnificent. They made me feel humbled and honored to know that I was once a contributor to their art and sport.

BIBLIOGRAPHY

Baiul, Oksana, and Heather Alexander. *Oksana: My Own Story.* New York: Random House, 1997.

Boitano, Brian, and Suzanne Harper. *Boitano's Edge: Inside the Real World of Figure Skating.* New York: Simon & Schuster, 1997.

Browning, Kurt. *Kurt: Forcing the Edge.* Toronto: HarperCollins Publishers Ltd., 1991.

Coffey, Frank, and Joe Layden. *Thin Ice: The Complete, Uncensored Story of Tonya Harding, America's Bad Girl of Ice Skating.* New York: Windsor Publishing Corp., 1994.

Coffey, Wayne, and Filip Bondy. *Dreams of Gold: The Nancy Kerrigan Story.* New York: St. Martin's Paperbacks, 1994.

Dean, Christopher, Jayne Torvill, and John Hennessy. *Torvill and Dean.* London: David & Charles, 1984.

Dean, Christopher, Jayne Torvill, and John Man. *Facing the Music.* London: Simon & Schuster, 1995.

Fleming, Peggy, and Peter Kaminsky. *The Long Program: Skating Toward Life's Victories.* New York: Pocket Books, 1999.

Hamill, Dorothy, and Elva Clairmont. *Dorothy Hamill On and Off the Ice.* New York: Alfred A. Knopf, 1983.

Hamilton, Scott, and Lorenzo Benet. *Landing It: My Life On and Off the Ice.* New York: Kensington Books, 1999.

Henie, Sonja. *Wings on My Feet.* New York: Prentice-Hall, Inc., 1940.

Kelly, Evelyn B. *Katarina Witt.* Philadelphia, Pennsylvania: Chelsea House Publishers, 1999.

Kimball, Martha Lowder. *Robin Cousins.* Jamestown, New York: Martha Lowder Kimball, 1998.

Manley, Elizabeth, and Elva Clairmont Oglanby. *Thumbs Up!* Toronto: Macmillan of Canada, 1990.

Money, Keith. *John Curry.* New York: Alfred A. Knopf, 1978.

Orser, Brian, and Steve Milton. *Orser: A Skater's Life.* Toronto: Key Porter Books Limited, 1988.

Reisfeld, Randi. *The Kerrigan Courage: Nancy's Story.* New York: Ballantine Books, 1994.

Sabovcik, Joseph, and Lynda D. Prouse. *Jumpin' Joe.* Toronto: Macmillan Canada, 1998.

Strait, Raymond, and Leif Henie. *Queen of Ice, Queen of Shadows: The Unsuspected Life of Sonja Henie.* Briarcliff Manor, New York: Stein and Day, 1985.

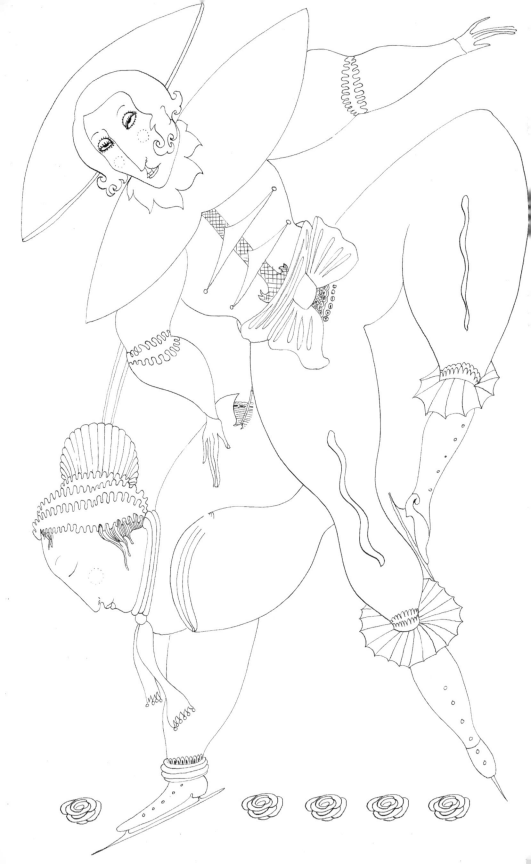